ESSAYS IN PHILOSOPHY

BY MEMBERS OF THE

PHILOSOPHY DEPARTMENT

THE PENNSYLVANIA

STATE UNIVERSITY

ESSAYS IN PHILOSOPHY

THE PENNSYLVANIA

STATE UNIVERSITY

PRESS

University Park, Pennsylvania

1962

PREFACE

The philosophical situation in the United States, determined for almost a generation by the marriage of empiricism and analysis, is once again in flux. A strong minority of American philosophers, dissatisfied with this new tradition, is turning once more toward the classical tradition of Western philosophy. Those of us who are a part of this movement have again come into direct contact with continental European thought, both to be instructed and to criticize, but essentially to engage in that dialogue which constitutes the development of philosophy. This return to a concern for the traditional ideas and problems of philosophy is not a jettisoning of logic and science or an appeal to the irrational, but rather a determined and rigorous effort to understand the various expressions of human life and history in terms of the Western spirit.

Since philosophy has always included the exploration of man's spirit, the present dissatisfaction with those views which reject the spirit expresses not a theological need, but rather a deep sense that philosophy itself has been mutilated by the analytical and empirical movements of the recent past. The authors of the following essays are united by nothing more than a sense of the importance and mission of a philosophy which assumes its total responsibilities. They wish to reaffirm the significance of certain kinds of problems and the value of a free and critical effort to deal with them. These essays are intended, then, apart from what-

694423 WITHDRAWN

ever individual merits they may have, to help focus attention on the concern for philosophy in its deepest and fullest meaning, and in that sense alone do they speak with a single voice.

The editorial committee wishes to acknowledge with thanks the generous support of Frederick R. Matson, Assistant Dean for Research, College of the Liberal Arts.

John M. Anderson
Henry W. Johnstone, Jr.
Stanley H. Rosen

Editorial Committee

CONTENTS

ESSAYS IN PHILOSOPHY

JOHN A. MOURANT

THOMISTIC EXISTENTIALISM

Many a philosopher, even a Thomist philosopher, may find the title of this essay rather provocative. His immediate reaction might well be that the very expression "Thomistic existentialism" is a complete contradiction. Certainly, Thomism has traditionally been identified largely with the rationalistic trend in philosophy, and this would seem to exclude it from anything remotely connected with what passes for existentialism since the latter is usually identified as anti-intellectualistic in spirit and certainly far removed from traditional rationalism. On the other hand, as we shall see, to oppose Thomism and existentialism as the antithesis of the rational with the irrational is not precisely accurate.

All great traditions in philosophy are subject to changing trends in philosophical thinking and accommodate themselves in greater or lesser degree to such trends. Yet it is the very strength of these traditions that they continue to stand out in historical thought, maintaining their historical identities even though they exhibit the influence of the successive currents of philosophical thought that move over them. What has been true of Platonism, Aristotelianism, Kantianism, and Hegelianism in their ability to withstand the eroding influence of diverse philosophical revolutions and innovations has also been true of the tradition of

[1]

Thomism. To define precisely the essential meaning of any one of these great traditions is not an easy task; and to define Thomism or distinguish Thomism from Neo-Thomism is no exception. Certainly, the Thomism of the early modern period is quite different from that of the nineteenth century and this again from what passes as present-day Thomism. Interestingly, the characterization so frequently made of thirteenth-century Thomism as reflecting a revolution in philosophy has also been stated of what is termed the "true existentialism" of present-day Thomism.

My principal purpose in this essay is to examine the meaning and the validity of this conception of a Thomistic existentialism. I hope to show that the so-called "revolution" in Thomistic thought today is not a warranted one and that a "counterrevolution" is in order. Such a "counterrevolution" will reaffirm the older tradition and interpretation of Thomism and reveal also the difficulties and the limitations involved in a Thomistic existentialism. Those who disagree with the conclusions arrived at in this paper may be more inclined to designate this as "reaction" rather than "counterrevolution."

Before undertaking our main enterprise, let us consider what possible features Thomism might have in common with the movement currently known as existentialism or existential phenomenology and the impact that this movement has had upon Thomism. The term "existential phenomenology" is broader and more representative than the term existentialism, for it connotes the fusion of the existentialism of Kierkegaard with the phenomenology of Husserl in the writings of such philosophers as Heidegger, Sartre, Merleau-Ponty, and others. Also it is the term used more prevalently by those Catholic philosophers who have been influenced by this new movement of thought. Dondeyne gives an excellent definition of this new philosophical movement: "Existential phenomenology appears in the history of philosophy as a manner of philosophizing centered around the notion of existence." [1] The very breadth of this definition indicates how it is possible for Thomists to accept in greater or lesser degree the basic orientation of this philosophy. Thus an outstanding philosopher like Dondeyne shows himself to be a very competent and sympathetic historian of the movement without abandoning in the least his own basic Thomistic principles and methodology. On the other hand, some Thomists are more committed to the methodology of the new movement and endeavor to combine basic Thomism with this new orientation and more particularly with the introspective insights and even the peculiar language of the new philosophy.[2] In no sense should this absorbing interest of many contemporary Thomists in existential phenomenology be considered as a retreat from Thomism or an attempt to compromise Thomism with the new movement. In contrast, there are a few Catholic philosophers, like Gabriel Marcel, who have felt the impact of the new movement so strongly that they have rejected the basic premises of Thomistic philosophy in favor of the existentialistic approach.

To narrow our own purpose, we shall consider neither a conception of Thomism which compromises Thomism with existentialism nor one which accommodates Thomism to the new movement. Rather, our concern will be with a type of Thomism which approaches the problem of being (esse) as identified with existence in the broadest sense of that term, i.e., as the "act of existence." Thomistic existentialism then is essentially a metaphysics of existence rather than of essence—a metaphysics which emphasizes always the priority of existence but which is completely divorced in virtually everything but the name "existence" from contemporary existentialism. The attempt to formulate a philosophy of existence in terms of human existence [3] and such categories as dread, anxiety, despair, etc., is foreign to the spirit of this present movement in Thomism. Some references to contemporary Thomists will clarify the orientation of Thomistic existentialism. Dondeyne declares: "It is characteristic of Thomist existentialism that it does not strictly speaking, separate essence and existence, nor make existence a useless repetition of essence; it gives existence a genuine primacy as the 'first intelligible.' " [4]

Both Gilson and Maritain have urged a new interpretation of certain Thomistic texts that would emphasize "existence" (esse) as virtually a new principle necessary for the explanation of reality. They affirm that St. Thomas has definitely gone beyond his Aristotelian origins in this respect and that we may speak accordingly of a Thomistic existentialism. "Yet, Thomistic philosophy is no existentialism, at least as the word is now understood, unless one prefers to say that it is existentialism as it should be understood." [5]

Fr. Hart regards this new approach to the metaphysics of existence as revolutionary:

This was something that Plato and Aristotle failed to do. This failure is also characteristic of many other historic metaphysical systems, not only of the Middle Ages but of modern times as well, all of which focus on the essences of things, what things are, rather than on such essences as exercising their respective acts of to be. Hence, these other systems can be called *essentialistic* metaphysics. The revolutionary character of Thomistic metaphysics then, in the whole history of this discipline, is its existentialism, making metaphysics an inquiry into the acts of to be of the various essences of things. Only within relatively recent times has this revolutionary system been fully recognized.[6]

That there is a measure of truth in this claim for a revolutionary metaphysics may be verified by a contrasting citation on being and metaphysics from one of the representatives of the older tradition in Thomism. Fr. Harper states:

> Being has two significations, according as it is taken nominatively or participially. In the former sense, it stands for Essence; in the latter, for *existing* Essence. These two are not contra-distinct concepts, but one and the same objective concept under more or less determination. The former includes the latter in the same sort of way as a Genus includes its Species; therefore the two are not reducible under a common and more universal concept.
>
> Being, in its nominative use, is the proper and adequate object of Metaphysics.[7]

From this background of the problem we wish to initiate now the following lines of inquiry: First, a consideration of the meaning that St. Thomas himself gives to the distinction between essence and existence and an examination of several of the more pertinent texts which appear to assert the priority of existence over essence and bear out the contention that we have here the opposite of an essentialistic metaphysics. After a brief evaluation of the conflicting interpretations we shall then assume the interpretation that Thomistic metaphysics is existentialistic and consider some of the consequences of such an assumption. Finally, we shall observe some of the implications of an existentialistic metaphysics for Thomistic epistemology and for the possibility of a science of metaphysics.

Turning to some of the more pertinent texts in the writings of St. Thomas, there appears to be little doubt that he is emphasizing both the priority and the importance of what he terms the "act of existence":

> Being itself is the most perfect of all things, for it is compared to all things as that which is act; for nothing has actuality ex-

cept so far as it is. Hence being is the actuality of all things, even of forms themselves. Therefore it is not compared to other things as the receiver is to the received, but rather as the received to the receiver. When therefore I speak of the being of man or of a horse, or of anything else, being is considered as a formal principle and as something received, and not as that to which being belongs.[8]

To be can mean either of two things. It may mean the act of being, or it may mean the composition of a proposition effected by the mind in joining a predicate to a subject.[9]

Since in everything which is there must be considered its quiddity, by which it subsists in a determined nature, and its act of existing, in virtue of which it is said of it that it is in act, this name *thing* is imposed on the thing from its quiddity, as Avicenna says . . . whereas the name *being* or *what is* is imposed from the very act of existence itself.[10]

And in holding that intellectual substances are not equal to the divine simplicity, he says: "For a certain composition is found in them by the fact that in them *being* is not the same as *what is*." [11] And: "Now, being, as being, cannot be diverse; but it can be diversified by something beside itself; thus, the being of a stone is other than that of a man. Hence, that which is subsisting being can be one only. Now, we have shown in Book I that God is His own subsisting being. Hence, nothing beside Him can be its own being. Of necessity, therefore, in every substance beside Him the substance itself is other than its being." [12]

In all of these passages, St. Thomas seems quite explicit in asserting that there is a real composition or distinction between essence and existence. That existence (*esse*) is to be taken in the participial rather than in the nominative sense. It is the to-be, the act of existing, the actuality of a thing in contrast to the essence which designates *what* a thing is rather than *that* it is. Yet as Fr. Clarke points out, there are a number of significant passages which have been interpreted as supporting the traditional or essentialistic view of metaphysics in St. Thomas.[13] And in fact, Fr. Conway is convinced that virtually all the texts quoted by Fr. Clarke in defense of his thesis are either misinterpreted or quoted out of context, and he feels that this is sufficient for the rejection of all validity to the existentialistic thesis.[14]

The interpretation of Thomistic texts has always been difficult and is never beyond dispute. The present instance is certainly no exception, and it is not my intention to adjudicate the exegetical dispute between Fr. Conway and Fr. Clarke. Rather than make such an attempt, I shall try to resolve the dispute on more dialectical grounds by exploring further the meaning and the consequences of the existentialistic view.

Returning to the meaning of the "act of existence," the "to-be-ness" of anything, the existentialistic view affirms the priority of existence over essence and asserts that there is a real distinction between the existence and the essence of any existing thing. Such a distinction is not an easy one to grasp. According to Fr. Harper: ". . . take any man of ordinary sense, and endeavor to persuade him that his existence is one thing and his actual nature or manship another thing quite distinct from the former; he would either think that you were treating him as a fool, or he would have serious doubts about your sanity." [15]

What, then, can it mean to say that existence (*esse*) is the "to-be-ness," the "act of being"? As some contemporary Thomists [16] have well pointed out, such a notion as *esse* is not required for the explanation of reality. An Aristotelian universe is adequately explained by the hylomorphic principle. But for Thomistic existentialists, since matter and form are not eternal but created realities, it is essential to introduce a third element or principle which will explain the actuality of things as formally and materially constituted, and this principle is that of the "act of existing." Such an act of existence, they hold, cannot be the form of a thing, otherwise it would be merely an essence and essences do not entail actual existence. Nor could it be matter, for matter is potentiality. As Maritain puts it: "The act of existing is the actuality of every form or nature; it is the actuality of all things, and even of forms themselves. The act of existing, which is not an essence, which is neither this nor that, and which could not be called act or energy of form or perfection if these words were univocal and could not designate something outside the whole order of essence, the act of existing is that which is most actual and most formal." [17]

That existence is not form, that it represents something over and above essence, matter, substance—in a word, that it is an element or principle added to the nature of any given thing —is brought out by another of the contemporary commentators on St. Thomas:

> What he has said, and more than once, is that existence is "formal" with respect to all that which is in the existing thing. What he means in such cases is that, analogically

speaking, existence is to form as form itself is to matter. In both cases, the relation is that of the "received to the receiver" . . . If form is supreme in its own order, existence cannot be the act of essence *qua* essence. In other words, existence does not monopolize the whole actuality of existing substance. Rather, just as essence is in potency to the act of its own existence, so also is the act of existence in potency to the formal act of its own essence. If existential actuality is higher than formal actuality, the reason for it is that the very core of reality is existence. Thus, existence may well be said to be "formal," but it is not just a form. Were it a form, it would be an essence which it is not. For, indeed, there is no essence of existence, although there is essence in each and every existence.[18]

These comments and others of a similar nature are based in good part on those passages we have already cited from St. Thomas. They are relied upon rather heavily by the Thomistic existentialists. But assuming that the interpretation of those passages by the existentialists is correct, certain observations are in order. For one thing, it should be noted that the more explicit passages from St. Thomas on this issue are rather limited in number. Also that they are to be found primarily in his expositions on the nature of God and on spiritual substances. Strictly speaking there is no definitive text on metaphysics by St. Thomas and consequently no pertinent and unambiguous statements on the general nature of reality with respect to this distinction of existence and essence. Certainly there is no empirical observation or warranty for the notion of existence (*esse*) as something other than the substantial nature of the individual thing. Rather, the notion of the act of existence is drawn first from the need to establish that God's essence is His existence, that in God there is merely a logical distinction between essence and existence, whereas in created beings there is a real distinction between the two and such beings merely participate in the divine existence. St. Thomas notes:

Moreover, being itself belongs to the first agent according to His proper nature, for God's being is His substance, as was shown in Book I. Now, that which belongs to a thing according to its proper nature does not belong to other things except by way of participation, as heat is in other bodies from fire. Therefore, being itself belongs to all other things from the first agent by a certain participation. That which belongs to a thing by participation, however, is not that thing's

[7]

substance. Therefore, it is impossible that the substance of a thing other than the first agent should be being itself.[19]

Now, what may be said in this way of Deity—namely, that His essence is His existence—is in a certain sense understandable. For in the light of a negative theology or any other method which seeks for a knowledge of God, we expect that much of this knowledge will be of so transcendent a character as to escape all determinate definition. It is when such descriptions are attempted for created beings that we immediately encounter difficulty, for their reality is designated and known by their essences and not the act of existence. With God we may simply state that He is, that He is good, wise, intelligent, etc. In such instances we are aware that we are not predicating attributes of Deity but identifying His nature with such attributes. This applies whether we are attributing the transcendentals to Him or the more determinate qualities we find in created beings, such as life, intelligence, etc. But with respect to created beings we cannot take refuge in the incomprehensible and mysterious nor look to a negative theology. Here our attempts to explain the nature of existence and to use such a term descriptively break down completely. For existence is a verb and cannot be used as a noetic category. Even a rather penetrating analysis by Gilson at this point is not very helpful. He declares:

> In the very formula, "that which is," there is the "that which," that is, the substance which is the proper receiver of existence, and there is the "is," which that substance receives. In other words, being is that which is "be-ing," in virtue of the very "to be" which it exercises. The noun *ens* (being) means *esse habens* (having esse, to be), so that it is derived from the very verb *esse* (to be). In such a doctrine the word "being" can never be used without meaning both the thing which a certain being is and the existential act which makes it to be a "being." [20]

This statement is as effective as it can be with respect to an explication of a being's existence (*esse*). By excluding from the meaning of being as *esse* any predicate or quality, by showing that *ens* means that which *has* being, we are left only with the verb "be-ing." And previously it was shown that existence is neither nature nor essence, neither form nor matter. Hence by a process of exclusion we arrive at the only possible meaning and status that existence can have, namely, that of the verb "to be."

But does this confer any real meaning upon being *(esse)*? If being in this sense is neither that about which something is affirmed or denied nor that which is affirmed or denied about *a* being, then are we not left with that which is in essence undefinable? Have we really accomplished anything more in such attempts at determination than to hypostasize the copula in the act of judgment, thinking thereby to arrive at something real and meaningful independent of that which is united in a judgment? True, a judgment should conform in some way to reality, but this should extend to the content of the judgment and not to the act of judgment. It would not be within the spirit of Thomism to infer that it is the act of judgment that constitutes the being of anything. On the other hand, it is not clear how the "existential act makes a thing to be a being," for the existential act is simply the "to-be-ness" of a being. At this point we seem not only to be multiplying entities beyond necessity but distinctions as well.

Also, in those passages from Aquinas where he is concerned to show that God is His existence, it is obvious that here there is merely a logical distinction being drawn between essence and existence rather than a real distinction which would destroy the divine simplicity. But surely in denying that there is a real distinction between essence and existence in creatures, in maintaining that their essence is one with their existence, we are in no way detracting from the Divine Omnipotence. In this connection it is interesting to note the comments of Copleston on the position of Suarez:

> Suarez . . . was convinced that the utter dependence which logically precedes any distinction of essence and existence is itself the ultimate reason of finitude. There is absolute being, God, and there is participated being. Participation in this sense means total dependence on the Creator. This total dependence or contingency is the reason why the creature is limited or finite. Suarez did not explain finitude and contingency in terms of the distinction between essence and existence: he explained this distinction, in the sense, that is, in which he accepted it, in terms of a finitude which is necessarily bound up with contingency.
> . . . Moreover, by refusing to admit a "real" distinction between essence and existence in the creature Suarez avoided the danger of turning existence into a kind of essence. Cancel the creature's existence, and its essence is cancelled too.[21]

To maintain only a logical distinction between essence and existence in creatures does not imply that their existence is in any way infinite and no longer received from the Divine existence. Certainly a doctrine of analogy would allow us to assert that the existence enjoyed by creatures is similar to that of the Divine existence without subverting the relationship of dependency of creature upon Creator. Creatures would still *have* their existence and would not *be* their existence. Such an assertion is quite compatible with a principle of logical distinction and does not necessitate that a real distinction between existence and essence in creatures must follow.[22]

In our opinion the type of solution offered by Suarez is conformable to the texts of St. Thomas. But even assuming for the moment that the existentialist interpretation of St. Thomas is correct, such an assumption, we believe, would raise epistemological difficulties of such magnitude as to leave little hope for the validity and the future of an existentialist metaphysics.

To put the matter as simply as possible, the epistemological issue facing us is the knowledge we can have of existence. How and what do we know of this act of existence, of the to-be-ness of anything? Again, the problem is placed before us rather vividly in some remarks of Gilson concerning the attitude of Suarez toward the real distinction of essence and existence:

> Their fundamental mistake, Suarez says, is that they are begging the question. When he asks them: "How can you know what existence is?" they answer by positing the distinction of essence and existence as a condition for such knowledge. But how can we distinguish essence from existence, unless we already know what existence is?
> . . . What he would like to know is *quid existentia sit:* what is existence, as if existence could be a *what*. Having himself identified being with its essence, he could not possibly find in it an *is* which, if it is, is neither an essence nor a thing. This is why Suarez does not know existence when he sees it. Hence his strange metaphysical notion of being.[23]

But perhaps Suarez cannot know existence because he cannot see it! How much more strange a metaphysical notion of being that escapes all definition and description. This seems even more apparent from some contemporary descriptions of our knowledge of existence. Thus Maritain speaks of existence as a concept and declares that "metaphysics uses the concept of existence in order to know a reality which is not an essence, but is the very act of existence." [24]

And more obscurely: "Thus existence is made object; but
. . . in a higher analogical sense resulting from the objectising of
a trans-objective act and referring to trans-objective subjects that
exercise or are able to exercise this act. Here a concept seizes
upon that which is not an essence but is an intelligible in a
higher and analogical sense, a super-intelligible delivered up to
the mind in the very operation which it performs each time that it
judges, and from the moment of its first judgment." [25]

Summing up this analysis he states that "all this simply
amounts to saying that the concept of existence cannot be detached from the concept of essence." [26]

In another work he moves away from this contention that
existence is a concept to what appears to be quite the contradictory: "True existentialism is the work of reason. The act by
virtue of which I exist and things exist, transcends concepts and
ideas; it is a mystery for the intellect. . . . The act of existing is
indeed the very object of every achievement of the intellect, that
is, of judgment. It is perceived by that intellectual intuition,
immersed in sense experience, which is the common treasure of
all our assertions. . . ." [27]

It may be that Maritain is unable to decide whether existence
(esse) is a concept or an object of intuition because he is
still vacillating between traditional Thomism and the new existentialistic Thomism. In any event his position is not a clear one.
Actually the Thomistic texts on the knowledge of existence (esse)
seem to be clearer. St. Thomas frequently declares that the first
intelligible known by the intellect is being. This is a logical
priority granted to being, for a thing can be known only in so far
as it is in act, hence to be, to be in act, must be known prior to
all knowledge. "That is prior in idea which is first conceived by
the intellect. Now the first thing conceived by the intellect is
being, because everything is knowable only inasmuch as it is
actually. Hence being is the proper object of the intellect, and
is thus the *first intelligible,* as sound is the first audible." [28]

Such being (*quod est*) is wholly indeterminate (thus not
an essence nor a proper object of knowledge) and has its source
in the physical universe surrounding us. The knowledge of being
on this level is analogous with the knowledge of the sensible and
the intellectual. Just as the knowledge of the singular and sensible
is imperfect and potential to that which is universal and more
perfectly known through the intellect, so the knowledge of being
in this first phase is imperfect and less known than the knowledge
of being as *quod quid est.* In other words, to use the formula of

St. Thomas, *proprium objectum intellectus est quod quid est.*
Strictly speaking, the proper knowledge of the intellect then is
not being in this wholly indeterminate sense. For being and its
transcendentals, although logically prior to a knowledge of
quiddities or essences, do not convey so much a knowledge to
the intellect as they provide a means of making such knowledge
possible. Perhaps being as the first intelligible may be said to
represent the *a priori* element in a Thomistic theory of knowledge.

It is at this point that Maritain's remarks upon the intellect's
intuition of being (*esse*) has a certain validity, although intuition
is a term rarely used by St. Thomas and then only analogously.
Certainly it should not be used in a literal sense here, for although there may be a sensory intuition of things, there is no
immediate and certain knowledge of being as such. There is an
awareness, an apprehension of being in our knowledge of things,
but being becomes known to us only through essences or quiddities, and such knowledge that the intellect obtains is never direct
or immediate but rather is always subject to that which the intellect is able to derive by way of phantasms from sense experience.
The Thomistic maxim that there is nothing in the intellect which
was not previously in the senses would apparently rule out rather
effectively any direct knowledge of being as such, for the proper
object of the intellect is being, in the sense of essence or quiddity.[29]

Father Regis points out that in several passages St. Thomas
explicitly states that essences or quiddities are the proper objects
of the intellect.[30] That the knowledge of a thing is consequent
upon the knowledge of being is brought out in the following
passage:

> In our intellect there are some concepts naturally known by
> all, such as the concept of being, one, good, etc., which the
> intellect uses as a starting point in seeking the *quiddity of
> each thing,* just as it seeks knowledge of conclusions starting
> from self-evident principles. This happens either with the
> help of what is perceived through the senses, as e.g. when we
> conceive the quiddity of a thing by means of its sensible
> properties; or by means of the spoken words we hear . . .
> or again, by means of truths revealed to us in faith.[31]

Being as first known, as the beginning of the knowledge of
quiddities, is neither a proper object of knowledge nor does it
terminate, as Gilson believes, in the perfection of all knowledge.
Speaking of the definition of truth as the adequation of intellect

and thing he remarks: "The definition is correct to the extent that the object of intellectual knowledge is supposed to be the thing *(res)*. In this case there is adequation between the intellect and the *essence* of the thing, but if truth is supposed to consist in a perfect correspondence between the known intellect and a known *being,* then it no longer suffices for knowledge to reach the essence. The act of being itself has to be reached, in and through essence, because this act is what makes the essence itself to be a being." [32]

But it is difficult to see how we can reach a perfection of knowledge, a "perfect correspondence between the knowing intellect and a known *being,*" when we cannot even describe this knowledge that reaches beyond all essences. Nor does it help to say that "the human intellect thus reaches, even in its most natural operations, a layer of being more deeply seated than essences." [33] For the metaphor of "a layer of being" would seem to presuppose some unknown differentiating principle within being. The metaphor appears to clarify the problem but actually renders it more obscure. Also, to conclude that "the act of being itself has to be reached in and through essence, because this act is what makes the essence to be a being," seems to beg the whole question. For to know that it is the act that makes the essence to be a being would seem to imply that I have a knowledge of *esse* as an essence. Certainly if it remains something hidden and obscure it cannot validate an existentialist metaphysics.

Hence if being as *act,* as *esse,* is distinct from every essence or quiddity and even distinct from the first known aspect of being as *quod est,* there still remains the problem of what can be known, if anything, of this mysterious something which is denominated *esse* or the to-be-ness of anything. Whether being in this sense can be considered an object of the understanding, and as such known, is a moot problem and one which, in our opinion, defies understanding. Even one of the most ardent supporters of this conception of being as *esse* admits that it is not something subject to demonstration: "What has divided the Thomist school from the other schools of theology, ever since the 13th century, is a general reluctance to conceive the act of being *(esse)* as a distinct object of understanding. To tell the whole truth even the so-called "Thomists" have been and still are divided on this point. No such disagreement would take place if the presence, in things themselves, of an act in virtue of which they can be called 'beings' were a conclusion susceptible of demonstration." [34]

[13]

Perhaps if being or the act of existence cannot be known through abstraction or demonstration, a more adequate solution might be found in something resembling a phenomenological approach, such as is contained in the remarks of Dondeyne when he speaks of *esse* as a "primary indubitable datum which human knowledge can never completely elucidate nor effectively escape in this life." And he remarks further: "In modern terms, one might say that this datum is nothing other than the experience of 'existence' as inseparable from the existential orbit that is ours. It is the experience of my existence as myself-with-others-in-the-world. . . . This existential experience constitutes our participation in being, our way of *having a part of and taking part in* the being that surrounds and bears us. It is at once the experience of our presence to being and of the presence of being to us." [35]

However, this notion of an "existential experience" seems not only difficult to adapt within the context of Thomistic thought and expression, but also poses added difficulties associated with the articulation and communication of such an "existential experience." Particularly when such an experience is structured into a philosophy which stresses the subjective values of knowledge. Also, it would narrow the conception of being or existence to human existence which is central to contemporary existentialism. Whether this is the correct approach or not, it is still not Thomism. Conceivably Thomism might be drastically modified so that existence would lose its universal character and become restricted to the existential categories, such as dread, fear, anxiety, etc., which are so typical of present-day existentialism. Some may regard this as constituting the correct approach for Thomism to take. But if it should be taken, explored, and validated within the context of what is proper to a Christian philosophy, the net result would be an even more revolutionary form of Christian philosophy and one that would lose entirely its Thomistic heritage and cast. Actually, the evaluation and the very future of what has been termed a Thomistic existentialism hinges not merely upon all the foregoing considerations, but also upon the consequences of a Thomistic existentialism for metaphysics itself. In conclusion, therefore, let us look to some of the implications of Thomistic existentialism for the possibility of a science of metaphysics and the future of a Thomistic metaphysics.

We have already observed that Thomistic existentialism is a metaphysics of existence rather than essence. St. Thomas himself indicates that the subject of metaphysics is simply *being as being.*[36] As Fr. Owens points out, however, there are no distinctive texts written by St. Thomas which are exclusively devoted to the problems of metaphysics nor is there a distinctively metaphysical procedure. And it is by no means clear as to the precise meaning St. Thomas would give to this definition of metaphysics as the science of being as being. The contemporary commentators on St. Thomas are more explicit, but apparently quite divided. Thus Gilson declares: "In metaphysics, the science of being *qua* being must be understood as the science of that-which-has-an-act-of-being." [37]

On the other hand Fr. Harper states: "For, as Being in its nominative acceptation is equivalent to Essence, it may truly be said that Metaphysics is the science of Essences. It is well to remind the reader once more, that Being or Essence which constitutes the object of Metaphysics, does not *exclude,* as neither does it *include,* existence. It prescinds from existence altogether." [38]

But Fr. Hart declares:

> Because it has for its proper object the natures or essences of all actual or conceivable beings from the common standpoint of the exercise of their respective acts of *to be* . . . we may define metaphysics very simply as that ultimate philosophy which considers all beings (essences) simply as being (existing) —*ens qua ens, ens ut sic,* "that which exists simply as existing." The first "being" in the definition is a noun meaning *essences* or natures of things. It is the material object of metaphysics, its matter. The second "being" is the present participle of the verb "to be" and hence means existing or exercising the act of *to be.* It represents the unique formal object of metaphysics, by which it is distinct from all other ways of knowing reality.[39]

And as Fr. Conway puts the matter: ". . . the basic point at issue is the metaphysical primordiality of the necessary and immutable order of essences, *whether viewed as actually existing or merely possible,* over the contingent order of actual finite existences. It is precisely for that reason that traditional Thomists maintain that the object of metaphysics is primarily the intelligible order of essences in so far as they prescind from their contingent actuality." [40]

Both traditional Thomists and existential Thomists accept the validity of metaphysics. They would insist that it is a science in the Aristotelian sense and that it is concerned with necessary

[15]

and immutable truths. This entails that as a science metaphysics must prescind from that which is individual and contingent because the individual, contingent thing is neither necessary nor immutable. However, it is extremely difficult to see how this position can be maintained from the existentialistic point of view. Fr. Clarke argues very ably in defense of this point of view. He declares:

> The permanent core of truth in the Aristotelian principle is that a science should deal only with necessary and ultimately constitutive, or nonaccidental, predicates. Now if the proper object of metaphysics is precisely existent being as existent, and if the substantial act of existence is according to St. Thomas the most intimate and most fundamentally constitutive element of every real being as long as it remains existent and the object of metaphysics, then the legitimate requirements for a science are met in a genuine, though analogous way.[41]

But the phrase "as long as it remains existent" by emphasizing the temporal seems to negate the requirement of necessity and immutability of metaphysical truth. Also, there is the apparent admission in the phrase "though analogous way" that metaphysics is not a science in its own right but only analogously a science. If metaphysics is a science merely in an analogous sense, it would then lose its character of being necessary and immutable.

Fr. Clarke does not help his case any by adding immediately after the above statement: "In other words, the true answer to this difficulty is simply to refuse to accept its premises in a rigid and univocal sense and to insist that the too narrow Aristotelian concept of science be enlarged to make room for the new *sui generis* element of reality brought into focus for the first time by St. Thomas and for the *sui generis* character of the science of metaphysics resulting from the nature of its object." [42]

For actually the new *"sui generis"* principle, instead of enlarging the Aristotelian conception of science, introduces added difficulties into the notion of an existentialistic metaphysics. One of these is the problem of our ability to know this *sui generis* principle—this act of being, this to-be-ness. As we have already observed, Thomistic epistemology holds that intellectual knowledge consists of essences abstracted by the active intellect from the phantasms presented to it through the senses. There is no intellectual knowledge, either intuitive or abstract, of singular individual existents. Since existence is not an essence it cannot be a subject of intellectual knowledge.[43] Nor is it a means to the distinction and differentiation of things in our knowledge, for as St. Thomas points out: ". . . things are not distinguished from one another in having being, for in this they agree. . . . It remains, then that things are different because they have diverse natures, to which being accrues in a diverse way." [44]

To follow a somewhat different but related epistemological approach to the nature of being, since all knowledge is expressed in the form of propositions following acts of judgment, we might ask whether metaphysics as the science or knowledge of being as being is concerned with the subject, the predicate, or the copula of the proposition. On an existentialist interpretation, being (esse) could not be the subject of a proposition for then it would be in individual substance. Nor can it be the predicate because being is not a predicate nor is it subject to differentiation. After a close analysis Fr. Owens points out that what we mean by the act of being corresponds best to the verb "is" rather than to the subject or the predicate, but, as though anticipating the difficulties this would lead to, he reaches the more modest conclusion that "the Thomistic being as being rather cuts across the logical elements of a proposition, and cannot be expressed adequately by any one of them." [45]

Fr. Hart puts the issue more confidently and forcefully (but less wisely we fear) when he says: "The act of judgment is the intellect's supreme function to which all its other acts are subsidiary. It is this judgment act that points to the intellect's own proper and unique object, namely, *the being of things simply as being*. The intellect can say: A Nature or essence *is,* that is, it exists." [46]

And Gilson is not very helpful when he says: "Since *is* does not mean either a predicate or a subject, its meaning must needs be wholly contained in itself." [47]

None of these comments really sheds any light on the nature of being (esse) as such. It is difficult to see how we can possibly establish a science of metaphysics on that whose meaning is "contained in itself," on that "to which the intellect points as its own proper and unique object," or on that which expresses "inadequately the Thomistic notion of *being as being*." Not only does such a notion of being escape all conceptualization and thus scientific knowledge, but, being precluded from conceptualization, whatever knowledge might be had of it would be impossible to communicate to others.

[17]

The analysis of being in terms of a Thomistic existentialism leaves us with virtually a meaningless conception of being. To contend that metaphysics must concern itself with the act of being and construct a science on this notion is to play into the hands of the logical positivists. For to say that metaphysical statements are nonsense because they cannot be verified in our experience is but one step further removed from the contention that being (*esse*), the object of metaphysics, is neither an object of understanding nor of sensory intuition but rather a veritable mystery for the intellect as Maritain has asserted.

And to say that metaphysics points beyond the subject and predicate of the proposition to the act of existence signified in the copula is to move beyond knowledge to what is ostensively merely the act of knowledge. With this approach the temptation might then occur to become more concerned with the linguistic analysis of the act of judgment, to develop perhaps some contemporary version of Thomistic Analysis!

On the other hand, for Thomistic existentialism to move in the direction of existential phenomenology would add to its difficulties rather than explicate its position. For Thomism is still basically rationalistic, whereas existential phenomenology is essentially a protest against reason. To treat of existence as a mystery and something exclusively human, to regard truth as subjectivity, and to exploit and give priority to all the categories of the irrational is completely foreign to the spirit of Thomism. Certainly no Thomistic science of metaphysics could be established upon such a foundation.

To conclude, Thomistic existentialism cannot move in the direction of logical positivism—it must accept the meaningfulness of being. It should not move in the direction of existential phenomenology. To continue to assert the priority and necessity of a metaphysics of existence leaves the scope of metaphysics hopelessly narrow, for neither a principle of participation nor any manner of analysis will add anything to the meaning and determination of existence as such—the inner nature of existence will continue to elude us. But the conclusion of our study is not as elusive. Contemporary Thomistic existentialism must abandon a metaphysics of mere undifferentiated existence and return once more to an essentialistic metaphysics with all the diversity and wealth of being contained in a world of essences, actual and possible.

NOTES

1. Albert Dondeyne, *Contemporary European Thought and Christian Faith* ("Duquesne Studies, Philosophical Series," No. 8 [Pittsburgh, Pa.: Duquesne University Press, 1958]) , p. 29.

2. See particularly the work of Remy C. Kwant, *Encounter;* William A. Luijpen, *Existential Phenomenology;* F. J. J. Buytendijk, *Phénomenologie de la Rencontre;* etc. For the effect of the language of existential phenomenology upon Thomism, note the following statement from Fr. Luijpen's *Existential Phenomenology* in which he is describing the meaning of existential openness: "But the existential openness which is characteristic of man can be satisfied fully only by the encounter with God. St. Thomas adds that we cannot bring about this encounter by our own powers, since God is beyond the range of human possibility. Encounter with God can only be the fruit of God's initiative, that is, in theological terms, of supernatural grace" ("Duquesne Studies, Philosophical Series," No. 12 [Pittsburgh, Pa.: Duquesne University Press, 1960], p. 163) .

3. Cf. the work of Merleau-Ponty, who opposes "being" to "existence" and uses the latter term as more proper to the being of man.

4. *Op. cit.,* pp. 159–160.

5. E. Gilson, *Being and Some Philosophers* (Toronto: Pontifical Institute of Mediaeval Studies, 1949) , p. 167.

6. Charles A. Hart, *Thomistic Metaphysics* (New York: Prentice-Hall, 1959) , p. 7.

7. Thomas Harper, *The Metaphysics of the School* (New York: P. Smith, 1940 [1879]) , I, 72. See also P. Dezza, S.J., *Metaphysica Generalis* (Rome, 1945) , pp. 24–25; and in general the works of Gredt, Marquart, Grenier, Gardeil, et al. For a full account of the pros and cons of this continuing debate see also the excellent article by Fr. W. Norris Clarke, S.J., in *Progress in Philosophy* (Milwaukee: Bruce, 1957) , pp. 61–90.

8. *Summa Theologica,* I–I, q. 4, a. 1, ad 3, trans. Fr. Laurence Shapcote, O.P., ed. Anton Pegis (New York: Random House, 1945) . Subsequent quotations from this work will refer to this volume.

9. *Ibid.,* I–I q. 3, a. 4, ad 2.

10. *In I. Sent.,* d. viii, q. 1, a. 1.

11. *Summa Contra Gentiles,* II, chap. 52, 1, trans. James F. Anderson (New York: Hanover House, 1956) .

12. *Ibid.,* II, chap. 52, 2.

13. *Op. cit.,* pp. 73–75.

14. James Conway, "The Reality of the Possibles," *The New Scholasticism,* July 1959, pp. 331–353. For Fr. Clarke's reply see "The Possibles Revisited," *The New Scholasticism,* January 1960, pp. 79–102.

15. *Op. cit.,* p. 104.

16. Notably Gilson.

17. Jacques Maritain, *Existence and the Existent,* trans. Lewis Galantiere and Gerald B. Phelan (New York: Pantheon Books Inc., 1948), pp. 36–37.

18. Gilson, *op. cit.,* pp. 170–171.

19. *Summa Contra Gentiles,* II, chap. 52, 8.

20. *Op. cit.,* pp. 178–179.

21. Frederick Copleston, S.J., *History of Philosophy* (Westminster, Md.: Newman Press, 1953), III, 376–377.

22. Some Thomistic existentialists support their position with an appeal to the principle of participation. The origins of this principle are found in Plato, and more recently the principle has been prominently developed by Fr. Louis B. Geiger, O.P., in his work *La participation dans la philosophie de S. Thomas* (Paris: J. Vrin, 1943). Fr. Hart terms this principle "the foundation of all Thomistic metaphysics" (*op. cit.,* p. 8). Whether such a principle contributes significantly to an existentialist metaphysics and adequately represents Thomist thought is still a moot question. For a recent discussion of the principle see Fr. Clarke's "The Meaning of Participation in St. Thomas," *Proceedings of the American Catholic Philosophical Association,* XXVIII (1952), 147–157. See also the remarks of Gilson (*op. cit.,* p. 104) where he observes that the Suarezian position is equally acceptable with the existentialist position to Christian theology, but that philosophically both positions cannot be true.

23. *Op. cit.,* p. 105.

24. *Op. cit.,* pp. 33–34.

25. *Ibid.,* pp. 23–24.

26. *Ibid.,* p. 25.

27. "A New Approach to God," *Our Emergent Civilization,* ed. Ruth Nanda Ashen (New York: Harper & Brothers, 1947), p. 281.

28. *Summa Theologica,* I, q. 5, a. 2. See also *Summa Theologica,* I–II, q. 94, a. 2c; *Summa Contra Gentiles,* II, chap. 83; *De Veritate,* q. 1, a. 3.

29. Fr. Louis Marie Regis notes in his recent text, *Epistemology* (New York: Macmillan, 1959, p. 513), that St. Thomas affirms the dependence of the intellect upon phantasms in more than 1,500 places.

30. *Ibid.,* p. 514, n. 141.

31. Passage from *Quodlibetales* quoted by Fr. Regis, *op. cit.,* p. 290.

32. *Elements of Christian Philosophy* (New York: Doubleday, 1960), p. 231.

33. *Ibid.,* p. 232.

34. *Ibid.,* p. 131.

35. *Op. cit.,* p. 147.

36. For the various textual references see Joseph Owens, "A Note

on the Approach to Thomistic Metaphysics," *The New Scholasticism,* October 1954, pp. 454–476.

37. *Elements of Christian Philosophy,* p. 233.

38. *Op. cit.,* p. 70.

39. *Op. cit.,* p. 4.

40. *Op. cit.,* April 1959, p. 141.

41. *Op. cit.,* pp. 79–80.

42. *Ibid.*

43. See Gilson, *Being and Some Philosophers,* p. 204: ". . . being is not and cannot become an object of purely abstract cognition. What is conceivable is the essence of *a being,* not that of *being."*

44. *Summa Contra Gentiles,* II, chap. 26, 3.

45. *Op. cit.,* p. 475.

46. *Op. cit.,* p. 3.

47. *Being and Some Philosophers,* p. 196.

STANLEY H. ROSEN

THALES: The Beginning of Philosophy [1]

τοὺς ἀνθρώπους . . . διὰ τοῦτο ἀπόλλυσθαι,
ὅτι οὐ δύνανται τὴν ἀρχὴν τῶι τέλει πρόσαψαι·

Alcmaeon, *Diels,* Fr. 2

INTRODUCTION

From the time of Xenophanes, mankind has been criticized for its tendency to conceive of the eternal in its own image. It is this tendency which Hegel praises as the necessary first step of a development culminating in the completion of man through an appropriation of the eternal: the form of the divine and the human becomes one and the same, through the unfolding of *Geist* as essential Time. In the nineteenth and the twentieth centuries, the Hegelian conception of the completeness of essential History or Time (and so of its formal determination and intelligibility) was discarded, but Hegel's interpretation of Time as the form or image of man has been retained. As a result, we now conceive of the eternal in our own image, but in such a way as to transform it into motion, change, history. This new version of anthropomorphism differs from its predecessors only in this respect: those who subscribe to the new version are convinced that they have freed themselves from the bondage of eternity, from the gods and the Ideas. If, as in Hegel's thought, man becomes a god, man *replaces* god in post-Hegelian philosophy, which is an entirely more radical matter. To say with Nietzsche that "God is dead" is to say that the divine has been replaced by the human. If God is dead, it makes no sense to speak of man as a god (except perhaps as a corpse-god) : the *Ubermensch* is delimited, and therefore defined, by a godless eternal return, eternal *in* its turning and so as the unending denial of eternity.

Nevertheless, the unending denial of eternity may be distinguished from an eternal denial of the end: from what is called the infinite progress or, less optimistically, the infinite change, of history. Nietzsche's "eternal return" is in a way intelligible as the infinite repetition of Hegel's uniquely unfolding History: all that was, will be ever again. Nietzsche is closer to Hegel, one may say, than to contemporary historicism, at least in this: he sees a limit or a boundary to becoming, for only the limited could occur again and again. If Hegel's thought is a circle revolving in its place, Nietzsche has set the circle rolling through the void. Nietzsche's successors, however, have set into motion what he himself left at rest. In removing the limit or boundary to becoming, they accelerated the rate of change; freed from its restrictions, "history" began to move ever more rapidly, until, indeed, in some quarters, man seemed to be standing still, to have lost sight of what was no longer visible because of its speed. The disappearance of the boundary between the local and the eternal led first to the illusion of the eternity of the local and then to what we may call *localism*. In this sense, the circle of history has been transcribed: we find ourselves in a postphilosophical condition which shares the deepest belief of the *prephilosophical* condition, the belief that, in Pindar's words, "custom is the king of all men." [2]

This juncture of the post- and prephilosophical conditions, even if fortuitous and partial, may serve at least to pose the opportunity once more to begin to reflect upon the origins of reflection itself. It may be that the coincidence of the beginning and end implies a condition inherent in the very form of the circle, which is not itself, as condition, in motion. It may be that the obsession with change and custom is itself neither changing nor conventional but the expression in human terms of nature as the *principle* of motion. And it may even be that a motion is visible, not merely by means of its direction or end, but through the *stillness* of the forms of the elements of that motion. In any event, the remarks which follow embody some reflections upon the possible meaning of the concept of the "beginning" or "origin" of philosophy. My point of departure, in beginning this reflection, was to consider the sayings commonly attributed to Thales, in order to determine *what they must mean, if they are indeed the beginning of philosophy.* It should be apparent that what I have done is to interpret Thales rather than to reproduce him. Thales spoke his own words, and our task is to understand the essence of these words in language which is both our own and adequate to his *logos.* Such an effort is no doubt hazardous, but in my view less hazardous than merely to reiterate the traditional accounts of Thales' sayings or to interpret them without admitting to ourselves that we are doing so—and perhaps interpreting them on the basis of assumptions which are themselves drawn from contemporary rather than Thalenic times.

In order to identify its beginning, we must have come to a decision as to the nature of philosophy. For this reason, the problem of the origin of philosophy is not at bottom a "scholarly" one. Or rather, the scholarly approach to the problem is itself already philosophical. To give one important example: F. M. Cornford claims that philosophy originated in a gradual evolution of religious mythology, whereas Karl Reinhardt denies such an interpretation altogether, and considers philosophy proper to begin in logical or metaphysical speculation.[3] By what criteria are we to choose between these rival accounts? The scholarly credentials of both men seem to be unimpeachable, their research laborious, and their documentation copious. Even were we to duplicate their professional attainments, we should have performed only an external act. At the radical moment, we should have to say, "I have studied the evidence as fully and as fairly as possible; I have tried to see the speeches as they were meant, and I take them to demonstrate the following. . . ." In this moment we act, not as scholars, but as philosophers. In other words: the origin of philosophy cannot be "scientifically" documented because what counts as evidence depends upon the philosophical assumptions governing our conception of scientific scholarship. But let us assume that the evidence *had* been scientifically gathered and had been agreed upon as being evidence. We should still have to understand it, and there is no neutral point, external to philosophy, upon which the "objective" investigator may build the foundations of philosophy itself.

We cannot, for example, say, "Thales was the first philosopher, and he speaks a modified version of religious language; therefore, Cornford is right, and Reinhardt is wrong." We should first be required to answer at least two questions: (1) how do we know that Thales *is* a philosopher, and (2) how can we demonstrate that the religious language used by Thales was intended by him to be understood in a religious sense? The answer to the first question manifestly depends upon our philosophical understanding, upon what we understand philosophy to be. It cannot be answered by scholarly evidence because it is not a question of scholarship. Consequently, "orthodox" opinions about the philosophical significance of scholarly evidence are no more compelling than the philosophical arguments upon which these opinions are based.[4] It is sad but true that we can never know whether Thales was a philosopher unless we ourselves are philosophers. If we place our trust in traditional agreement upon his status, we are behaving in a manner which is just the opposite of the traditional account of philosophers as men who examined tradition or put it to the torture. If on the other hand it is self-evident that Thales was a philosopher, one may say that philosophy is itself unnecessary. But the character of Thales' remarks could hardly be said to be self-evident, unless we mean by "self-evident" the findings of common sense or of modern science; in either case his words (if they are his words) are self-evidently untrue. If by this criterion it is self-evident that Thales is *not* a philosopher, one requires a demonstration or defense of the viewpoint from which he is so condemned, and this brings us back into philosophy.

As for the second question: the orthodox or conventional method for deciding whether a man is religious consists in asking him, if he is accessible to direct questioning, in reading his books if he is not, or in studying reports of the man's views if he wrote no books or if they have been lost in time. It should be easy to see that this conventional procedure possesses no philosophical status whatsoever. To begin with, men may lie and have often done so. They may lie for compelling social and political reasons, from pride, or even from mere playfulness. This possibility has been stated publicly throughout antiquity and even before the time of Thales; it suffices to mention the wily Odysseus. Plato and Cicero among the ancients treated at length the ambiguous status of religious professions by the wise men of the past, and the theme has been much discussed throughout the history of European thought.[5] But apart from the possibility of lying, which may strike some as frivolous, let us consider the point raised by Reinhardt in his work on Parmenides. Reinhardt reasonably reminds us that, at the beginning of philosophy, there could not have existed a previously developed set of technical philosophical terms.[6] Therefore, the first philosophers were forced to make use of available language to express their meaning. Since religious language was normally employed to speak of exalted matters, they understandably used religious words, albeit in a new sense, for their own purposes. Reinhardt continues by showing how the context in which these terms are employed rules out the possibility that they possess an orthodox or even a religious sense. He is primarily concerned with Parmenides, but why can we not adopt his suggestion in the case of Thales (or anyone else)?

If we reject this suggestion, and argue that the speech of Thales and the other pre-Socratics is just like that of modern savages or of primitive people who are just emerging from a condition of totally mythical belief, then we are asserting a *philosophical* rather than a scholarly or scientific view. We mean to assert that, regardless of the identity of the first philosopher, he *must* have spoken like Thales, and Thales' speech is like that of the cited primitives, a development from religion to philosophy. It should at least be mentioned that this hypothesis can *never* be empirically confirmed and is therefore scientifically worthless. In the first place, the superstitions of modern primitives do not "congeal" into philosophy by themselves; if any "primitives" go on to become philosophers, it is by leaving their tribes and studying at universities staffed by men who have already been formed by the prior emergence of philosophy. Nevertheless, philosophy must have begun prior to the existence of universities, so let us assume that a savage in some primitive tribe now accessible to us suddenly became a philosopher, entirely unassisted by outsiders. How could we prove that what he had done was merely to develop, step-by-step, the superstitions of his tribe? Exactly the same problems would arise as have already been mentioned. We might ask him (perhaps in the form of a questionnaire submitted by a team of sociologists), but he in turn might be as scornful of our ignorance as Francis Bacon, among others, tells us that the ancient philosophers were. Or he might share Socrates' views on the utility of noble lies, or the belief of Odysseus that one's speech should be relative to the kind of man one is addressing, or Spinoza's conviction on the advisability of speaking *ad captum vulgi*. We should once more be thrown back onto our philosophical understanding of philosophy.

It is in this vein that I ask the reader to consider the following reflections upon Thales. Thales, whoever he may actually have

[27]

been, is for us philosophy making its appearance in human history. The question of the historical accuracy of the opinions and sayings attributed to him is in one sense unanswerable. What I should rather wish to do is to justify this attribution by discussing the philosophical content of these fragments. I believe that this content is accessible to us, despite the ambiguities, the encrustations of history, and the reason for this belief constitutes my understanding of the nature of philosophy. Thus, a complete interpretation of Thales' sayings would be identical with a complete philosophical speech, even if Thales' sayings were in themselves incomplete, provided only that they were indeed philosophical. Philosophy, if it is an activity distinguishable from others, with a form and so an essential nature, must originate essentially (as distinguished from accidentally or historically) for each of us as it did for Thales. I shall therefore restrict my interpretation to the problem of the necessary conditions which make possible the origin of philosophy. I shall try to suggest how the speeches of Thales explain themselves by explaining the possibility of philosophical speech. In one sense, the speeches are self-explanatory; that is, they are, as reproducible by us in our own thinking, essentially intelligible apart from their original historical context. If this is so, the question at once arises why we should read Thales at all and not rather simply ourselves. Therefore, my interpretation must begin with a defense of the study of history.

THE DESEDIMENTATION OF PHILOSOPHY [7]

It is sometimes the case, and especially since Descartes, that men turn away from history and "l'étude des lettres . . . me résolvant de ne chercher plus d'autre science, que celle qui se pourrait trouver en moi-même, ou bien dans le grand livre du monde," to discover philosophy within themselves.[8] It might seem to some that they are thereby following the example of Thales by turning directly toward ideas, questions, and answers in their eternal purity rather than in their historically encumbered form. And so, in addition to the excitement aroused by the notion that one may himself originate philosophy, it seems that the first philosophers live again in the return of the modern thinkers to the self. Of course, the self in question must be something more than the

[28]

conclusion of one's personal history.[9] But even if the self is transformed into the transcendental ego or absolute Geist, the danger arises that such a transcendental or absolute structure may be historically modified, perhaps even a historical construction. For the structure of the self is extracted from self-introspection; and do not selves present themselves to themselves as historical crystallizations, as *results* of the forces of time? We must ask how it is possible to grasp a self whose structure permits the presentation within it of eternal ideas, a structure which underlies, but is sedimented over by, history. We must decide whether "the origin of philosophy within the self" means the discovery by each self of the *same* philosophical origin, or whether it means the "original" creation by each self (as a new moment of history) of a fundamentally new philosophy. How, for example, can one recognize the origin of philosophy within one's *own* experience? Is not the experience of the individual a microcosm of human history, with the same ambiguities and contradictions that serve as obstacles to precise identifications? Entirely apart from the difficulty of locating the self, who of us could dare to say, after an honest assessment of his own experience, "For me, philosophy began with event X or condition Y at age Z." And is such an "honest" assessment of our experience even possible? Do we not carry it through in the distorted light of our already past, and so determined, experience? Is not our view of our own past therefore *obscured* by its progressive accumulation or sedimentation? At the moment when we begin to wonder about the origin of philosophy, have we not already become alienated from this origin by the relativism of historical experience?

In view of these objections, it has often been suggested that a theory concerning the "origin" of philosophy is nothing more than a conjecture about history, with the added inconvenience that the theory is about one's *own* history, of which we have the least possible perspective or "objectivity," and about which we are most certain to be biased. If we nevertheless insist that philosophy originates in a specific way, which is elaborated by us as individual philosophers, we find that there is a wide variety of such theories and that the variety is characterized, not simply by disagreement, but by contradiction as well. If we say that all these theories are correct (or irrefutable), we say in effect that philosophy has *no* origin because it originates everywhere and in every way: this is to say that its origin is *ex nihilo,* since "everything" is obviously "nothing." Contemporary "sophisticated" relativism, which takes for granted the impossibility of establishing the relative satisfactoriness of philosophical positions—or, more radically, of conceptions of philosophy—terminates in the conclusion that Being, which is defined by our philosophical language, is Nothing.

On the other hand, to substantiate our own theory, we should have to refute those of our contradictors. Each contradictor represents a historical generation, and each generation mirrors the confusion of history as a whole. We face the same problem: we should have to know what philosophy is, which is to say that we should have to know our own history. Is not our own history, despite the illusions of propinquity, considerably more obscure than human history? What else did Thales mean when, in reply to the question, "What is hardest of all?" he answered, "To know thyself." And when Socrates, in obedience to this maxim, advises us to study the psyche by way of its more easily visible paradigm, the *polis,* have we understood anything if we dismiss his words as a "fallacy of composition?" [10]

Perhaps the most usual counterobjection to the difficulties just sketched would be something like this: I agree that knowledge with respect to the origin of philosophy is included within knowledge of what philosophy is. I further agree that I am circumscribed by my own experience and that this propinquity raises difficulties of perspective. But philosophy is in fact nothing more nor less than the thoroughgoing attempt by the individual to understand his own experience and whatever that experience touches upon or implies. On the basis of this attempt, each philosopher arrives at a decision concerning the origin of philosophy which he must defend against opposing decisions as best he may, i.e., on the basis of how he understands his experience of himself and of others and, so, of how he understands not merely his own decision, but the reasons or experiences of others, whereby they are led to reject *his* decision. What more could any man do?

On the face of it, this counterobjection seems eminently sane. The problem lies in understanding more precisely what it means. Has it not merely accepted our earlier diagnosis of the issue of origin? We have now been told that the decision with respect to the origin of philosophy not only faces the difficulties which were previously raised, but is intrinsically impossible to make because it depends upon a never-ending attempt to certify the soundness of our understanding of experience. We are like hoops rolling through history, with each hoop itself a micro-history, obsessed with questions of origins which cannot be found, because of the circularity of our obsession. To ask, "How does philosophy originate?" is to ask, "What is philosophy?" If we do not know what philosophy is, we cannot locate its origin. If knowledge of what philosophy is depends upon a sound understanding of our experience, then we are perpetually immobilized by problems of historical interpretation. If philosophy *is* just this perpetual immobilization, then again, *it has no origin,* except perhaps in so far as consciousness deteriorates into self-consciousness. Then philosophy is just the decay of non-Being into the Becoming of Being. It is the bracketing of the "non" by a progressively more paranoiac Historicism. That is to say, there is no such thing as philosophy except in the sense of helplessly self-critical *opinion.* But why is one opinion better than another? Again, a matter of opinion. *De confirmatione non disputandum est.*

If man is radically historical, then self-understanding is historically conditioned understanding of history. Within this decisive perspective, the original objection against the relevance of the historical investigation concerning the first philosopher is a historical error. The definition of the self can only be accomplished by establishing the perimeter of the self's history, that is, by the invocation and articulation of the historical continuum within which the self emerges and through which its experience is illuminated and obscured. In this case, the statements of the first philosopher, say Thales, are of decisive relevance with respect to our own statements about philosophy. Indeed, they are even *more* relevant to the question of the origin of philosophy than are our own statements concerning that question, in as much as it is precisely the statements of Thales which originate the philosophical mode of historical existence. We exist philosophically relative to Thales. We see the world from the perspective illuminated by Thales' vision: Thales' vision is the origin, not just of philosophy but also of the world which we see, and so of us as philosophical selves.

Suppose, however, that man is *not* radically historical. If the roots of the self are embedded in an eternal order, in an ahistorical ground of history, then self-discovery depends upon a perception or grasping of, which is also a standing upon, this ground. Such a discovery requires a movement away from history, a moving through history to its conditions. But if the self is the theatre of philosophy, then the movement is also toward philosophical origin. As independent of historical modifications, the origin of philosophy is *ex nihilo;* its source is timeless, without location,

[31]

always accessible to man just because it is nowhere, utopian, ideal. Thales, therefore, makes manifest this *ex nihilo* origin better than any subsequent philosopher because in him the origin is less obscured by historical sedimentation. That is, the obscurity of Thales is not historical, but entirely philosophical. In order, however, to rid ourselves of the detritus of history, we must master it; we cannot return to the pure obscurity of Thales without recovering him from impure obscurity. And, since we are ourselves determined by history, such a recovery cannot be accomplished merely from our individual resources. We must think our way to the conditions of the self by thinking our way back to Thales. The accuracy of self-knowledge must be confirmed by an understanding of Thales.

THE DISCOVERY OF NOUS

Diogenes Laertius records the views attributed to Thales by tradition; they may be summarized as follows: [11]

1. "According to some, he was the first to call the soul deathless."

2. "Some say that he was the first to speak of *physis.*"

3. "He established water as the beginning of everything, and made the cosmos ensouled (*empsychon*) and full of daimons."

4. "*Nous* is quickest of all things, for it runs through everything."

5. "He said that there is no difference between life and death."

6. "When asked, 'what is the most difficult of all things?' he replied, 'to know thyself.' "

If we interpret Thales either as a primitive mythologist or as a primitive physicist, it is immediately apparent that the notions attributed to him possess little if any *philosophical* significance, unless we assume (as most modern men, following Descartes, would do) that philosophy begins with the discovery of physics, although this discovery is initially couched in mythical terms.[12] Even then, of course, Thales would have only minimal substantive importance for philosophy. However this may be, philosophy is, under this assumption, if not physics itself, what we may call "meta-physics" (to be distinguished by the hyphen from what is traditionally known as "metaphysics"), or speech *about* physics. But speech about physics must have a foundation which is not merely physical, for the simple reason that matter is itself *mute:* electrical charges, for instance, *qua* electrical charges, are unable to measure themselves and speak of the results.[13] Meta-physics is based upon a monist materialism which cannot account for its own speech. The relationship between physics and meta-physics depends upon a *metaphysical* structure within which matter and speech find their place: their possibility and their intelligibility. The speech about the metaphysical structure is not the same as meta-physical speech, and the difference between these two kinds of speech is recognized (if not understood) by those who themselves speak of the "mythical" character of Thales' speech. But the conception of "myth" here employed is itself determined by the acceptance of scientific or meta-physical speech; in referring to the "mythic" elements in Thales' speech, such an interpretation refers to the imperfectly or partially *scientific* character of his speech.[14] That is, the "mythic" element represents the incursion of ignorance into a recognition of the road to knowledge, if not of knowledge itself. Therefore, in so far as Thales speaks "mythically," he is speaking *nonsense* (since attempts to interpret this nonsense make use of concepts themselves derived from the scientific conception of significant thought). Mythical speech is therefore speech about nothing, and the transition from mythical to scientific-philosophical speech is a transition to a speech about something.[15]

According to this view, talking about the mythical component in Thales' speech is just a polite way of referring to his ignorance. To the extent that he is *not* ignorant, he is assumed to be speaking meta-physically or scientifically. But meta-physical mythology cannot explain the *difference* between knowledge and ignorance which it purports to discover. Assuming that Thales is really a physicist [16] (or a meta-physicist), the difference between his (physical) knowledge and (mythical) ignorance cannot be explained in terms of the physical structure which his meta-physical speech attempts to describe. The correspondence between metaphysical speech and physical structure can only be measured from a third point, or rather from a third structure which encompasses the two, and is therefore a *superstructure.* Knowledge is not explained by ignorance nor ignorance by knowledge. But the two are explained by an understanding of their difference, and an

[33]

understanding of their difference lies in the recognition that the *condition* for the possibility and intelligibility of each *is* the superstructure encompassing the two. In other terms, the difference between knowledge and ignorance is that between a positive and negative quality. If there were nothing else, the positive and the negative would cancel each other out, or in effect the negative would negate the positive. The presence of different qualities is proof of the reality of their difference, and so of the "difference" between them and it. The recognition of the reality of the difference is the origin of philosophy as the recognition of the accessibility of the superstructure within which knowledge and ignorance themselves become evident.[17]

If the "mythological" interpretation of Thales is correct, then he is certainly not a philosopher. For we may certainly say that philosophy, as the love of wisdom, *cannot* be present where there is no recognition of that which makes such a love possible (namely, the recognition of the difference between knowledge and ignorance). Such a recognition is *ex nihilo* in an ordinary, even common-sensical understanding of instantaneous illumination. One does not see that one is beginning to see: when we begin to see, at any moment of this "beginning," we *are* seeing. So we cannot recognize by stages or degrees the reality of the difference between seeing and not-seeing, between knowledge and ignorance; in order to recognize this difference, one must *already* know it. In order to see its "origin," one must be able to see, *one must be seeing*. The mythological interpretation is at bottom identical with the interpretation of Thales as a physicist or a meta-physicist. The "mythologist" assumes the emergence of philosophy from superstition or religion to be a partial repudiation of mythical in favor of physical speech because he is at bottom convinced of the identity between philosophy and meta-physics. Whether or not the ostensibly "mythical" elements in Thales' speech are really mythical elements depends, in effect, upon whether he is speaking, or attempting to speak, as a meta-physician rather than as a metaphysician. Thales is considered to be by intention a meta-physicist because of Aristotle's somewhat professorial remarks (which seem to reveal his lack of interest in Thales) on Thales' image of water. But if Thales understands water in the "physical" sense as the term is used by modern scientists (although not by Aristotle), what are we to make of his speech about souls? If the speech about souls is just myth, then Thales is not a philosopher. The question is whether Thales is using mythical terms in a new, philosophical sense (analogous to the procedure which Reinhardt attributes to Parmenides) and so, in consequence, whether he is performing the same liberating or originating function with respect to the vocabulary of the physical universe (as must be the case if he is a philosopher and if Reinhardt is correct about the "origin" of philosophy). The philosophical dimension of physical terms used to discuss the cosmos need not conflict with what we may call their "scientific" dimension; indeed, we may say that, at any epoch, no term can be *scientific* if it does not also have a philosophical dimension not simply identical with its function in describing the extended universe. And it is an error to assume that all speech about the physical universe is speech about physics in the modern sense, or meta-physics; we fall into this error by assuming that the use of mythical terms is in every case an adherence to myth, only partly mastered by the recognition of science. In other words, we interpret Thales in a circular fashion, a circle which has as its center our own acceptance of the identity between science and philosophy.[18] This is inadequate, not because it is circular but because it makes philosophy impossible by transforming it into an ungrounded metaphysics. Thales' cosmology may well be what tradition tells us it is, but it hardly follows from this that his cosmology is identical with his philosophy or that we have adequately understood the traditional account of his cosmology.

We must therefore see whether the notions attributed to Thales can be so interpreted as to make possible the recognition of the reality of the difference between knowledge and ignorance and, so, of the origin of philosophy. It goes without saying that our words will be different from those of Thales: but their difference must be contingent, or due to the difference in the time and not to the difference in the nature of philosophy itself. Our interpretation is perfectly justified in translating the speech of Thales into another idiom in order to make his thought more explicit; it is not justified in distorting the thought itself. We may begin by observing that there is a connection between the discovery of *physis* and the attribution of deathlessness to the psyche, and that this connection indicates the recognition for which we are searching. When Thales says that there is no difference between life and death, he means that the superstructure of the difference between knowledge and ignorance is independent of, or unchanged by, the phenomenal or historical appearance of the psyche. The becoming of the psyche, its physical manifestation as an incarnate soul, is the temporal reflection of the being of the

[35]

psyche, its form or intelligibility, and so its áctuality. The identity of life and death is the difference between Being and Becoming, and this difference is the superstructure within which Being *and* non-Being (represented by knowledge and ignorance) find their place and are revealed as intelligible.[19] Being and non-Being, when mixed, produce Becoming (opinion) : the three are separate from each other, or different, and the articulation of their differences is the superstructure of the Whole.[20] The superstructure of the Whole is reflected in the psyche of man, the structure of which (the psyche) mirrors the articulations of the superstructure. Not only does the psyche imitate or "become" the superstructure (and, through this becoming, achieve immortality in the form of wisdom) , but the superstructure itself, as the paradigm of the human psyche, is a kind of psyche.

Thus the identity of life and death means not merely that Becoming differs from Being, but also that life is death and death is life: Being, in opposition to Becoming, is dead; but this death constitutes true life, for it is the total actualization of all possible forms.[21] This total actualization is expressible in an *arché* or principle: water is the *arché* of all things. Thales comments upon this principle by adding that the world is *empsychon* and full of daimons. There is a connection between water as the *arché* or *physis* of all things and the psyche. World or cosmos is an order; it cannot be characterized by the fluidity of water. The sense in which water is the structure of the world-order stems from the structural analogy between water and psyche or *nous*.[22] Order in the world stems from the immanent presence of psyche and daimons: daimons are everywhere because the ordering principle in the cosmos is *psychic:* e.g., it is the metaphysical superstructure (describable only by analogy with the human psyche) which is the condition for the possibility of meta-physical speech about physics. Water becomes the structure of the world-order by submitting to the immanent *nous*-psyche which is the form of order. And water is, not matter in the ordinary physical sense, but the content of intelligible form, the principle of the differentiability of intelligibility.[23]

If we wish to understand Thales by means of an Aristotelian interpretation, then we cannot simply think of water as prime matter and psyche as form. Water is more like psyche than like matter; it is not a prime but a *formal* matter, or another way of expressing form-psyche itself (though both are analogies or metaphors with reference to the actual superstructure of the Whole) :

there is a fluidity in psyche itself, *an ability to assume all forms.*[24] As Thales says, *nous* runs through all things; it is quickest of all. This means that everything is (in principle) intelligible because of the fluent character of psyche. Water is the middle-term between *nous*-psyche and *anthropopsyche,* and, regarded in this sense, it is the expression of the *difference* between them: that is, a metaphorical expression of the superstructure of the Whole, within which cosmic order is structurally analogous to the articulations within the order of man's psyche. Water is both psyche and nonpsyche; it is the *same* and the *other,* the representation of the differentiability (and so of the intelligibility) of the structure of the Whole. The compatibility between *nous* and man's psyche, the ability of the latter to assume all forms generated by *nous,* makes philosophy possible. Thus, the cosmos is daimonic because it is in principle intelligible. The principle of this intelligibility is expressed in the deathlessness of psyche and so in the identity of life and death. Just as the daimonic is deathless, so too is the order within the cosmos of *nous* a "fluent" or fluid order, in that it assumes all forms (and so there is movement within the eternal) ; so, too, is the psyche of the knower "deathless" in so far as it also assumes the forms of the cosmos by virtue of its quickness or fluency. The deathlessness of the psyche is philosophy, made possible by the accessibility of the cosmos to the psyche, because of the common aqueous content of the cosmic *nous* and the human psyche.

"Becoming" (Being differentiated by non-Being, or the difference of one intelligible structure from another) is the serial appearance of cosmic psyche assuming its infinity of forms, as perceived by the man whose own *nous* runs through these forms simultaneously with the cosmos.[25] To understand the cosmos or order, i.e., to philosophize, one must go beneath this Becoming (into the difference) , one must ignore the apparent difference between life and death; and so, one must ignore oneself as a historical, mortal self. Philosophical concentration upon the self (i.e., the psyche) results in a laying-bare of the structure of the self as the visible reflection of the structure of the cosmos (and of the difference between the two, which is the superstructure of Totality) . The hardest of all things is to know oneself, because one's historical self is the most insistent obstacle to the perception by human *nous* of the cosmic order, in terms of which the self is alone intelligible. The *arché* of this order, fluid psyche, is indifferent to the historical peculiarities of our individual lives. It is

[37]

deathless: in order to be perceived, it makes us die as individuals because it requires us to run through *all* of its forms. It requires us to imitate its fluidity and so to cease to be *ourselves.* Thus, philosophy *originates* in death; or, as Socrates put it, philosophy is the preparation, i.e., the beginning or origin of death. And so the relevance of history to philosophy is contained in the need to desedimentize the psyche of its temporal accretions in order to begin to die philosophically. Thus, philosophical death, although dependent upon history, is essentially different from it and from the history of philosophy (and the reality of the difference between the two is the superstructure of the Whole) .

Deathlessness (Thales' equivalent of Socratic death) is the eternal swiftness of *nous.* And it is an *immediate* swiftness; it has no "beginning" but is immediately present: it is *we* as historical selves who are *absent,* i.e., not present before the eternal presence of *nous.* The cause of our absence is the difference between us and eternal *nous,* and we become present to philosophy as we enter into the difference. Philosophy is the selfless expression of the swiftness of *nous* within the aperture of the historical self, opening into the difference between the self and *nous,* running forever, in *some* historical self or other, throughout the cosmos.[26] Philosophy is *ex nihilo* because it is *ab initio:* philosophy has no origin, but is rather itself the origin or *arché* of every finite activity.[27] In the same sense that there is no origin for philosophy, we may say that there is no *need* for philosophy. Philosophy is the origin of need because, as the love of wisdom, it is the expression of the eros whereby the psyche imprisoned in each of us strives for completion by escaping from the "life" of history into the "death" of the eternal running of *nous.* Within the perspective of history, philosophy is the *arché* in the same sense as water: it flows most swiftly, it assumes all forms, it permeates everywhere. In the words of Pindar, "water is best."

Aristotle, after interpreting the doctrine of Thales in a physical-materialist sense, makes the following observation: "There are some who believe that the ancients who lived long before the present generation, and who first theologized, supposed something similar about *physis;* for they made Ocean and Tethys the fathers of genesis, and water what the gods swore by, which the poets called *Styx:* for the most honorable is the oldest, and what one swears by is the most honorable." [28] The eternity of water is traditionally associated with the divine: water is the *arché* because it is *empsychon* and full of gods. From the very beginning, the

[38]

excellence or divinity of the origin or principle made manifest the relationship between philosophy and religion. How we understand this relationship depends upon the way in which we interpret the statements of the first philosopher. It depends upon our understanding of the psyche, and so, upon how we interpret *religio:* scrupulousness, exactness, respect for the sacred. In conclusion, let us recall the viewpoint of Socrates, who, in the *Theaetetus,* repudiates the explicitly theological interpretation of water because it leads to the dissolution of all things.[29] The theological interpretation, in other words, is the mytho-physical interpretation which we have already noticed. For Socrates, the problem of philosophy is to cultivate the divine madness, which comes *ex nihilo* like a spark that sets fire to the psyche. The problem is to mix the fire of philosophy with the fluidity, the fluency, the water, of the psyche. To "cultivate" (*colo, cultus*) is both to "adorn" and to "worship." The cultivation of divine madness is then the adornment and worship of the highest part of the psyche, the part which is *afire,* so that the fire is not extinguished by the very fluency and quickness of the psyche. The proper mixture of fire and water depends upon the proper adornment of worship. The "religion of the philosophers" resists that disgust for the sacred which is a consequence of antitheological ire, but it replaces the *creatio ex nihilo* of the world in the theological sense with the *ex nihilo* appearance of philosophy as the eternal accessibility of the world.[30] Philosophy replaces the chaos of religion with the water of Thales. It is not God, but Thales, who hovers over the waters. Thales is the purification of history by philosophy, the transformation of the waters of chaos into the waters of *nous.*

NOTES

1. I am indebted to the editors of *Arion* for permission to reprint this article, which appeared in a slightly revised version in the September 1962 issue.

2. Or at least in the interpretation given to these words by Herodotus.

3. F. M. Cornford, *From Religion to Philosophy* (Harper Torchbook, 1957) ; Karl Reinhardt, *Parmenides* (Klostermann, 1959) .

4. It is possible to deny that there is any such thing as an orthodox or generally accepted interpretation of *any* great thinker. One need consider only the history of Aristotelian scholarship, for example,

to say that no such agreement exists in his case, and in the same sense, the soundness of Aristotle's remarks about Thales can hardly be self-evident.

5. For extensive documentation, see Leo Strauss, *Persecution and the Art of Writing* (Free Press, 1952). As examples of discussion by philosophers on this topic, compare Francis Bacon, *Advancement of Learning* (Spedding, Ellis, and Heath), Vol. 6, pp. 217, 290, with J. J. Rousseau, *Les Rêveries du Promeneur Solitaire*, Quatrième Promenade. Montesquieu's views on the political origin and function of religion among the ancients are too well known to require references. Whether he was correct or not, depends precisely upon how we understand the speeches in question.

6. *Op. cit.*, pp. 23–24. For the priority of logic and metaphysics to physics and religion, see pp. 74 ff., 250 ff.

7. It will be apparent to the reader that, in the few remarks of this section, I am making use of the notion of desedimentation developed by Husserl in *Die Krisis der Europäischen Wissenschaften* (Martinus Nijhof), e.g., pp. 372 ff.

8. Descartes, *Discours de la Méthode*, ed. Gilson (J. Vrin, 1947), p. 8.

9. Consider the closing words from the Introduction to Hobbes' *Leviathan* (Oxford, 1947, p. 10): "But let one man read another by his actions never so perfectly, it serves him onely with his acquaintance, which are but few. He that is to govern a whole Nation, must read in himself, not this, or that particular man; but Man-kind: which though it be hard to do, harder than to learn any Language, or Science; yet, when I shall have set down my own reading orderly, and perspicuously, the pains left another, will be onely to consider, if he also find not the same in himself. For this kind of Doctrine, admitteth no other Demonstration." Compare Kant's comments on the empirical procedure of Locke in the *Kritik der Reinen Vernunft*, B118–119. Bacon's initial emphasis upon history as the source of human, worldly, or practical wisdom (*op. cit.*, pp. 102, 190, 359), even further, of the importance of "particulars" for metaphysics, to which he adds, "knowledges are as pyramides, whereof history is the basis" (p. 221), passes through the critical purification in Kant to re-emerge in Hegel.

10. The Socratic analogy between the *polis* and the psyche is based upon a structural isomorphism which is not itself a stage of historical development, but the condition for the possibility of historical development. Thus the Socratic concern for political phenomena is in a sense analogous to the Kantian concern for sensible phenomena: for Kant, the categories of pure reason, although not themselves sensible, are "visible" in and through their presence in (the structure of) sense-objects; one must move "upwards" from the empirical or phenomenal world to the conditions for the possibility of this world; and in this sense one cannot see these conditions directly or in themselves. For Socrates, the structure of the psyche cannot be seen directly or in itself, but only through or in political experience (that is, in the fundamen-

tally political structure of experience). The latter constitutes a Whole or Totality of possible human experience: politics is the architectonic art, and the *arché* of politics is the psyche.

11. I. 22–44; Diels, Vol. I, pp. 67 ff. Perhaps I should emphasize that my argument is in no way dependent upon, or concerned with, the historical authenticity of these attributions. I wish rather to deal with the significance of such attributions.

12. The pre-Socratics were by no means exclusively interested in cosmology, as is sometimes maintained; we know from such sources as Herodotus and Plato of their concern with politics (See Plato, *Protagoras*, 343 ff.). Diogenes Laertius says of Thales: Μετὰ δὲ τὰ πολιτικὰ τῆς φυσικῆς ἐγένετο θεωρίας. (I. 23)

13. The common sense difference between matter and speech is presumed by the controversy between materialism and idealism. The same arguments might be employed on behalf of either position. Thus one may speak of the two positions, inspect them and contrast them, only because of a prior distinction which renders either position more than questionable. The question, then, is not whether electrons think, but rather of the difference between the electron and its thought. I should wish to argue that the distinction between matter and thought is the form of ordinary experience as such. No "fundamental" explanation of the form of experience which renders that form inexplicable (the form upon which the fundamental explanation is itself based) can be considered a satisfactory explanation. This necessarily oversimplified statement of the issue may be more adequately seen when compared with the essentially Socratic conception of "saving the phenomena." In classical materialism, this question is discussed in terms of the distinctions between the form and mere extendedness of matter on the one hand, and between motion and rest on the other. It also underlies the problem of the swerve of atoms, necessary for the creation of the cosmos, but not intelligible in terms of the properties of the atoms alone (e.g., the necessity of physical reality is derived from an initial chance).

14. Contemporary thinkers, under the influence of science (in the modern sense of the term) even when they fancy themselves most sympathetic to the prescientific myth-makers, mean by "myth" not rational speech of a specific kind, but rather primitive or *prerational* speech: "Myths are original revelations of the preconscious psyche, involuntary statements about unconscious psychic happenings. . . . Not merely do they represent, they *are* the mental life of the primitive tribe . . ." C. G. Jung, *Introduction to a Science of Mythology* (Routledge, 1951), pp. 101–2. For another influential contemporary account of myth from a scientific viewpoint, see Ernst Cassirer, *The Philosophy of Symbolic Forms*, Vol. II: *Mythical Thought*. As to why contemporary men have become so obsessed with myth, a word which is now applied to science, religion, and art, consider M. Heidegger, "Die Zeit des Weltbildes" (*Holzwege*, Klostermann, 1952), p. 70. For a philosophical discussion of the meaning of myth in Plato, see Gerhard Krüger, *Einsicht und Leidenschaft* (Klostermann, 1948). Krüger's argument is perhaps too "religious," but, when corrected from a balancing, secular viewpoint, it

becomes most suggestive, and may be applied by extension to the pre-Socratics.

15. Thus the movement from myth to science is a secular imitation of the "movement" from nothing to Being involved in the Judaeo-Christian *creatio ex nihilo*.

16. That is, a physicist in the modern sense of the term. When considering Aristotle's interpretation of Thales as a physicist, it is essential to consider also Aristotle's concept of *physis*. See *Metaphysics* 1014 b16 ff. *Physis* is not just growth or formed motion, but it is also the *arché* of growth. It is true that Aristotle's account of Thales is limited to a consideration of water as the material cause. But it does not follow that an *Aristotelian* consideration of Thales must be so restricted. (I do not imply, of course, that my interpretation is Aristotelian.)

17. In the formulation of this point, as in many other ways, I am indebted to Alexandre Kojève for conversations concerning the Hegelian notion of the difference between Being and non-Being. I do not, however, believe that this notion is *restricted* to Hegel, and have tried to state it in terms of the origin of philosophy simply.

18. On the hypothesis, frequently made in our time even by "philosophers of science," that science is itself a form of myth or that key scientific terms are mythical, there must obviously be a difference, *within* rational discourse, between scientific myth and nonmythical science or between scientific and nonscientific myth. Further, if science and philosophy are identical, then it is meaningless to speak of a philosophy *of* science.

19. Being and non-Being are compatible and coactual; neither is derived from or subordinate to the other. We need not look merely to Hegel for such a notion. It is implied in the parricide committed by the Eleatic stranger in Plato's *Sophist* at 240 e1 ff.: the stranger points out that, in order for falsehood to be possible, we must think that non-Being somehow is, and that Being somehow is not. If non-Being is actual, then it "is" in a sense, and, since it "is" not Being, Being is less than itself, and so in a sense is "not." Not only do Being and non-Being make each other intelligible; we must ask *how* it is that both are intelligible.

20. The trinity of Being, non-Being, and Becoming (analogous to the trinity of One, Unlimited, and Many in the *Philebus*) does not alter the fact that, between any pair of opposites, the superstructure is manifest as the reality of their difference. (Aristotle at least touches upon this notion when he observes that knowledge is knowledge of contraries. Being and non-Being are contraries in the sense that Becoming is neither the one nor the other.) This superstructure is none of the three, and presents a *different* problem from that of the relationship between Being and non-Being as manifested in Becoming. Or, put differently, the difference between Being and Becoming *is* non-Being, and the difference, *qua* superstructure, is indeed *nothing*, neither Being nor Becoming.

21. Greek philosophy begins with the concept of an intelligible cosmos and therefore of an isomorphism between psyche and cosmos.

It is interesting to compare with this initial version of Greek thought its final form in the words of Hegel: . . . die Idee ist selbst die Dialektik, welche ewig das mit sich Identische von dem Differenten, das Subjektive von dem Objektiven, das Endliche von dem Unendlichen, die Seele von dem Leibe, ab- und unterscheidet, und nur insofern ewige Schöpfung, ewige Lebendigkeit und ewiger Geist ist. (*Encyclopädie*, par. 214) For Hegel, the isomorphism is developed into a concrete actuality: Greek philosophy is mediated by Christianity, and man becomes God.

22. On the other hand, the difference between water and psyche-*nous* is the actuality of the Whole, within which each element exists and is intelligible and which may be itself expressed only through concrete or partial analogies.

23. Compare perhaps Aristotle's conception of *pneuma* as the divine matter, akin to the element of the stars, within the sperm, and the carrier of psyche: e.g., *Generation of Animals*, 736 b30.

24. For a Greek expression of the "theological" view that not everything is thinkable, see Xenophanes, e.g.: ἔφη δὲ καὶ τὰ πολλὰ ἥσσω νοῦ εἶναι. (Diogenes Laertius, I. ix. 19). This is connected with his view that πᾶν τὸ γιγνόμενον φθαρτόν ἐστι καὶ ἡ ψυχὴ πνεῦμα.

25. For a development of Thales' position, one must turn to his student, Anaximander: οὗτος ἔφασκεν ἀρχὴν καὶ στοιχεῖον τὸ ἄπειρον, οὐ διορίζων ἀέρα ἢ ὕδωρ ἢ ἄλλο τι. καὶ τὰ μὲν μέρη μεταβάλλειν, τὸ δὲ πᾶν ἀμετάβλητον εἶναι. (Diogenes Laertius, II. 1) The Whole is an eternal order of changing parts; the boundless is the infinity of forms through which *nous* runs. See also, Plutarch, *Strom.* 2 (Diels, p. 83): ἀπεφήνατο δὲ τὴν φθορὰν γίνεσθαὶ καὶ πολὺ πρότερον τὴν γένεσιν ἐξ ἀπείρου αἰώνος ἀνακυκλουμένων πάντων αὐτῶν. Thus is described the eternal (and so cyclical) procession of forms: *phthora* "comes to be" when the form is invisible (because of the rotation of the circle); and because of the cyclic progression, the form (as distinct from its material manifestation) cannot be destroyed.

26. See Heracleitus, Fr. 50 (Diels): οὐκ ἐμοῦ, ἀλλὰ τοῦ λόγου ἀκούσαντας ὁμολογεῖν σοφόν ἐστιν ἐν πάντα εἶναι·

27. Cf. Heracleitus, Fr. 60, 103 (Diels).

28. *Metaphysics*, 983 b6 ff.

29. 180 c7 ff. According to Socrates, the ancients concealed their actual meaning from the mob by speaking in theological terms. This actual meaning is the metaphysical conception of the universe as fluid or moving. If, however, my interpretation of Thales is correct, then the theological doctrine (or its public metaphysical counterpart) cannot be attributed to him; his own thought comes considerably closer to that of Socrates than is indicated by Socrates himself in his own "poetic" statements.

30. See Heracleitus, Fr. 18 (Diels) for a beautiful expression of the classical conception of the "religious" aspect of philosophy: ἐὰν μὴ ἔλπηται, ἀνέλπιστον οὐκ ἐξευρήσει, ἀνεξερεύνητον ἐὸν καὶ ἄπορον· For a modern statement of the same issue by a famous atheist, see Nietzsche, *Jenseits von Gut und Böse*, par. 58.

[43]

ALBERT TSUGAWA

THE INTENTION OF A WORK OF ART

The title of this essay is not meant to imply the personification of works of art, although only conscious beings can be said to have intentions; nor is it meant to be a solecism.

We would shake our heads at someone whose chief reason for praising a certain Botticelli turned out to be "the human and compassionate eyes of the centurions' horses, which reminded her of the eyes of her own Great-Uncle Graham, whom she had adored as a child," or whose chief delight in a Crivelli madonna was "the peaches in the back-ground [that] looked exactly like marzipan." [1] A critic with greater solemnity points out certain features in the work he is discussing as irrelevant or extraneous because they are contrary to (or do not add to) the tenor of the rest of the work considered as a unity. He may boldly open a discussion of a novel by announcing that *"Hard Times* is not a difficult work; its intention and nature are pretty obvious." [2] He presupposes then that we can discover what the nature of a particular work of art is and that we already know the answer to the question "What does it mean?" What is the meaning of *King Lear* that allows us to condemn a happy ending in which Lear lives on, surviving his patrimonial folly, and in which Cordelia

[45]

and Edgar are happily married? [3] Why do we say that the movements in Schubert's Symphony in C are not too long,[4] or that the melody of the aria "Che farò senza Euridice?" is too happy and mellifluous to fit into the opera (*Orfeo ed Euridice*) at this point? [5] In these contexts, it is not to the point to argue (few critics do so) that Shakespeare originally wrote the play with quite a different ending or that Schubert did not think the movements any too long.

These arguments are all familiar. They refer to different sorts of features and in important ways have distinct logical functions. (One way in which they differ will be elaborated upon in relation to the concept of form.) But they are all alike in presupposing that in some definite way we can know or come to know what the work of art is and what it intends to be. That arguments of this pattern are much stronger than any I have mentioned so far is seen most clearly in Shaw's idiosyncratic defense of his Fabian interpretation of the *Ring of the Nibelung*. Wagner said that, although he did not know it while he was composing the work, after the event he could see clearly that all along Siegfried was meant to be the embodiment of a Schopenhauerean pessimist.[6] What Shaw says is clear enough. "These works must speak for themselves: if The Ring says one thing, and a letter written afterwards says that it said something else, The Ring must be taken to confute the letter just as conclusively as if the two had been written by different hands." [7] In discovering the nature of the intention of the work of art, then, the intention of its creator, or its psychological motives (albeit unconscious), or its social origins, though all interesting and illuminating, are logically irrelevant. They are logically irrelevant because if what we find to be the intention of the work of art and the latter should conflict, so much the worse for the latter.

When we say that a work of art is autonomous we may mean two different things: (1) that it can "stand on its own"; that we can "get to know it for what it is"; or (2) that it is unique; that nothing else in the world is like it (as against the doctrine that there are art types). I want to show in this essay how the notions of autonomy and uniqueness are crucially related; and how the assertion of autonomy (a doctrine that is related to the slogan "art for art's sake") is based on a sort of formalism. I believe that there is much truth to this slogan, but I want to show the limits of formalism as an esthetic theory and the modification that the theory requires to be wholly satisfactory.

[46]

I

When a critic discusses a work of art, he may refer roughly to two different sorts of things: (1) its referents (meaning or sometimes content); and (2) its formal features. The distinction is an uncomfortable one, and at first glance one would not expect the doctrine of autonomy to make much sense in connection with the representational arts. It might even seem wrong-headed to begin with this dichotomy at this late date in the history of esthetics when we all know that form follows content and that in successful works of art, the two must be organically united; and when we further know that with the prevalence of nonobjective art, if anything *is* important at all, it must be the formal expressiveness of a work of art. But the case is not so simple; for it is possible to insist on the importance of the meaning of a work of art. We say that a work of art need only *be*. Yet even when a work of art is formally perfect and beautiful, it is possible to criticize it as being thin—that it has no depth. In asking that the work of art amount to something, we seem to be looking for something that the work of art (which is one thing) refers to (which is another thing). And we find that it is not easy to explain what we mean when we say that form must be united with content.

I wish to show how we have passed from autonomy to formalism. And I do this by taking the territory of representational art first—assuming that once I have done this, we will be able to move about on the map of the nonrepresentational arts readily enough (where the doctrine of formalism makes complete "sense," we say, anyway). In order to show the road travelled, it would be enough to indicate some of the features of the terrain that drives one, even while discussing the referents of a work of art, to resort to its formal features to bring off one's critical arguments. The following selected points, though very brief, must serve as the sign posts along the way and show why formalism is so convincing.

On one prevalent theory of meaning, a meaning relationship is at least a relationship between two entities.[8] Thunderclouds mean rain; a rash means measles; breaking a treaty means war; the *fleur-de-lys* means the kingdom of France. The relationship may be simple or complex. In the case of works of art, meaning or referring to something is not always the same as having a content, although content is usually understood as something representational. Many works of art with recognizable events and objects (surrealist novels and apocalyptic paintings) are still very opaque

[47]

in their intentions. A nonobjective work of art may mean something and not refer to anything. But at least it might be said in favor of the dependence of representational art on the world of nature that, when we praise a portrait for capturing the subtle psychological traits of the sitter or a novel for capturing the mood and feeling of a locale, the very term we use, "capturing," suggests that what it captures (and thus what is contained *in* the work of art) was nevertheless originally "outside" of it. The very notions of identity and similarity presuppose the knowledge of an original (at some point in the past) —or else there would be no resemblance. An imaginary landscape does not resemble anything. But if we can praise a novel or a painting for its realism or its verisimilitude,[9] the entire logic of this manner of talking presupposes our world and our knowledge and experience of this world.

(1) In the course of his discussion, a critic may point out a factual error in a work of art, inept distortions in the representations, an unconvincing aura of local color, etc. In being able to make such comments, the critic obviously must have been forearmed. The fact that we will not find a beach in Bohemia is something that we learn not from *The Winter's Tale* (III, 3) but from our geography lessons. The clue to the fact that a painting is about Columbus planting the flag of Castille on the beach of his first island is not contained in the painting.[10] Titles of works of art (when it is not the name of the form) usually indicate their "subject matter" by way of a brief résumé of its content. It would be convenient to discuss the representational content and meaning of a work of art in terms of the notion of the title of a work of art. Persons inexperienced with works of art frequently ask for a brief summary, a verbal paraphrase, of the content or the intention of a work of art. It is not always easy to give such a summary. But to refuse to give one often leaves us with the suspicion that perhaps we have failed in our comprehension of the work. We know that such a suspicion is unwarranted. Still works of art come with "subject matter" titles; and in what follows, I go on to discuss the function of the titles of works of art, keeping in mind that works of art may refer to something and yet may be unsummarizable.

Clues given by titles are often helpful. Though they reach us from outside the work of art, their primary function is to aid the viewer in adjusting himself to the work of art. It facilitates matters to have works come to us with names already attached to them like *Pride and Prejudice*, "Trojan Women Setting Fire to the Grecian Ships" (Claude Lorraine), "Romeo in the Vault of the Capulets" (Berlioz), for we can then channelize our responses appropriately. Such clues are, of course, extra-esthetic. They are dispensable. They can, for example, get lost. There are names of sitters which have been misplaced, and books of emblems and iconography have disappeared. Artists often find that the title of a work of art hardens a viewer's response. If he fears this strongly, then he sometimes simply calls a poem "Poem" or "Song" (even giving it the name of its form, like villanelle, ballade, etc.), and a painter his canvas, "Study No. 5." Since such titles are minimal in their suggestion, the reader is forced into paying maximum attention to the work of art itself in order to get an inkling of what it is about. Any artist first of all wants the attention to be focussed in this way. No matter what the subject matter, we need to discover what is meant there; and to do so is in accordance with the doctrine of autonomy.

Cutting down on the connotation of the title is, however, not the only way to compel the percipient to focus attention on the work. One can confuse the audience. The following experiment was performed by a musician who wrote a ballet that he called a "dance-satire." He provided elaborate, complicated and obscure program notes on the proceedings of the music and the dance. The notes were long; of such a length that few in the audience were able to read them through before the performance. And even if someone had done so, he could not have understood much of them on first reading. The result was that a great number of persons shrugged their shoulders and relaxed, fortunately having decided that, since the notes were so perplexing, the ballet and the music must yield up their own meanings.[11]

(2) To remove the title or in any other way to insist that the viewer forget that there are external references to a work of art is not to reduce the meaningfulness of a work of art. Though a work of art may have no specific subject matter statable in a title, it may still resemble something or other. Just because an object looks like something, we do not say, thereby, that it ceases to have an interest and a meaning of its own. If a person examining a work of art claims that it is faulty because some factual element in it is mistaken or that the figure represented is distorted, the discussion need not end there. He might be asked to see if esthetically, in terms of the intention of the work itself, it works or not. What matters is the fit. Then whether what is presented in the work accurately resembles anything or not becomes irrelevant.

(3) If a work of art has "intrinsic meaning," it must be intelligible on its own. What if the work of art is opaque like the poetry of Ezra Pound or barely looks like anything at all? To

what extent can we afford to dispense with meaningfulness (where we expect it) and frustrate the respondents? To take a case in point, how can we respond to a passage of poetry like the following?

> . . . nor that *Nyseian* Ile
> Girt with the River *Triton,* where old *Cham,*
> Whom Gentiles *Ammon* call and *Libyan Jove,*
> Hid *Amalthea* and her Florid Son
> Young *Bacchus* from his Stepdame *Rhea's* eye:

> (*Paradise Lost,* IV, 275–79)

The allusions are not easy; one needs the aid of notes. And sometimes we are given notes, such as that by Marianne Moore for the following:

> If 'compression is the first grace of style,'
> you have it. Contractility is a virtue
> as modesty is a virtue.

She lets us know [12] that the quotation is from "The Treatise on Rhetoric by Demetrius Phalerius, or a Late Alexandrian?" One knows in this case that the citation is unnecessary: these limpid lines can stand on their own. (And anyway, if we were to take note, who is Demetrius Phalerius? One needs to have more told in order to understand.) Although modern readers are willing to wrestle with difficult lines (for example, in the writing of G. M. Hopkins, Ezra Pound, James Joyce), they are dubious about the annotations of their poetry that some poets provide. Some of these notes verge on the personal and the esoteric; and in many ways the notes are inessential. In regard to T. S. Eliot's notes to *The Waste Land,* one critic writes that the way in which the poem is organized "should be obvious without the aid of notes."

> *The Waste Land,* then, whatever its difficulty, is, or should be, obviously a poem. It is a self-subsistent poem. Indeed, though it would lose if the notes could be suppressed and forgotten, yet the more important criticism might be said to be, not that it depends upon them too much, but rather that without them, and without the support of *From Ritual to Romance,* it would not lose more.[13]

The argument seems to have taken a curious turn. This comes of taking the notes as an organic part of the poem. If they are a part of the poem, then they should be indispensable. But the notes and

[50]

explanatory apparatus seem to be dispensable. We believe that poems, including notes if they are an integral part of them, should present an organic unit. This criticism is thus seen to be a formal criticism.

(4) We must still rely on the subject matter and the meaning of the work in order to catch its mood and tone. If we ignore the subject matter, how can we tell that a poem, for example, is ironic or satiric in tone? If we mistake the mood, we misread the poem.

There might be an easy way of identifying the mood, as in the case of *MacFlecknoe, a Satire* or the *Faerie Queene*.[14] These are instances in which what is said is accompanied by an external gesture (or a tone of voice, a broad grin) to show that what is being said is not to be taken at face value. (It is like winking and saying to a child, "Of course, Santa Claus will not come this year.") But we cannot always trust to external clues. How do we know that *Candide* is a satire? The title makes one suspect, for *Candide*, it says, *ou L'optimisme*. The more certain indications are internal; the tone of voice of the prose (there is a gay sneer in the style), the juxtaposition of the various ingredients of the tale— high cheerfulness in the presence of great suffering, submissiveness in the face of the most incredible disasters and the most extreme acts of violence—and all of these topped off by the most platitudinous ameliorism. All together they constitute what we call the tone and the style, and they form the texture of the work. The tone and mood which a work presents act as the prime factors in determining the appropriateness and the organization of the parts. Anything which jars against tone and mood (barring some overriding factor) is likely to be judged irrelevant. Whether the relevance of parts is determined by the subject matter or the texture-mood, any criticism alleging irrelevance of parts clearly cannot be wholly grounded on the subject matter alone. If details and parts are irrelevant, they are said to be esthetically irrelevant, and by "esthetically irrelevant," then, we mean "formally irrelevant." The supersensitivity of Spanish mysticism, for example, is esthetically irrelevant to an estimate of El Greco's paintings.[15] What matters is what is in the paintings: the form, the organization which is presented in the work. What is irrelevant is not essential to this organization.

So it begins to appear that the assertion of the autonomy of a work of art, while granting the distinction between form and the content, places a priority on the formal, organizational aspects of the work. All the arts, to paraphrase Pater, seem to aspire to the condition of music in this way.

II

By "form" we may mean two different aspects of a work of art: its shape and pattern in the large; or its texture, its organization in detail from point to point, moment to moment. The very usefulness of the term (and thus the strength of formalism as an esthetic theory) is derived from this ambiguity; but at the same time, the limits of formalism also spring from it.

When we say that a feature of a work of art, a detail, is formally irrelevant to it, we are speaking of the general structure, the pattern of the object. Statues have a shape, an organization of masses and movements. The parts of a painting too are organized in fairly recognizable schemes. The binary form, the sonata-allegro form, the rondo, are names for such shapes in music. Details of a work either fit this scheme or do not. In this first sense of form, there is a further ambiguity; one which is important for anyone attempting to describe the ontological nature of a work of art. Statues have a form, filling out three dimensions in space; so do Greek vases. Paintings in a flat plane present visible shapes. Such are spatial forms. When Plato speaks of the form of the world's body, or when geometricians speak of the forms of circles and spheres, they mean these. But not all shapes are spatial. The notion of temporal shapes is more difficult to describe. Temporal shapes as remembered patterns seem to depend metaphorically on the notion of spatial form. (Are temporal forms conceptual in a way that spatial forms are not?) Form in music, or the seeing of form at least, seems to be aided by the seeing of the printed score. We might image the *basso ostinato* melody as an undulating black mass in the bottom portion of the visualized music. The dynamic ranges are thought of as widening or broadening the music (is this a sculptural image?), and we say the writing is full or thick, that music is a fabric and has texture. At any rate, we seem to use curiously visual metaphors and feel most comfortable about discussing the form of music in terms of the printed score. Which is the primary notion of form? That which we can grasp all at once, visually, or that which hinges on memory and seems somehow fugitive? Few of us can, as Mozart is said to have been able to do, see "music spatially, i.e., like a picture, all at once." [16] There are also combinations of the two types of form. Mobiles have a form though a changing one from moment to moment. But as the articulated parts etch out lines and arcs in space, the changing shapes of the mobile form a second order shape; and these shapes we must be able to remember in order to grasp. They are like the gesture of a *corps de ballet* in action. It is also like the organization of the persons on a stage in a play or an opera as they individually move about.

The concept of form as shape looms large in critical discourse. Knowing that a composition is a symphony (i.e., a classical symphony) a critic may indicate how the work under discussion is more like a rhapsodic fantasia. Tovey demonstrates how Beethoven failed to observe some of the tricks of composing a concerto as discovered and developed by Mozart, and how this failure accounts for the ineffectiveness (or lessening of expressive power) of two of Beethoven's early piano concerti.[17] Arguments concerning tragedy (the structure of the events, the peripety and discovery, the reversal, etc.) may be cited.[18] And if these arguments help, they help the cause of comprehension and appreciation *because* there are such shapes and organization schemes. The task of discovering such shapes is a part of the study of literary history and the science of musicology. Teachers of literature may therefore speak of the serial organization of the picaresque novel, the geometrically well-foiled personages of *Tom Jones,* the "tear drop" shape of *Pamela,* to help students see and enjoy the coherence of the objects before them.

The notion of form is then granted to be an important one; for works of art display shapes which can make comprehensible an order and form in the flux of events that we never see because we are too deep in our quotidian bread-winning to notice. But how do we learn to see these forms in works of art? Here is the dialectic of form as we find it in art criticism. Suppose that we have been acquainted only with paintings that are like those by Giotto or Carpaccio. And then, for the first time, we encounter a painting by El Greco or Rubens. The natural response would be a confusion, a sense of uneasiness—and one of the things we would say (assuming that we have a negative response) is that the painting is ill-organized. "It has no form" in this context means, primarily, "it is ill-organized." Then, of course, it is open to the artist to say the following: "Well. You must learn to see a new kind of organization. Study, and you will see it. Life and beauty do not have the repose and the static regularity of a receding series of planes as in the world of Giotto. This painting, look, has this organization—a spiral, a dynamic fluctuation of curves and masses in movement." The artist may have so intended and failed; but before we can say so, we must acquire this new way of seeing. The artist may be wrong, but there is, at least, this new way of shaping. The shock felt by the judges of the academic salon of 1863, the confusion and irritation that we experience on viewing the canvasses of Pollock, de Kooning, Still, Hartigan, all have to do with our inability to organize the ingredients of the painting. If it is disorganized, then surely this is a negative criticism that is relevant. (Though how telling is it?) But if the shape is something new, how much time must we allow ourselves in finding it? (Not forever; yet see how long El Greco had to wait.[19]) When can we be certain that a failure to discover the "form" of a work of art is due to a fault in the work of art itself, and not in our myopia and short patience? The answer is difficult to formulate, and this surely shows how unreliable the notion of form (as shape) is in the criticism of a work of art.

The process of understanding a work of art (of which seeing the form constitutes an important part) takes time. But if the process is one that might be claimed to be endless (a possibility which the above discussion indicates), then the notion of form is one that might not help the critic at all.[20] It is at this juncture in the dialectic that the second notion of form creeps in. Someone might point out while looking over a sonnet that each of the lines in the poem has more than the requisite number of syllables and that there is something odd about the rhyming words:

> I caught this morning morning's minion, king-
> dom of daylight's dauphin, dapple-dawn-drawn Falcon,
>   in his riding
> Of the rolling level underneath him steady air, and striding
> High there, how he rung upon the rein of a wimpling wing
> In his ecstasy!

Can a respectable sonnet proceed in this manner? Well, what is a sonnet? We usually ask this question with the idea of shape in mind. If we manage to answer this question then we can go on to see whether the object at hand actually succeeds in exhibiting the necessary shape.[21] We need to be, out of necessity, a bit arbitrary sometimes in answering questions like "What is a sonnet?" At present, we go to some sort of authority, say to an encyclopaedia.

The answer we get may not be clear cut. There are, of course, several kinds of sonnets. That the answer is not clear cut and that we cannot decisively establish what a sonnet is (or what a symphony is) is not crucial. Even if the object at hand (in this case the poem by Hopkins) fails to meet the criteria with flying colors, we may still be able to notice the particular qualities of the "object," the way in which the parts interact to form a coherent whole.[22] We can ask if the entity is fitted well. We can try to see how the parts from moment to moment create a tension and how these tensions are resolved. If somehow the work can stand on its own, then even if it is not a good sonnet, it is a good poem, and to that extent we esteem it, even if no other poem is like it in shape. Notice that we have resorted to what we can still call formal features to argue our case, though what we call form is the particular and minute texture of the work of art.

This is the second meaning of the word "form," a use which began to predominate in esthetics with the advent of modern art. And why this was so is easy to see. What after all is the form of an impressionist painting, like the dazzling mosaic of colors we find in a late Monet? The whole surface of the canvas, the minute arrangement of the parts constitute both its substance and form. So naturally form and content are inseparable. But this sense of form is a different thing from the shape of a work. It is allied with the idea of style and enters into discussion of the late novels of Henry James, the poetic novels of Virginia Woolf, James Joyce; even in the sort of style that is Jane Austen's, which we say so perfectly mirrors her intellectual and moral universe; or the craggy, rough style of John Donne that goes so well with (because it *is*) the crabbed, tortuous thought sequences, the painful emotions of the Holy Sonnets. We now say too that categories like the canon, the fugue, the passacaglia are not forms in the first sense because they do not dictate a shape; they suggest how notes may be combined to form textures of the requisite sort.[23] And so on. It is in this context that the untranslatability of works of art acquires meaning. For if form and content are inseparable, then we wouldn't expect them to be translatable either. A novel of Virginia Woolf is what it is (being a unique marriage of style and thought), and a canvas by Monet, though a piecing together of paint, is not something that can be disassembled and reassembled. The autonomy of a work of art and its uniqueness go together. Form and content are one; this statement now has the status of a dogma.

[55]

But wait. Is this dogma any help in criticism? No matter how "unshapely," any object must have a form in the second sense. The content, no matter how thin, will be presented in a certain configuration, the textural-form that cannot be separated from the content. How does this help us to pick out successful works of art from anything else in the universe? We are left with an impasse.

III

Can we, in any way, salvage the notion of form from this stalemate? Two paths have been taken by critics.

(1) The meaning of the word "form" *is* ambiguous. This is admitted. But this very ambiguity is its virtue. The form of a musical composition, as Tovey suggests, "may be considered in two aspects, the texture of the music from moment to moment, and the shape of the musical design as a whole." What we frequently call the content or the substance of the music [24] is this fabric, woven out of the ingredients of sound. What more is there to music, once we have related the concrete, minute detail to the design as a whole by the expectations we have of how these fragmentary shapes should be organized?

There is something else in music, one may say, without which no musical composition is worth anything. That is its expressiveness. But where may we locate this element? There are, of course, melodies (and themes and motifs), and these are variously melancholy, gay, elegant, attractive, or dull. To seek still other components of music: there are harmonic sequences and the interplay of the tensions among these harmonic sequences. Or there are dynamic ranges and subtle inflections. Or orchestral color. All cr any of these may account for the expressiveness of the music; and apart from the skill with which the material of the music was originally arranged, we may say the expressiveness is a result of phrasing. It may be a function of the manner in which the musical texture was created: its harmony, contrast, tensions. Or it may be a function of its re-creation. Phrasing is "the art of relative emphasis by which important notes are distinguished from less important ones, so that stresses and accents fall in their proper places and the meaning of a melody or a passage of music is made evident to the listener." [25] Two repetitions of the same melody, uttered with different accents, may sound sufficiently unlike each other so that the listener may altogether miss the import of the form (the repetition). The properly emphasized and articulated parts must be placed in their correct context so that the whole architectonic of the composition is dramatically presented. That is what expressiveness and appropriate phrasing is: and described in this way, they are primarily matters of articulation or proper *forming*. A good conductor, for example, is one who is capable of paying close attention to the work to see what it is and of being sensitive to the logic of the structure of the work.

The above discussion has been focused on music. But a close analogy to phrasing in music may be found in the declamation and pacing of the action in drama. And here is an example from painting (though in painting we no longer have the distinction between creation and re-creation). Cezanne, says Kenneth Clark, evolved a unique style in his late watercolors which embodies an attempt to "record for his own satisfaction the nodal point in a composition, and by nodal points I mean those places where the junction of the planes is of the greatest importance. The direction of these planes he represents by touches of pure color, pale blue, pink, sienna, and green and . . . few of such transparent touches are sufficient to create an effect of great solidity." [26] Speaking of works created by such a free technique, one which led to a "spontaneous looking expression of his sensations," Cezanne is reported to have said in 1906, "je deviens comme peintre plus lucide devant la nature." By this, Clark says, he meant that "his own passionate imaginative life" could now be "revealed in every stroke with which he recorded his visual sensations." He had, that is, "created a harmony parallel with nature." [27] This is the achievement of expressiveness by means of texture and overall design. Much is in the hands of the artist or the performer in their acts of arranging or performing: but what results is an integrated texture either in time or in space. It is a matter of form, and form can move us. [28] Form as shape and form as texture are also form as expression.

(2) The second way out takes on the note of desperation. It is to deny that "form" can mean "shape" or the apparent structure and organization of a work of art. What is it then? It has been said to be the life-enhancing values that peer through the sensuous surfaces of a work of art; [29] the communication of an "essential reality, of the God in everything, of the universal in the particular, of the all-pervading rhythm." [30] It is the expression of

"that which gives to all things their individual significance, the thing in itself, the ultimate reality." [31]

The consequence of making this distinction, other than a certain intractability and opaqueness, is that "form" now becomes something which must be imaginatively grasped; [32] and the danger is that one is tempted to say that a special faculty is required to do this, or that what is so grasped may not be in the work of art as a publicly inspectable entity. Berenson himself seems to suggest this in saying that "ideated sensations [i.e., significant forms] . . . are those that exist only in the imagination." [33] He does not mean to be mysterious; rather he emphasizes, quite legitimately, the difference between the physical properties of a work of art, our physiological reactions to these physical properties, and a controlled esthetic response to the work of art. But he says too, "Form must not be confused with shape. Form is never a shape—that is to say, a geometrical object looking the same to everybody. Form is a quality beyond common cognizance." [34] To ascertain that anyone has accurately perceived this uncommon "form" of a work of art becomes difficult. For the workings of the imagination are frequently devious and deep; and we sometimes say of that which we merely *imagine* that it is not real.

The whole question of form has actually revolved into the question of "significance" or meaning of a work of art. Berenson betrays this in employing the terms "tactile *values*" and "ideated sensation" interchangeably and in saying that they are chiefly produced by animate and human figures. What the artist does is to "organize and harmonize" various stresses and strains "into an equivalent of what he feels the object to be intrinsically, and what at the same time it says and means to us." [35] Formalism, at its core, thus reverts to a consideration of meaning and content, though the significance of a work of art is independent of the world surrounding it. The argument has made a full circle.

The questions that may be raised about such significances (life values or depth meaning) [36] in works of art are enormously complicated, and I cannot begin to do them justice in this context. But that depth meaning, life values, etc., may be communicated by the work of art is in no way incompatible with the assertion of the autonomy of a work of art. Music, according to some critics, "communicates valuable spiritual states," [37] and presents a "vision of life." [38] Clark says of landscape painting that "like all forms of art," it constitutes an act of faith.

From Leonardo to Seurat painters, as well as critics, have maintained that the rendering of light is part of the science of painting; but Hubert van Eyck, John Bellini, Claude, Constable and Corot show us that the representation of light owes its aesthetic value to the fact that it is the expression of love. "As the air fills everything and is not confined to one place, as the light of the sun overfloods the whole earth, so God dwells in everything and everything dwells in Him." Now it was this mystical sense of the unity of creation expressed by light and atmosphere which, however unconsciously, provided a basis of pictorial unity. . . .[39]

Can this be? Can such profound and metaphysical assertions be communicated by a musical composition or a painting? One can perhaps believe that Hubert van Eyck and Bellini had such notions in mind, since we know something about the times they lived in; but can such theses be presented in a painting and of all things in a landscape? When a critic speaks in this vein, we try to make sure that he has not "read into" the work of art; that the rich plethora of significance is really there. (We do not look elsewhere.) That such seeing involves an active use of imagination, sensibility, and heart need not be denied. Nevertheless the value of such critical communication depends on whether it enriches the responses of the listener, and much of the credibility and reliability of such critics lie in whether we, rescrutinizing the work of art, are helped in our efforts or not. The attention must be refocused on the work of art.

IV

The doctrine that works of art are autonomous consists in the claim that works of art are independent, free, self-contained entities. They are, we have seen, self-contained because they are formally complete and well rounded. There may be works of art that are formally incomplete. But if a work of art is incomplete, this feature (which would be taken as a defect) must be compensated for by some other feature (usually its meaning or significance). We then value it for its "message." But oddly enough, the meaning, the "message" need not be extrareferential. Any work of art must be an entity which can be understood on its own terms, and its meaning must unravel from within like an act of revelation. It may then in addition look like something, preach, cajole, shock, astonish. These functions, though important, are extraesthetic. Toward an esthetic evaluation of the work, these do not count, though they may be true about a work of art and even, *in their way*, contribute to our comprehension of the work of art.

Of what significance, of what help and use is the doctrine of autonomy? Suppose that works of art *can* be taken autonomously. Why should they be? There are two possible reasons. First, because if a work of art is not given full free play to work its own influence on us, we are not in any way connected with it essentially. Not to take it *as it is* would be to see it as we, subjectively, wish to see it: to impose our will and desire on a segment of reality. Second, because the autonomy of the work of art ultimately results in the exercise of *our* autonomous natures. Both answers, because the question is about the place of art in the spiritual economy of human beings, point to, and are stated in terms of, human effects. Works of art in common speech are said to have intentions. But we also know that only persons (and rational creatures possessed of a will) have intentions. The implicit analogy between works of art and persons is worth pursuing in some detail.

The principal meaning of the autonomy of a work of art and of a person is that both are independent and free, requiring, even demanding, treatment as self-contained, sacred beings possessing an intrinsic worth. All persons are unique. It is only the requirement of ethics (and the contingencies of social existence) that compels us to treat human beings, and then only in relevant moral contexts, as commensurate equals subsumable under universal principles. There remains the inward, non-rational ego, which is always incompletely understood, infinitely complex, various, and inexhaustible. This is the self that is particular, changeable, existing within and beneath the ethical and rational self—and which conceptually ejects the shell of the symbolic self. A work of art too is unique—just in the respect that its substance is inseparable from its form. I have already indicated how the doctrine of autonomy is related to the uniqueness of a work of art. The connection should not be surprising. If a work of art is free, independent, worthy of treatment as an instance of intrinsic value, it would be incommensurable with any other object. In saying that its substance is inseparable from its form, the theorist is also saying that the work of art is particular, its existence grounded on its manifestation here and now. If the work happens to be complex, then we can never have an ex-

[60]

haustive description of it and our comprehension of it must remain incomplete, even perhaps always inadequate, because the work is absolutely concrete and multifarious. So it is with persons. Their uniqueness requires that our treatment of them should preserve their separateness and differentness; that we hold in abeyance our will to simplify, unify, to label things with categorical terms. No concept should be adequate for them.

Formalism (and the doctrine of autonomy) as usually interpreted, however, leads to consequences that are different. In treating a work of art as independent, we emphasize its formal completeness and we especially value the clarity that comes with it, be it clarity of form, clarity of meaning, or clarity of vision. The ambiguities of intent, the messiness of relationships, the incomprehensibility of content, the sheer density, complexity, and unreason of experience are things we would like to see left out of art, if possible, just as we would like to see them left out of human society and, ultimately, the human spirit. We want to understand fully, to speak out completely in finite terms. But the particularity and the uniqueness of works of art (and persons) should forbid the fulfillment of such a hope.

A formalist would reply that life and persons are inexplicable, uncontrollable, infinite. But can art be incomplete, contingent, formless? The very notion of a work of art is that it should have a form even if we must admit, regretfully, that it is form not based on a concept. While it is possible for a work of art to present the contingency and muddiness of life artfully, in practice the formless contingency tends to destroy the form. And that is why even the content, ideally, must be self-contained, necessary, highly articulated, and independent. Art is, in this sense, form; in ethics it is analogous to the willful subsumption under the universal of something that is intrinsically and thoroughly particular and contingent. However, art is so much more stringent and ruthless in its demands that we learn to take *it* just for what it is (at the peril of otherwise never seeing it and understanding it), while, on one view of the moral life, morality consists in the opposite activity of subsuming the subject under the rule of reason. (After all, there is a difference between treating an object esthetically and morally.)

Formalism in its drive for clarity and simplicity, then, tends to work against the uniqueness and particularity of a work of art. This paradox, or better yet, double drive, must be left as it is. For that is the nature of a work of art. To be particular, multi-

[61]

farious, concretely sensuous; to be formed, clear, self-contained, independent; these are the intentions of a work of art.

V

Works of art communicate, and the commerce between objects of art and persons ought not to be overlooked. The above unravelling of the concept of autonomy may be amplified in two further ways.

(1) Works of art express emotions and spiritual states. The account so far given misses the affective aspects of art altogether. Human beings respond to works of art in various ways; and what is more, works of art evoke all sorts of practical responses depending on social context. They are never found in isolation. The essence of art is the ability to move us.

I do not underestimate the affective and evocative nature of a work of art. Still, from the viewpoint of criticism, it is not enough simply to be moved; one needs to know why we respond in that manner, i.e., what about the work of art makes us respond in such a manner. The study then should refocus itself on the object. Why do I set off these objects by themselves and treat them as works of art? It is the reporting of countless reflective, controlled responses that is relevant in the criticism of the arts. Without critical scrutiny, any response would be tantamount to the undiscriminating saying: I know what I like even if I don't know why; but I know what I like by how I feel. While it is certainly a good thing to know what one likes, this is only a beginning. Further, the response must be one common to a fairly large group of persons. It is not enough merely that *I* should respond in a particular manner. There must be a sizable group that does so for good, relevant reasons. It makes no sense to say "this is a work of art, but only for me."

(2) We need to examine more closely, the nature of the practical commerce between the viewer and the object of art.

> . . . there is good reason to believe that every artist works with ideas or facts and tries to alter behavior, thereby employing, in some measure, the aims of both the philosopher and the moralist. Every artist, however much of an abstractionist he may be, conveys ideas and expresses imperatives. The abstract painter does not merely present a medley of

lines and colors. He also asserts something and commands attention in a certain way. Far from making a sensuous presentation that is to be enjoyed out of relation to everything else, as the Art for Art's Sake theorists suggest, the painter is engaged in telling us something about these lines and colors—at the very least, that they are in these relations to one another, that they are lines and colors of the sort that they are, and that they do not, perhaps, represent any particular objects in nature. Likewise, he is exhorting us to behave towards his production in a certain way—we are not to react towards it as we would towards a bowl of spaghetti or a streaked wall that needs cleaning; instead, we are merely to *look* and enjoy what we see. To the extent that he makes these assertions and commands, the painter is conveying ideas and expressing imperatives, and to that extent his aims overlap those of the philosopher and moralist. He is an *artist* once again, only to the extent that he is able to integrate these various aims by means of artistic criticism.[40]

I cite this passage as a sample of how artists and critics reply when they have been pushed into justifying the uses of poetry or painting; when they must defend the conviction that works of art do and must have a direct influence on human conduct. So one might claim that works of art command; or that they make assertions. But claims of this sort are usually Janus-faced (as even the quoted passage shows), for they usually withdraw with one hand what they originally gave with the other.

From the very terms selected, it is clear that the passage claims too much. Does every artist express an imperative? Perhaps at some time or other in his life he does, being a human being with practical needs. But does every work of art that he creates express an imperative? We need to proceed more slowly here. Imperatives, of course, express commands. " 'Break it,' she whispered. 'It will be locked, nailed. You have the hatchet. Break it.' "[41] This is an urgent command. It occurs in a novel, one character issuing it to another; but it does not seem correct to say that the novel itself is issuing it. And this is questionable both for verbal as well as nonverbal commands—like gestures, a wave of the hand that sets a class free to go.

Optatives are not always clearly imperative in function. "Hurry, it is late. You will have to go or you will miss the train." If I must go because the train mentioned is the last train of the day and I must get to my destination on time, then the facts (and my intention) make me hurry, not the will of the

[63]

speaker or *how* he said what he said. What the words do is to call my attention to these prior facts (i.e., prior to the command). Many moral commands function similarly. "You ought to be more gentle to Jane because she is in pain." So informed, I notice that Jane is indeed in pain, her eyes swollen, her arm in a sling, and I see that I must not be harsh. The force of the *ought* (if it is a command) differs from that of a direct command. I am not being told directly to be kind and gentle, but by way of the facts of the situation, seeing which I would be gentle whether I am commanded to be so or not. Simply being told "Jane is in pain" would have been enough. We may call these indirect commands, issued by way of pointing out facts.

While Singer says that works of art command, he seems to mean an indirect command, for he rests his case on this: that the painting tells us (asserts) something about lines and colors and their interrelationship—i.e., they tell us just what they present on their surfaces. First it must be admitted that there is much representational art which seems to affect us overtly. Daumier's satiric prints of lawyers, Goya's frenetic series of prints on the disasters of war, sundry propaganda art (*Uncle Tom's Cabin*), Toulouse-Lautrec's advertising posters, pornographic works of art,[42] all of these are examples. These works move by presenting a vision. But even so, are we presented with an imperative, direct or indirect? Just how they work is therefore important to see. A painting may present the suffering, the misery of the poor (some of the graphic work of Käthe Köllwitz). A novel may depict the wages of hasty judgment (*Pride and Prejudice*). But do these works of art in their totality assert anything? It seems to me misleading to describe the manner in which works of art present something as the saying or the asserting of it. It makes little sense to wonder of a portrait or a landscape: what is it telling us? Showing and stating are not identical acts. If it is difficult to say that works of art assert, then it seems implausible that they should make an indirect command by way of an assertion.

Perhaps an indirect command can be issued in another way. In the act of presentation, the artist may also be saying, "This is the way I felt." Can he be saying (to paraphrase R. L. Stevenson), "Do so as well!"? That any sort of imperative content (even if intended by the artist) cannot be the central business of a work of art is shown by the examples of poor works of art containing commands that we approve of. If the intention is good, we accept

[64]

the message, but it is still open to us to say that the expression is faulty, if it is. It is not always easy to separate the artistic function from some other function (it is sometimes psychologically difficult), and that is why, as in the case of pornography, we may put them away in toto. We may still say that they are fine works of art but that their influence is pernicious. This is a moral decision and not an esthetic one. Some people avoid the religious mannerist paintings. They admit that they are, many of them, fine paintings, but their "commanding" puts them beyond the pale because the message gets in the way (psychologically) of the full esthetic play of the work. So also with works that are sentimental. The ways an object of art functions esthetically and as a work of propaganda are two different and sometimes incompatible ways.

Even when works of art do not have an imperative content, it might still seem natural to describe the way in which we relate ourselves to them as a result of a command from them that we do so in that special (esthetic) way. The existence of a painting apparently *implies* this command. While our relation to a work of art does involve our assuming a certain disposition, it is still not the result of a direct telling. At best, it is indirect. To construct an analogy between the esthetic and the imperative mode is wrongheaded (unless we use the word "command" in a very loose way). The relevant treatment that we are to accord a work of art is presupposed and is prior to the emergence of an esthetic object. The objects do not *tell* us to approach them in a certain way. Rather, we approach them in a certain way, and lo and behold, works of art emerge, if we happen to be in the presence of the right sort of objects. This manner of approach is in part a result of previous training. We have learned to respond in a definite way to objects in a museum or to objects with frames around them. But the response is up to us. Theoretically speaking, we can respond to anything esthetically (though there may be practical limits, to be mentioned later on). The manner of approach cannot be solely a result of a command from the object of art.

The two points involved are different enough to warrant keeping apart. (1) The way in which "works of art command attention" involves a number of clues and conventions which we learn from an early age.[43] The esthetic mode of responding is a difficult and complex one which requires a godlike objectivity and steadiness of perception from us. What we might avoid staring at or savouring in a garbage heap (or in a diseased, disfigured human body) we scrutinize and contemplate in a painting.

[65]

We eavesdrop on conversations in a novel which in all decency and modesty we would hurry away from in real life. At a play, we do not rush on the stage to prevent Othello from strangling Desdemona, though in all charity, if our neighbor were doing so, we would rush to the rescue of the innocent and noble lady. (Don Quixote ran onto the stage to save a damsel in distress.) The context of the opera house, the concert stage, and the church make us respond differently to the same music.[44] In themselves, works of art are sublimely indifferent and independent of how we treat them. They simply *are* (to use a Platonic turn of phrase), and keep their status in their own realm.

(2) The second point is related to the first. Theoretically it is possible to respond esthetically to almost anything in the world. But practically it is impossible. To be esthetic about human cruelty, for example, would be difficult and undesirable. Some objects block off an adequate esthetic response: works of pornography and works of horror. (Could we ever consider lampshades made out of the skins of exterminated Jews or instruments of torture as objects of art?) Then how does it come about that certain objects and certain sequences of actions can be and are regarded esthetically? First we approach objects esthetically and then, if we are before works of art (i.e., things that are autonomous as described earlier), the experience rounds itself out satisfactorily. It is clear that certain objects are easier to respond to in this special manner: a lovely piece of stone, the graceful motions of a young girl, etc. And it is common knowledge that we fashion certain objects especially for the purposes of this special treatment. But that they are created for such purposes (and are intended to be so treated) in no way assures their getting such treatment. To begin with, our responses to objects (even so-called works of art) are not always clear-cut. We look at vases differently depending on the occasion. Some vases we would not dream of using (like Sung vases) and others we do not see at all—we only notice the flowers in them. And they may be the same vase. Religious objects and symbols affect us differently depending on whether we encounter them in the church or in a museum. Further, works of art draw out different responses from different people. What insights we take away from any experience of a work of art (what preparatory sets for future action) depend on subjective predispositions. A novelist and a literary critic may both acquire an insight into the nature of the novel (or of a particular novel), one to further his craft and the other to deepen his critical

expertise. A movie director, reading the same novel, may get the germ of an idea on how to structure images and scenes in a future film. But if the cognition is a full and adequate one, in all these cases the focal point would have been the object observed as an entity of intrinsic interest and as a source of value.

A successful work of art is one which, when scrutinized esthetically, is seen to be complete and autonomous. We can ascertain the range of its meaning, the relevance or the irrelevance of its parts, regardless of tradition, the intent of the artist, or factors external to the work, but merely in terms of its own nature. (Textural scholarship, the biographical and historical studies are all aids to seeing the work for what it is, completely and clearly.) Works of art themselves intend something because they can be treated in this way. This is what we mean when we say works of art simply are: and if they moralize, propagandize, or command, they are works of art in spite of these functions. The mode of communication of a work of art, if communication is the right term for the sort of commerce we have with works of art (and they *say* something, don't they?) is *presentation*. We need to take them as they are, just as we need to learn to take persons as they are, and that is possible because they are both unique and free. Works of art, in this respect, are like persons after all.

NOTES

1. Jean Stafford, *Children Are Bored on Sunday* (N. Y., 1952), p. 245.

2. F. R. Leavis, *The Great Tradition* (London, 1948), p. 227. One is reminded of I. A. Richards' famous remark, "It is never what a poem says which matters, but what it is."

3. Nahum Tate's "Tatefication of Lear" in 1681. See David Nichol Smith, *Shakespeare in the Eighteenth Century* (Oxford, 1928), pp. 20 ff., for details, esp. p. 380.

4. Donald Francis Tovey, *Essays in Musical Analysis* (London, 1948), I, 207 f. See also p. 203.

5. Eduard Hanslick, *The Beautiful in Music* (London, 1891), pp. 48–49. See also Joseph Kerman's remarks on Hanslick in *Opera as Drama* (N. Y., 1956), p. 43.

6. Wagner himself vacillated on his interpretation. For details see G. B. Shaw, *The Perfect Wagnerite* (N. Y., 1907), pp. 121 ff.

7. *Ibid.*, p. 130.

8. It is when this relationship is given up that the notion of self-reference is adopted. Cf. Susanne Langer, *Philosophy in a New Key* (Cambridge, 1932), in which Mrs. Langer develops the notion of "presentational symbols." entities that are symbolic in function but refer to themselves.

9. The notion of verisimilitude has sometimes been described not in terms of correspondence to an external reality, but in terms of internal consistency and the right balance and emphasis of its internal parts so as to suggest a harmonious and self-subsistent entity (without reference, however, to the balance and harmony that one may find in nature).

10. How can this clue be contained in the painting? The figures may wear what looks like fifteenth-century armor and there may be three galleons in the bay, but how do we know that this is Columbus and the three ships *Santa Maria, Niña* and *Pinta?* In this case, the three ships function as an iconographic symbol of Columbus, like the position of the right hand for Napoleon. But images are not always so accommodating.

11. An actual occurrence as related to me by John Garvey of the School of Music of the University of Illinois. The "dance-satire" (there was, I think, a pun in the title) was "The Bewitched" by Harry Partch, performed at the Contemporary Arts Festival in the springs of 1957 and 1959 and later performed in New York City.

12. "To a Snail," *Selected Poems* (N. Y., 1935), p. 99; notes, p. 123.

13. F. R. Leavis, *New Bearings in English Poetry* (London, 1938), pp. 112–113. (A footnote to the first sentence has been omitted.)

14. The poem is preceded by a letter from Spenser to Sir Walter Raleigh "expounding his whole intention" in which the work is described as a "continued Allegory, or darke conceit." *The Poetical Works of Edmund Spenser*, ed. J. C. Smith (Oxford, 1908), III, 485.

15. "With [the] rather facile ecstasies and the orthodox Counter-Reformation theology in terms of which they could be interpreted, El Greco has nothing to do." Aldous Huxley, "Meditations on El Greco," *Music at Night* (London, 1949), p. 63.

16. Donald Francis Tovey, *Musical Articles from the Encyclopaedia Britannica* (London, 1944), p. 208.

17. Tovey, *Essays*, III, 68 ff.

18. For a discussion of the grounds on which certain plays have been denied the name of tragedy, see Cleanth Brooks, ed., *Tragic Themes in Western Literature* (New Haven, 1955), pp. 154 ff.

19. Or, for a more contemporary example, Ezra Pound.

20. For works of art will have a form, and none can be said, clearly and certainly, not to have a form at all (since we may not have discovered it yet).

21. Ivor Brown says, for example, of Shakespeare's sonnet no. 126 that it is "not a sonnet but a dozen lines of rhymed verse." *Shakespeare* (Garden City, N. Y., 1946), p. 155.

22. In the case of most of Hopkins' poetry, we need usually to learn to read his lines in a new way: to count the stresses instead of the syllables per line, for example.

23. Tovey, *Musical Articles,* p. 19.

24. See A. C. Bradley's use of the term "substance" to contrast with two terms, "form" on the one hand and "subject matter" on the other, in "Poetry for Poetry's Sake," *Oxford Lectures in Poetry* (London, 1909), pp. 12 f.

25. Winthrop Sargeant, *Listening to Music* (N. Y., 1958), pp. 8 f.

26. Kenneth Clark, *Landscape into Art* (London, 1952), p. 127.

27. *Ibid.,* p. 129.

28. See also Clive Bell, *Art* (London, 1924), pp. 9 ff., 62 ff.

29. Bernard Berenson, *Aesthetics and History in the Visual Arts* (N. Y., 1948), pp. 65 f. Berenson goes on to identify those life-enhancing values with what he calls tactile values (see p. 63) and to assert that these are what "significant form" means (p. 65).

30. Clive Bell, *Art,* p. 69.

31. *Ibid.,* pp. 69–70.

32. Berenson, *Aesthetics and History,* p. 67; Bell, *Art,* pp. 56 ff.

33. Berenson, *Aesthetics and History,* p. 67.

34. *Ibid.,* p. 65.

35. *Ibid.,* pp. 67 f. It is, for Berenson, the chief concern of the visual arts to represent human forms (see also p. 86).

36. John Hospers, *Meaning and Truth in the Arts* (Chapel Hill, 1947), pp. 11–14.

37. J. W. N. Sullivan, *Beethoven* (N. Y., 1957), p. 55.

38. *Ibid.,* p. 231.

39. Kenneth Clark, *op. cit.,* pp. 131–132.

40. Irving Singer, "The Aesthetics of 'Art for Art's Sake,'" *Journal of Aesthetics and Art Criticism,* XII, 355.

41. William Faulkner, *Absalom, Absalom!* (N. Y., 1936), p. 367.

42. I am supposing that there may be items of pornography which are bona fide works of art, but fashioned with the arousal of sexual passion as their purpose, just as wartime posters may be drawn to increase military enlistment. One of the rare discussions of purely erotic art is J. Hillier's comments on Utamaro's "The Poem of the Pillow," in his *Utamaro Colour Prints and Paintings* (London, 1961), pp. 55–58.

43. We learn, for instance, to stand a certain distance away from a painting—which is unfortunately not always a satisfactory way of viewing many paintings. We also learn to see depth in a painting.

44. The tune of the sextet from *Lucia di Lammermoor* (Donizetti) has been heard in some Roman Catholic churches, fitted to the text of "Tantum Ergo," with little public cognizance or surprise.

[69]

JOHN M. ANDERSON

MAN AS DOUBTER

My philosophy begins in doubt, but it is directed toward being. Its path is traced through an affirmation of man, an affirmation which initial doubt makes possible. In this sense doubt is not an accidental trait of my views, but an essential ingredient. Thus it is important for me to make clear the manner in which doubting opens the path to an affirmation of man which, in its turn, leads to being. I understand doubt as an attitude which man chooses in the expectation of developing his own nature in relation to being.

Doubt is often thought of as disbelief, as doubt of claimed truth; the doubter is frequently viewed as a disbeliever, as one who denies the possibility of knowledge. There is some truth here, but this is a superficial view which obscures the real point of doubt. After all, a doubting attitude is not exceptional in human life. Quite the contrary, it pervades living experience; sometimes it is in abeyance and at other times in human life it comes to a focus to play its essential role. Thus the pattern of a normal life is a progression of certainties, if we see it positively; or a progression of doubts, if we emphasize the changes. The child turns to its parents; the youth is committed in romantic attachment and patriotism; the mature man believes in his family and his profession; the old man is oriented toward religion. In this very general way all men are much alike in the design which their history weaves. They are much alike both in the passionate certainty which attaches them to each in the sequence of their living beliefs; and alike in the doubt which dissolves each attachment in its turn so that it may be succeeded and the life show growth.

When we review the panorama of human intellectual history we may be impressed with the commitments which are typical of the beliefs in it. We may see man's political action expressed in the different forms of monarchy, democracy, tyranny and the variety of states and governments which mark political history. Surely each of these forms has been the focus of passionate political commitment in the name of which men have fought wars, exercised their ingenuity and stood forth as heroes or cowards. The same comment could be made concerning the diversity of social patterns. If these are less consciously the products of individual action, they nonetheless serve as the center of allegiance and certainty. In societies we find matriarchies and capitalism, feudal groups and agricultural organization, as well as many other dominant social structures. In religion the centers of human attachment are even clearer and, of course, in every aspect of the life of the human race there are to be found similar foci, similar viewpoints which hold man's commitment and guide his actions. When we look at these foci we may feel that the record of revolution, reformation and change which marks history is a defect; we may see the diversity of the foci as a defect leading to doubt and disbelief. Yet doubt and disbelief, modification and change are but the other face of man's intellectual history.

We unwarrantably deprecate this aspect of man's history when we speak of the element of doubt, pervasive of human life as it is, as if it were negative and had no part to play other than to lead back to commitment and certainty. In this way we speak of doubt as thrust upon us; we are plunged into doubt, we say. Yet are we really? The variety of belief and orientation is a positive characteristic of man's life and his history, but it is a characteristic which need not be accepted. Indeed, those zealots whose careers mark the human past have refused to note this diversity. It is only when we are not zealots that we become aware of other beliefs, that we analyze these beliefs and that we may come to entertain them. We might reject as false all alternative beliefs to the one we hold; that we do not suggests that our doubt and our disbelief are of our own choosing.

What do we gain by accepting doubt? Why should doubt be sustained, nourished and chosen? To accept doubt means to view human beliefs and orientations as restrictive and limited; fundamentally it means to stand in revolt against the apparent certainties of human life. This is something which men do as a quite typical aspect of their lives. Every adolescent lives a life of revolt against the restrictions of the patterns and channels of life which his parents and elders would impose upon him, against their beliefs and their certainties. Why? Because through this revolt is to be found a heightened sense of himself and a growing confidence in his own powers. In general this is the point. When men come to be sceptical of belief and outlook, when they revolt against traditional patterns, they are not turning toward some new version of the old pattern, although they often come to this; rather they are seeking themselves. That doubt is the obverse of certainty in human life, that it pervades human life as much as certainty, is evidence for the importance of its function. We doubt, we search out disbelief, we deliberately revolt because in these moments we stand revealed as men—this is our nature, a nature freed from a particular kind of dependence upon certainty.

To be thrust into doubt, to lose belief, is merely to have chosen certainty and to have failed to achieve it. To choose doubt is to claim that man has a part to play; it is to claim that man's nature as essentially human is a condition of whatever truth there is. To choose doubt is to raise the question of man's being, to ask more fundamentally than any possible specific answer, *what is man?* Since my philosophy begins in doubt, it begins with this question, what is man?

SECTION 2

Let us begin with an account of some of the usual views of doubt and doubting, which although wrong may suggest the correct analysis.

It is not unusual to suppose that the doubter is a man of common sense. The man of common sense we can imagine, at least, as a complete participant in the world of the plausible, the apparent and the practical. Such an individual deals with and in the obvious; we can picture him living a life in which he claims no certainty, in which he has no specific forms or ultimate commitment. In our imagination he becomes an "ordinary" man concerned with everyday experience, the proverbial man on the street. Whether there really are men of this sort is a question. To imagine men of an untroubled and direct nature, living completely in the scope of ordinary experience, is such an old and perennial dream as to warrant discount of any new version of the story. Sophisticates have always thought with nostalgia of a "noble savage," of primitive openness, of the uncomplicated peasant, of the honest workingman. Such vignettes are certainly the expression of a sophisticated ideal, but perhaps not drawn from reality.

Yet even if the simple untroubled life depicted in this ideal existed as a real possibility of which there were good examples, it would not be an instance of doubting. *We* may see it as a sceptical life because we see it as devoid of complicated commitments to beliefs and orientations which involve and disturb us. The "ordinary" man who did not believe or half believe in these would not doubt them either. The man who is untroubled by a network of allegiances and the complexity of the claims and counterclaims of beliefs will be no doubter; there is nothing for him to learn about doubt, for it is an activity which is not his at all.

Very likely the actual man on the street is ourselves; we are all ordinary men and the myth of the untroubled man of nature is merely an expression of an ideal state in which *our* doubts are resolved. But genuine doubting surely involves explicitly setting aside claimed certainties. Perhaps the prototype of the doubter is to be found in a man like David Hume rather than the hypothetically untroubled natural man, real or imaginary.

Hume's intentions seem to have been good; that is, he set out to discover the foundations of our knowledge of cause and effect, of the self and of real objects. The rare acuteness of his intellect is attested in the carefulness with which he surveyed the field and pursued his argument until, almost in spite of himself, he was forced to conclude that he had no knowledge of uniform conjunction, of the self and of matters of fact. We can see clearly that he arrives at his negative conclusions in the process of setting aside the claims of common sense and sophistication to have certainty of knowledge. In the appendix to *A Treatise of Human Nature,* Hume, expressing his difficulties, says, "I had entertained some hopes, that however deficient our theory of the intellectual world might be, it would be free from those contradictions, and absurdities, which seem to attend every explication, that human reason can give of the material world. But upon a more strict review of the section concerning *personal identity,* I find myself involv'd in such a labyrinth, that, I must confess, I neither know how to correct my former opinions, nor how to render them consistent. If this be not a good *general* reason for scepticism, 'tis at least a sufficient one (if I were not already abundantly supplied) for me to entertain diffidence and modesty in all my decisions." We hear in his own words the sense in which he sets aside claims to knowledge and we hear as well the assay of where this leaves him—not in an affirmed scepticism but in "diffidence and modesty."

What is a diffident and modest man to do? Is he to await, as Hume implies in the last sentence of the appendix, that individual of more mature reflections who will justify claims to knowledge? If this is so, then Hume's setting aside of such claims is not a positive choice which he makes. His doubts are not of his choosing, and they result not in a definite activity on his part but in diffidence. If this is the result of Hume's concern with claims to knowledge it is almost as negative as the orientation of the natural man; it, too, is an orientation without content of its own. No better example of a man explicitly preoccupied with the complications of human belief and knowledge could be found than David Hume. When we see that the results of his "doubting" are nothing at all we must conclude finally that a negative preoccupation with belief and knowledge cannot constitute doubt.

Perhaps, then, we should admit that the activity of doubting must involve truth, that it originates in the claim to certainty rather than in setting certainty aside. The natural man cannot doubt because he is unaware of certainty; and a man like David Hume is reduced to diffidence rather than achieving doubt because he does not recognize the claim of belief as the motivation for doubt. If this is so, then Descartes might provide the answer as to the name and nature of doubt, for Descartes is explicit in recognizing the claim of truth. He understands doubt as directed against false belief and knowledge. For Descartes, doubting sets aside the veil of error in order to reveal truth. It strips away illusion in order to focus attention upon being.

This is quite a different view of doubt from that of David Hume or that of Descartes' predecessor Montaigne. Montaigne, like Hume, would prefer to see doubt as an active and dynamic process, and yet as an activity which was continually pushing on

[75]

in search of truth. He says, "Whoever is searching for something comes to this point: either he says he has found it, or that it cannot be found, or that he is still in quest of it. All philosophy is divided into these three sorts. Its object is the search for truth, for knowledge and certainty." Like Hume, Montaigne cannot find the truth and like Hume he refuses to say that it cannot be found. Like Hume, he avows a continual quest, identifying his views with those of the Pyrrhonians as "bolder, and at the same time more probable" than those of thinkers who claim that the truth cannot be found. Yet surely Montaigne's "boldness" is Hume's "diffidence and modesty." Whatever name be used, boldness or diffidence, there is no dynamic and active process of doubt on this view. It is this lack which Descartes seeks to meet by orienting doubt upon truth.

Descartes observes, "not that indeed I imitated the sceptics, who only doubt for the sake of doubting, and pretend to be always uncertain; for on the contrary, my design was only to provide myself with good ground for assurance, and to reject the quicksand and mud in order to find the rock and clay." Such a method of doubt he thought to be successful in arriving at truth and indeed to appeal to reason as the ultimate authority. The Cartesian scepticism is founded on an insight into the truth, and a clear understanding of Descartes' method of doubt depends upon the nature of this insight.

There are two ways in which Descartes' expression of the nature of insight into the truth may be interpreted. One interpretation is that insight into truth is a kind of intuitive apprehension of ultimate content. Such insight is a direct apprehension, in the "light of reason," of whatever is to be known. Descartes describes this apprehension in "The Rules for the Direction of the Mind" as "the conception which an unclouded and attentive mind gives us so readily and distinctly that we are wholly freed from doubt about that which we understand. Or, what comes to the same thing, *intuition* is the undoubting conception of an unclouded and attentive mind, and springs from the light of reason alone . . ." (Rule III) . On this view intuition becomes a standard of knowledge; that is, the *content* of intuition becomes such a standard. Descartes cites some examples of this kind of certainty: knowledge of one's own existence and thought, knowledge that the triangle has three sides, that a sphere has one surface; but our interest here is not so much in the examples of intuitive apprehension as in the implications of such apprehension for doubt.

On this view doubt becomes a turning away from illusion and error in response to the standard which intuition provides. Doubt is a negative activity; it is directed against the training Descartes received in school at La Flèche, against the patterns of ordinary practice, and against the apparent truths of the imagination and the senses. Descartes finds these wanting and he speaks explicitly of their faults, for example, of "the fluctuating testimony of the senses, . . . the misleading judgment that proceeds from the blundering constructions of the imagination." He remarks that although "I was studying at one of the most celebrated Schools in Europe . . . yet I found myself embarrassed with so many doubts and errors. . . ." These doubts and these errors engender in Descartes a state of mind which is unacceptable and to which response must be made. Descartes' response is *doubt,* that is, a positive and dynamic procedure which takes the place of hesitancy and vacillation. The evidence of his writing is that he pursued this method of doubt with persistence and determination and, in his own view, success. He says, "I succeeded pretty well, since in trying to discover the error or uncertainty of the propositions which I examined . . . I encountered nothing so dubious that I could not draw from it some conclusion that was tolerably secure."

To doubt, for Descartes, is to assume the authority of knowledge, it is to say I do not know, but should. Doubt is, thus, the exercise of reason itself. When man doubts in the Cartesian sense he examines the claims of various knowledge using clear and assured reasoning in this examination, proceeding by the light of reason and so coming to definite conclusions, that is, to the certainty of intuition. Doubting, for Descartes, is clear, accurate thinking. As he says, in order to discover the error or uncertainty of the beliefs he examined he proceeded "not by feeble conjectures, but by clear and assured reasonings." This kind of doubting is an active and dynamic procedure only in the sense that it is the activity of sound reasoning. It is not a positive activity in its own right, it is not a chosen attitude or a learned technique in itself.

Yet there are aspects of Descartes' thought in which this metamorphosis of doubting into reasoning has not yet occurred and aspects of his thought in which the metamorphosis seems a

[77]

feat of magic. Descartes' initial perplexities with the claims and counterclaims of the various teachings at La Flêche can hardly have been expressed in clear and assured reasonings into the sources of their errors. We can imagine him setting aside these teachings in a mood of disgust at the deception practiced by his tutors, and he says, "I left as soon as age permitted." But his account of this in the "Discourse" suggests a rationality in the decision which must surely have come into existence as a result of his later reflections. There he speaks as if he turned to "the great book of the world" in order to analyze the claims of the people practicing in it, to use reason to see through these claims.

There is a similar injection of rationality into Descartes' account of his certainty concerning his own existence. He is led to discover this certainty by his doubts which suggested "making myself an object of study." There is nothing unusual in moving from doubt to a focus of attention upon man's nature. Through the whole history of doubt its advocates have been led to suggest that man is the measure of certainty. When Descartes says that in doubting he becomes aware of his own existence he reflects this perennial insight. But when he sees "clear and assured" reasoning in doubting and concludes that his existence is established as a thinking being because of his doubt, then the peculiarity of doubting has vanished and in its place Descartes has enthroned reason. Still, if there really is a positive and active doubting (if Descartes is not warranted in restating the nature of doubt as reason), doubt is not to be found in terms of negation.

Doubting is neither the negation of claimed certainty as Hume and "the man on the street" imply, nor is doubting the negation of the apparent and obvious as Descartes says it is. Hume and "the man on the street" imply that all experience is apparent or, what amounts to the same thing, that we are unable to distinguish between appearance and reality—even that the motivation to make such a distinction is illusory. But doubting, as a positive activity, insists upon this distinction; it expresses the fact that things *appear* to man. In the terms of Descartes, this distinction is made, but it is made on the assumption that doubting is reasoning. Thus Descartes distinguishes appearance from reality in terms of reason, not doubt; and in doing this he negates appearance.

There is a third alternative for an analysis of doubt which is able to distinguish appearance and reality without negating either. This alternative is to make of man the standard of such a distinction. The formulation of this alternative, however, is not simple. The typical statement, as attributed by Plato to Protagoras, for example, amounts to the observation that man's nature is a condition of his knowledge and, in consequence, his knowledge is relative to this nature. Thus, it has been observed that the conditions of perception are the possession of certain kinds of organs and that the content of perceptual knowledge is determined by these organs in relation to whatever is presented. Such a view of perceptual knowledge makes it relative to the perceiver and so appearance. But on this view all such knowledge is apparent in the same sense and hence there is no distinction possible on this basis between false perception and veridical perception. To speak of appearance in such a case is not meaningful: the assertion of the relativity of knowledge to man does not make of man a standard.

The formulation of man's nature as a standard requires a subtler analysis. The possibility of distinguishing between appearance and reality on the basis of man's nature is also a thesis developed by Kant. Kant argued that we can be aware of *appearance* because our analysis reveals in experience a formal structure and an ideal of unity contributed by the transcendental ego. In Kant's view, however, it is the *transcendental* status of the ego which enables it to function as a standard.

The development of this view is initially stated by an analysis of the formal structure of experience which is revealed to be the contribution of the transcendental ego. Such an analysis, called the critical method, proceeds by an internal investigation of the fact of noetic experience to determine what is necessary for such experience to occur for the thinking subject. Looked at from this perspective, noetic experience has a fundamental depth. It is revealed as a synthesis of content, that is, as an integral inter-relationship and organization of given materials which is productive of experience. Once we become aware of the two elements, structure and content, in noetic experience, and once we recognize the important fact that in the knowledge of mathematics and natural science this structure is universal and necessary (a priori) we are close to the conclusion that the transcendental mind is the source of antithetic structuring. This is the conclusion Kant draws. He tells us that the synthetic forms of space and time are introduced into experience as the structures relating material of sense by the transcendental mind. He presents a parallel argument in the case of the laws of nature which he views as categorical forms

[79]

of thought relating the material of sense presentations and ultimately deriving from the unity of consciousness. The details of his argument are well known and at any rate of no special importance here. What is significant is the claim that the transcendental mind in contributing this formal structure to noetic experience indelibly marks this experience as *phenomenal* in character, that is, as explicitly appearance.

We might at first suppose that any attribution of the formal structures of noetic experience to the human mind implies that such experience is subjective. This is far from the case. Kant is quite clear in pointing out the fact that what is subjective is relative to the inner existence of a psychological being and that the awareness and knowledge of such inner existence is consequent upon a spatial awareness which includes the inner self. That is, noetic experience is objective experience; it is that experience which is prior to any distinctions between subjective and external experiences. It is phenomenal and apparent not because it is a part of the internal life of a psychological individual, but because it is relative to a transcendental ego.

This distinction is important because it indicates at once that the critical method reveals the *appearance* of noetic experience not by relating it to the psychological individual but by expressing its relation to an individual of a radically different sort. Thus we see that Kant must clarify the nature of the transcendental ego in order to show how the critical method is successful in its function of revealing the phenomenal world as phenomenal. Certainly there are various emphases in Kant's thought as to the proper classification. At first glance it is easy to say that the transcendental ego, for Kant, is describable only in the terms of the forms of noetic apprehension, that is, the forms of space and time and the categories of scientific understanding. On this description, however, it is difficult to see what has been gained in Kant's account over the theory of the relativity of knowledge to the psychological individual. If the conception of the transcendental ego is really significant, we must suppose that there is more to it than a doctrine of the knower as a contributor of the forms of knowledge.

Perhaps the conception of knowledge formulated in terms of the forms of intuition and the categories as a systematic representation of reciprocally determining substances in space and time is satisfactory if it is regarded as a phenomenal account. Yet such a representation dissolves into infinity along lines in which it might be extended; that is, such a representation regarded as knowledge is radically unfinished. The active pursuit of unfinishable knowledge constitutes an activity without direction and so an activity which does not express even the appearance of its results. It is only when man's development of knowledge is guided by the concept of totality, as with the ideas of reason, that it could be called progressive and so have the kind of definiteness and cumulative significance which is satisfactory. Kant presents the transcendental ego not merely as a contributor of the forms of knowledge but as a contributor of the ideal standards for the development of knowledge. Thus his conception of the transcendental ego includes a statement of its contribution of the ideal of unity, expressed in the ideas of reason, to the nature of knowledge.

Traditionally these ideas, that of the soul, the world as a whole and of God imply a metaphysical context in which man has a derivative being. The theory of the soul as a spiritual substance, of the world as a cosmological whole and of God as the creator or ground of existence defines a specific context in which man plays a derivative part. In place of this Kant offers the theory that these ideas are expressions of the transcendental ego. He gives his theory plausibility by showing that the metaphysical account leads to paralogisms, contradictions and invalid proofs of God's existence. He elaborates his theory by formulating the ideas of reason as ideals which regulate the development and accumulation of knowledge within the forms of intuition and the categories.

Even when the conception of the transcendental ego is seen to include this reference to the ideas of reason, however, it does not obviously serve as the basis for judging knowledge to be phenomenal, that is, judging noetic experience to be *appearance*. Certainly the recognition of noetic experience as appearance is not possible in terms of the structure of intuition and the categories of the understanding. In these terms it is not possible to designate the merely apparent. Yet a reference to an ideal of unity which the transcendental ego contributes constitutively is equally useless in judging appearance for the same reasons. Undoubtedly this is why Kant insists that the ideas of reason are not constitutive but function as regulative of the development of knowledge. As regulative these ideas might well function effectively in some cases, but ineffectively in others, thus providing a basis for designating the nature of appearance.

[81]

Clearly Kant says that in terms of the ideal of unity which the transcendental ego contributes in the ideas of reason there is a basis for recognizing appearance. This basis is to be found when the particular and contingent material of experience comes to be organized more fully in accordance with the ideal aim of reason. It is a fact that this organization of the particular does occur, and its occurrence must be judged as a sign of reality. It is also a fact that this organization of the content of experience may fail to occur, and experience must then be judged as appearance. The essential point here is that the judgment of reality or of appearance is grounded in the ideal of unity which man contributes to the knowledge situation.

In drawing this conclusion Kant may be said to state the postulate that the content of experience is to some extent adapted to man and the conditions for the possibility of experience which his individuality imposes. In general man's individuality imposes the requirements of form which the particular contents of experience do not meet; yet in some cases these contents have the form which they must have or be given if noetic experience is to result. From Kant's perspective man stands, because of his own nature, as unable to solve the problem of gaining experience of reality. Thus the conditions of experience are the conditions which the transcendental ego imposes and not always those which the con ent of experience meets. Man is able to formulate the ideal of a solution to this problem, however, and to be aware that there do exist contingent solutions.

This is the situation which we have called that of doubt. Man as doubter is aware both of appearance and of reality. He is able to recognize that noetic experience which is appearance because he can state as an ideal, if not a fact, the conditions under which appearance can be overcome. In this sense man doubts appearance. But man is not in the position where he can set appearance aside. In Kant's terms, the ideas of reason which serve as ideal for the solution of the problem of knowledge are not constitutive of experience. This is to say that man is able to state an ideal, but not to achieve it with finality. Doubting, then, is that human activity which, while recognizing the inapplicability of the human conditions of experience to reality, is working toward an ideal that would overcome the limitations of these conditions without finally achieving this goal.

SECTION 3

When we doubt we call attention to the integral and essential place which man's interpretive and creative powers play in the construction of his knowledge and beliefs. To do this is to point to man as a source of human experience, but it is also to run the risk of conceiving this experience to be subjective, that is, as a kind of reinterpretation of the given in human terms. In this sense doubting is characteristic of many human activities. Indeed, in the contemporary world it is often the most dominant activities of man, such as science, politics, art and religion, that emphasize the human sources of human experience. In their dominance, however, they also suggest that this human emphasis is not subjective, but claim, for example, to express an ideal of progress and so to warrant a claim to objectivity. Thus such activities as these make clear man's claim to interpret situations and also affirm man's right to do this. Let us examine contemporary science and art as illustrations of these points.

Clearly, science today may be understood as essentially those technics and applications which give to the world a human significance. That many people today do view science in this way is evident in the approval of research in medicine and in the widespread use of scientific enquiry for industrial ends. To see scientific enquiry in this way is to see it as an expression of man's interpretive and creative response to given circumstances. So understood, science constitutes an interpretive and humanizing enterprise. It makes of the given something after the fashion of human judgment. This is to give to science a role of doubt for it definitely assigns to human powers a fundamental position.

The question we need to ask is whether this emphasis upon man's part in science is such as to make the whole enterprise subjective. Prima facie the answer to this question is *no,* for this view of science as a humanizing activity is one which we choose explicitly. Scientific enquiry need not be conceived as a kind of creative activity; in other ages and even today it has been understood differently. To prefer this conception of science is to claim for man the right of creative interpretation, to intend to accord to him the right of judgment. Such a claim might be wrong, but it is made and it is intended to be made, for example, when we speak of scientific progress. The claim that science progresses formulates the condition under which man's judgment is freed from subjectivity. In these terms the activity of science exemplifies a role for man which makes of him the measure of things, not in the subjective sense in which there is no measure, but in the fundamental sense in which man's being serves as standard. The whole positive tone of science and the sense of affirmative enterprise which attend it convey something of the ultimacy of this assumption and the fact that it is grounded in man's being.

An analogous point may be made in terms of a contemporary view of art. Today the function of art is often enough described as rendering man's natural and cultural environment significant for human experience. Not all artists today think of their efforts in this way, but many do; and certainly many of those who are not artists but appreciators see art in this way. Certainly art can and does serve this purpose, as for example when it shows the beauty in the endless repetition of mass produced articles and as aiding us to penetrate to the meanings of the shapes and colors of our cities. In such ways art represents to us, in the quality of our living experience, the world in which we live. John Dewey sees the function of art to be this, for example, when he says "The existence of art is the concrete proof . . . that man uses the materials and energies of nature with intent to expand his own life."

This conception of art sees it as a humanizing activity. In part a humanizing activity is interpretive and creative; it reflects man's powers as expressed in his ability to modify the world. Yet implicit in the emphasis on the humanizing function of art is the assertion of man's central status. The emphasis in art upon a humanizing function is intended to call attention to man's competence as a judge and creator, to accord to art something more than the temporary dominion of man over the present. It is intended to suggest that man is a pivot upon which whatever is ultimate turns. The artist as creator is not a producer of irrelevant and subjective results. His stature as creator is that of a hero who discovers new lands which reflect his objective competence and which he as creator opens to other men, thus revealing their competence as well. What makes the artist a hero and what transfigures the experience of the appreciator is the claim expressed in art that man has being.

Art and science not only do interpret and reconstruct man's environment in such a way as to augment his life, but in doing this they constitute affirmations of man's central importance. These claims are widely accepted in the culture of today. In large measure they typify our culture, setting its tone and orientation. How are these claims warranted? Too often the only warrant for them seems to be the creative and constructive elements in science and art, that is, their expression of man's creative powers in their modification of human environment. Yet this emphasis on creativity might deny the human centrality it is intended to re-enforce. If the constructive results of creative action reflect only the temporary dominion of man then the claim for human central-ity is the snare of egoism. Creative action which is not confirmed in its intention by the evidence of being cannot attest man's being. The warrant for man's central place is to be found only in that being which is opened to him by his creative arts.

When we choose and develop our human modes of action in terms of science or of art, we demand that given data be interpreted. We insist that what is given to us must be modified and that failure to do this is a mistake. There is a parallel to this demand in the context of man's perceptual and conceptual re-sponse to given situations. In this context the problem of how man's creative response may open being to him can be dealt with more briefly and in a way more suitable to an introductory statement than in the cultural context in which art and science have their place. For this reason we formulate the positive nature of doubt in perceptual and conceptual terms.

The importance of an interpretive response is clear enough when we view the contribution of conceptual thought to sense perception. Conceptual categories extend the range of perception, and they elicit patterns and connections which are not a part of perception as such. Yet it is true also that perception itself is an interpretive activity and that the results of conceptual analysis are subject to reinterpretation.

Perceptual data are given relative to conceptual analysis, but perceptions themselves are complex responses to circumstances which they interpret. Perceptions are the result of a learned re-sponse of the organism. They involve not only the physiological but the psychological pattern of the behavior of the perceiver and they change as these patterns change. Such patterns are the results of a learning process; in this sense, the individual learns to perceive, and what he perceives may be said to be a result of his learned responses. A part of what the individual perceives is a result of his own development and effort in learning. Thus the child comes to perceive spatial relationships over a period of years, the result of this maturation being his awareness of space, which varies from individual to individual. Similarly the individual may learn to see colors, to recognize forms, to hear sounds, which he has not been able to perceive before and which other men do not perceive.

A part of what the individual perceives is a result of his social environment. Spatial perception varies from one age to another and from one society to another. Thus there is a marked difference in spatial perception between the Middle Ages and Modern Times. This difference is reflected in the introduction of perspective and nature into modern painting and in the elimination of the hierarchical symbols and temporal events which are a part of medieval painting. We may cite the varied perception of sounds among different societies in the present as another example of social influence upon perception.

Perception is an interpretive, creative act; but so is thought. If the data which perception gives to us are not final because they may be changed, one of the functions of thought is to modify these perceptual results by analysis and conceptual interpretation. Such conceptual handling of the results of perception is a means to its change. The results of conceptual analysis are themselves not final, however, for whether these results are perceptual or ideas and theories they are subject to renewed analysis. Certainly the results of thought are often enough the data upon which thought operates. The attitudes and orientations of one historical epoch become the subject of criticism and analysis of the next. The intellectual fashions and the theories of an age are rarely repeated in the next; they are analyzed, criticized and superseded. The ideas and beliefs of an individual at any period in his life are subject, similarly, to reformulation as the result of his critical thought and meditation.

Thus what is given is mistakenly accepted if accepted as given. The apparent sense perception, the obvious thought, the patent social pattern, all such preanalytic data, need to be subjected to relevant analysis and are mistaken if taken for what they seem to be, that is, in their preanalytic meaning and significance. On the other hand, however, the results of interpretive analysis are not final. Whatever interpretation leads to can be reinterpreted; whatever analysis arrives at is subject to further analysis. Precisely because what is given is subject to analysis, regardless of the level of the terms in which it is given, so the results of analysis cannot be accepted as final. These results, in their turn, constitute the beginning of reinterpretation. Creative interpretation, perceptual or conceptual, introduces organization and system into the responses which it forms. But such organization and system are relative to the starting point and this relativity prevents acceptance of the system as final.

This analysis of the human perceptual and conceptual response exemplifies the negative aspect of doubting. We doubt what is given and we doubt the results of reinterpretation as well. What, then, is the aspect of man's perceptual and conceptual response which exemplifies positive doubting? In a preliminary sense, the positive aspect of doubting is to be seen in the assertion of man's right to interpret. Yet this right is suspect if interpretation means that what is given must be interpreted and that the results of interpretation must be based upon the given. This kind of interpretation may involve man as measure but it does not give him the right to serve as measure.

There is a part of creative interpretation as found in perception and conceptual analysis which suggests the sense in which man rightfully is the measure of things. One effect of interpretive schemes, perceptual or conceptual, is that they organize the situation which they interpret. In this they reflect man's dominion. This is not their only effect, however, for they also serve as the means of discovery: Our ability to perceive opens to us a world of perception to which we should otherwise be blind, and our capacity to conceptualize in a certain way affords us an awareness of interrelations of which we should otherwise be unconscious.

This aspect of interpretation is clearest in the realm of conceptual interpretation. When a scientist succeeds in interpreting a situation, his interpretation serves to make him aware of new subjects, it functions as an agent of discovery. This function of conceptual interpretation is not peculiar to science, although it is consciously used there. This function is fulfilled also in common sense; for in common sense experience we accept fads and fashions (which are interpretive schemes) in part because they open our consciousness to new areas of content in which we may move and experience.

The conceptual schemes of science are developed in order to open our experience to new realms. The discoveries which such schemes afford us occur within the scope of the interpretive response. They are unexpected and particular; they are contingent and yet they fall within an interpretive scheme.

The same aspect of interpretation is evident in the realm of perception through art. Art, like the fads and fashions of

[87]

common sense experience and like the interpretive schemes of science, provides a mode of perceptual interpretation which makes for perceptual awareness in new areas. Art has many functions: it enables us to play, it teaches, it serves as catharsis for repressed emotions. Whatever else it does, art awakens us to heretofore unperceived areas. When an artist makes a new use of color and light, we begin to see, through his art, the color and light in our environment of which we had been unconscious. When the artist initiates the use of common men as the heroes of his novels, we begin to observe such men; only then are we *able* to observe such men. In this sense art through its organizing use of concrete media functions as a means to perceptual discovery.

The discoveries which the perceptual schemes of art open to our perception are unexpected and unanticipated. But although contingent they fall within an interpretive scheme. I shall call such discoveries, whether perceptual or conceptual—in fact they are always both—by the name of *encounters*. As the examples of scientific conceptions and artistic creations testify, encounters are fairly common.

The significance of encounters is to be understood in two ways. First the occurrence of encounters is evidence that the interpretive schemes of perception and conception do not actually organize the whole of our awareness. These interpretive schemes are constitutive of parts of human awareness; they are in fact the structure of this awareness. The occurrence of encounters, however, suggests that these schemes are illustrative of ways in which the given can be brought into awareness, and a grasp of their illustrative character enables us to regard them as possible organizing patterns. Such patterns, as *possible* patterns, may be used or not. Therefore they can function as ideals for organizing the given material of awareness. In this function, although these patterns may be effective organizers of awareness, they must be held independently of their effectiveness, and in this sense they constitute a plurality of ideals which man formulates as guides for his perceptual and conceptual activity.

Second, the significance of encounters is to be found in their warranting of these ideals, for they evidence the adaptation of given circumstances to the schemes of man's interpretation. The content of an encounter occurs within the scope of an interpretive schema. Yet since this content is not the result of interpretive action, since it falls freely into the schema, it may be accepted as measured *in itself* by this schema as ideal. So far as its contingent occurrence in an encounter goes, this content may be accepted as what it appears to be, for it appears in encounter without distortion and as it is. In such undistorted appearance the content of an encounter testifies both to man's potential openness and to his centrality, for it warrants the ideals he formulates.

When man measures circumstances as he has the right to do, the warrant of his measure is found in encounters. These do not testify that man is a universal measure of things. On the contrary, both the contingency of encounters and their transiency testify that man's centrality is also contingent and possibly transient. Thus encounters demand that man see himself as central and that he understand his own centrality as requiring care and effort in order to be maintained. In this sense encounters are the positive aspect of doubting, for they reveal man's significant place and his limited and free powers. The being other than man's to which he is related in an encounter enables man to recognize his own being. In the contingency and transiency of the content of encounters, man sees reflected the contingency and transiency of his own being. Under the stimulus of this awareness he must act to preserve his own status, act to maintain and preserve his being.

The implicit mode of this action to maintain and preserve his own being is doubt. Doubt is directed against the claims of a unifying interpretation in which man would be lost as a central actor. But doubt is also directed toward the enhancement of a creative interpretation which makes man open to the being that warrants his freedom. This means that man doubts the very nature of his interpretive schemes and so himself. It is only through a fundamental doubt of whatever he is that man can hope to maintain and preserve his own centrality. Thus while man discovers his own importance through doubt of interpretive schemes, he also preserves his importance through doubt of himself and of his contributions to the being that appears in his encounters.

RICHARD GOTSHALK

REFLECTION AND SEEING

Philosophical reflection, in its aspiration for what is fundamental and universal, has its roots deep in the individual person reflecting. Whatever else this rootage may involve,[1] it involves the fact that reflection is the activity of a person whose being essentially involves temporality and whose activity is thereby permeated by an essentially temporal or historical character.[2]

A conditioning temporality shows itself, for example, in the deceptively simple fact that philosophical reflection emerges in the course of living one's life. This could mean simply that reflection occurs at a certain time in a person's life. But though in a sense this is true and pertinent, it does not exhaust the temporality involved. For thought also arises in such a way as to involve all three dimensions of time as they constitute a framework of one's life. Reflection occurs out of the background of a person's past, amidst the present affairs of the situation, in a life whose movement is always towards the future. Such emergence at a certain moment unites the life of the individual, continually spread out in all these dimensions, by giving that life a definite focus in the present situation. At the same time that uniting and focusing act itself incarnates and achieves much of its definiteness from the temporality and temporal content which it renders determinate. This is one way in which man's temporality constitutes an intrinsic condition entering into the nature of philosophical reflection.

[91]

There is a further way, arising out of this first and inseparable from it. For the moment of reflection emerges as immersed in materials already available because the individual stands as one human being interacting with others and finds himself at some location in the stream of human generations. Thus the person lives out of a past which, while his own, embodies what is not simply his but the gift of others who have preceded him. In short, he lives in history.

While philosophical reflection is temporally-historically so conditioned, its aim is the universal and eternal. These however are, and are reflectively discernible, only in and through the individual and temporal. Or better: since the universal and individual, eternal and temporal, are not distinct things or opposites, but constitute reflectively characterizable aspects of the concrete situation of being, reflection must break forth out of non-reflective immersion in the present actual situation. In so doing, it does not leave that situation but constitutes that altered mode of absorption within the concrete situation which attempts to elicit in conception the universal and eternal accessible to it.

Now this situation of the individual reflecting, being such as to involve time and history in the above indicated ways, may involve contemporary individuals living out of a historical past in great measure common among all. This past is not something gone and left behind, but is still integral to the present situation as its past. Thus, for example, we in the West live today in a present situation defined among other things by its emergence within a tradition of philosophy. More than that: we find our reflection growing in relation to a tradition which appears to have arrived at a dead end. We find our contemporaries generally expressing the feeling that something is fundamentally awry in the philosophical tradition. The course of events seems upon reflection to have suggested that there are fundamental limitations to previous thought, assumptions and simply temporally conditioned features which appear to have led reflection astray.

In this situation, many thinkers today have felt the need not simply to consider what other thinkers in the past have said (this is essential to reflection of any fundamental significance), but also to return to the past with the deliberate aim of eliciting what in general led to the situation of apparent sterility, what constituted the pervasive limiting and warping assumptions and conceptions embedded in past reflection.

The following pages seek to sketch certain facets of what has developed in my attempt to return to the philosophic tradition in this specific way. Since the aim of this essay is simply to indicate something of the direction and character of my thought along these lines, the sketch is deliberately limited in several respects. First, I will consider only one point which seems to me indicative of a pervasive limitation in past philosophic thought, namely, the manner in which traditional philosophy has tended to consider the central question, "What is thought and how is it related to reality?" Second, I will discuss individual philosophers (Aristotle, Descartes and Kant) only on a general level, without the detailed references needed to do more than merely state my point. Third, the consideration of the thought of others in this limited respect actually has grown out of a way of thinking which should be understood in its own terms if the considerations presented are to be fully clear and intelligible. But since the development of this essential background would lead far beyond the compass of an essay such as this, I will limit myself to occasional suggestions intended to convey the general drift of my thought but not expected to stand as any more than indicators whose elucidation would require bringing to bear much that is left untouched here. Finally, I will say much that parallels in a number of ways what contemporary thinkers such as Heidegger, Jaspers, and Dewey say.[3] I shall leave aside discussion of the extent and nature of any such parallels, lest the sketch become sidetracked in a discussion of points which are significant but not directly relevant for the aim of this essay.

Before I begin, a warning is in order. What I shall do in the following pages is attempt to indicate, in brief consideration of the thought of three men, a continuity of framework within which much of traditional thought has been worked out. In making explicit this more or less implicit framework, I am not suggesting the *irrelevancy* of the thought in question to what is problematic, but pointing to the presence (in a variety of ways) of a formulation and development of thought which by their very nature are incapable of *adequately* reflecting what is problematic. Thus I shall be suggesting how what is genuinely problematic in the thought of each man considered is obscured or distorted by the explicitly formed conception of the problematic.

Traditionally, thought has been taken, implicitly or explicitly, as a subjective apprehension of reality as object. Thought

[93]

which is to have any claim to attaining the truth of realities is taken as *knowing* an *object,* and what is *known* is formulable as knowledge gained or possessed. Underlying the conception of knowing an object has been a metaphor which conceives knowing on analogy with a detached seeing of a physical thing. What of the subject who apprehends objects? Traditionally, the conception of subject has been made intelligible simply as correlative to the objectively known, and the subject has been represented in distinction from the object by means of notions deriving their essential import either from their relevance to objects or from the analogy of the act of knowing to the act of seeing.

Now the analogy which underlies the development of the conceptions of both subject and object is one that grasps seeing (and thus knowing) only abstractly. Thus, in addition to the limitations to the metaphor due to the irrelevance of the whole analogy, there are those due to its abstractness. So far as traditional modes of thought take the nature and import of reality as man may understand and act upon these to be construed solely in reference to the subject-object dichotomy, these limitations are not clearly recognizable. To the extent that this is so, the problem as to the nature of reflective thought and its relation to reality has been posed in such a way as to distort its character even though the questioning has by no means been insensitive to the experiential matters pertinent to what is here problematic. It is this distortion involved in the traditional "spectator theory of knowledge" [4] that I should like to consider briefly.

In the remainder of this essay, I want (1) to suggest the nature of the metaphor of thinker as spectator, (2) to indicate several elements of traditional modes of thought directly reflecting this metaphor, (3) to consider certain important traditional figures so far as certain aspects of their thought are defined by these and other spectatorial elements, and (4) to suggest in a summary way the basic limitation of the metaphor, particularly in respect to the relation of philosophical understanding to being.

1.

The term "object" has a long and varied tradition of usage in philosophy, but one of its essential uses has been to indicate the possibility of thought's obtaining relevant purchase upon reality.

But reality as object is reality only as it can be gotten out in front of the mind's eye and formulated with reference to what confronts one. For ob-ject is reality as it is "thrown in front" of one, as it "stands over against" one (*Gegenstand*). Moreover, as the parallel between *gegenstehen* and the Latin *obstare* might suggest, an object is reality as an obstacle, a center of resistance, something with an independent localized nature that resists action upon it. Offering resistance to human manipulation, an object stands outside man as something essentially physically separate, "out there" in respect of me "in here" or localized in my body. In addition, an obstacle, if it really is taken as an obstacle, must be noted and taken into account, and being something physically separate, vision (rather than touch) provides the essential basis for orientation. For within the temporal and changing spatial situation, sight, with its detachment and "action at a distance," is of primary importance in timely adjustment. Certain characteristics of this vision in this pragmatic situation—its separation from the object physically, its lack of obvious bodily sensation and feeling in the exercise of the power of seeing, its awareness of something localized "out there" and explicit for attention—have been translated into the knowing act when this has been taken in analogy with sight. That such a translation is natural and far-reaching is suggested by the fact that we find throughout language words referring to the cognitive situation in terms with underlying visual connotations (for example, in English, theory, speculation, evidence, demonstration, intuition) or else metaphors and phrases such as "seeing the point or meaning," "gaining enlightenment," "seeing the light," "dawning on me," "seeing a demonstration to be valid," "seeing what you are driving at," and so forth.

2.

In general, when seeing is taken as paradigm, cognitive apprehension of reality is knowing it as it is "in itself": the object directly present as there in its own independent nature.[5] Secondly, reality in itself, as envisaged, is describable and fixable in thought in terms of the characters of its presentation: the independent object as apparent and as obstacle offering resistance to manipulation. Philosophy is the description of the characteristic features of reality as such, a description of what ultimately exists (for example, the elemental) rather than an elucidation of realities in their ultimacy. Thirdly, description of what exists in itself (and verification of such descriptions and/or explanations) fastens upon what is explicit through intuition (intellectual and/or sensuous) and/or demonstration (intellectual pointing out which receives its grounding in reality intuitively apprehended) : the independent resistant object as "seen."

3.

The first thinker I should like to consider is Aristotle. The oft-repeated opening lines of the first book of Aristotle's *Metaphysics* (980a 23–28) suggest a kinship between knowing and seeing. This kinship is developed in later books of the *Metaphysics,* where the analogy of knowing to seeing is sometimes supplemented by a reference to touch.[6] This reference is subordinate [7] and seems to provide the sense of immediacy and reality involved in apprehension but not conveyed by the metaphor of sight alone.[8]

How does this conception of knowing in general enter into and color Aristotle's conceptions of reality (being and substance) and of the reflective unfolding of thought (first philosophy or theology) ?

Aristotle characterizes philosophy (more specifically, first philosophy or theology) as a theoretical science and thus places it together with "physics" and mathematics in a group distinct from the practical sciences and from the forms of productive knowledge. First philosophy thus has certain features in common with the other theoretical sciences, among which are the possibility of demonstrative and certain knowledge and a foundation in specific ultimate and nondemonstrable principles directly intuited by reason. (Note the visual reference in all this.) But first philosophy is distinct from the other two theoretical sciences because it is universal and they are special.

In accordance with its definition (*Metaphysics* 1026a 31–32) first philosophy is the study of "being *qua* being—both what it is and the attributes which belong to it *qua* being." Such a study is essentially a study of substance, since substance is what fundamentally is. What is substance? The term *"ousia"* is used in a variety of ways in various contexts, but central to its meaning when the reference is to what is and the manner in which it is, is its

[96]

reference to a determinately characterized 'this' (individual)
which exists independently. From this we might be led to expect
that first philosophy is the study of independently existing individual things as independently existing and individual. But this is
not the case. Instead existence (so far as this is the existing of the
individuals which are ultimately real) and individuality are virtually ignored.

How is this the case?

Aristotle's development of the conception of being takes place
through the categories and such notions as form and matter,
actuality and potentiality, change or motion, and cause. What
emerges seems to be something like the following. That which
most fundamentally is—substance (in opposition to what has
dependent existence) —*is* (as primary substance) only through or
by means of secondary substance. For example, any particular tree
is only as it is a *tree,* only as it emerges into being as something
with characteristic modes of appearance and activity. Secondary
substance, as the essence of primary substance, thus achieves for
Aristotle a primacy with respect to being, even as primary substance is that which fundamentally is.

Now the notion of secondary substance renders intelligible
what is only in the sense that it defines *what* the being is in
descriptive terms, that is, as it may be "seen." Taking the multiplicity of beings in this way, their being is absorbed wholly into
the essential and universal. The being which is—the individual—
is not thereby rendered intelligible at all, but rather becomes an
instance of a kind instead of an individual.[9]

Further, the notion of existence which here emerges is one
also absorbed into secondary substance, as the presence [10] of a
distinct something, which is definable and intelligible in universal
terms as this distinct thing and which functions as ultimate reference point for the attribution of characters (which are, but in
dependent fashion) . Further than this, "existence" has no meaning.[11] This, of course, means that Aristotle has missed existing as
the mode of being of individuals. Existence rather is the fact that
there is something of a certain kind there to be seen.

That Aristotle's reflection grew within a sensitivity to individual beings in their being is abundantly testified to in his
thought; for example, his conceptions of philosophy as beginning
in wonder, of an unmoved mover, of a direction in the course of
the existence of each thing. But that his thought did not bring
forth in an explicit and satisfactory fashion what he was sensitive

to and seeking in a groping fashion to clarify is equally clear. That this happened is due in some measure to the spectatorial elements in his thinking.

Perhaps the point I wish to make concerning Aristotle's thought can be reinforced if we approach it from another angle. Let us attempt to look to the legitimate experiential applicability of the explicitly developed factors in his conception of substance. A substance is a thing, determinately characterized, with a localizable and knowable nature, etc. This conception of beings receives its *prima facie* applicability within the context of a way of taking things which is essentially objective and nonreflective. This way of taking things is exemplified within modern science— physical science in particular—and I think it is no accident that from Aristotle on, philosophy and science (however the conceptions of these changed) were not clearly distinguished or distinguishable. Nor is it an accident that with the rise of modern science and its success in the 19th and 20th centuries, philosophy found itself apparently at the end of its tradition, replaced by a more effective mode of knowing. Nor is the change in the meaning of "theory," and its almost exclusive appropriation by science in modern times, an accident.

Without developing in any measure a conception of science, I think it would be well to note the following in order to clarify what I have just said. It is fairly widely acknowledged that the (natural) scientific approach to things leaves the individual as such unintelligible; what has significance is at best the particular, the exemplar of general characters. This incapacity of natural science to understand the individual as such is inherent in the very framework which constitutes the possibility of such science. For involved in this form of scientific endeavor is an abstract mode of consideration of realities presented and received, one which allows for the possibility of grasping general characters as such. The abstraction involved is essentially the ignoring of the being of individual things as existing. Not only is the individual as such unintelligible and in fact ignored, but the nature and meaning of *his* existing *as individual* is as well. At best there is abstract reference to this.

Perhaps the meaning of the last statement may be suggested as follows: for the most part in our experience, the meaning of the existing of things is absent or not to the foreground. Only at times does it come home relatively explicitly and with it some basis for speaking of existence in a concrete manner. For example, the

[98]

sense of wonder with which natural things may be contemplated at times is one experiential ground for suggesting that the existing of things, when concretely appreciated and rendered intelligible, is indeed an ex-sisting, a continuous standing forth out of nothing towards other things. Within the context of the sense of being come alive, there is no purchase for speaking of independent (or dependent) existence; at best one could speak of "independent" (that is, distinct) existents or centers of existence. Yet when a human being is active with respect to other beings in such a way as to abstract from their being as such and to consider beings in an attempt to elicit a describable character—in other words, to grasp them objectively, as if they *were* "in themselves"—the definitive presence or the meaning of the presence of ex-sisting of things is— if present—dismissed as irrelevant. Givenness becomes, as referred to within this context, simply the fact of the localizable presence of what is a distinct entity with a determinable nature. In fact, then, the basis in experience for the explicitly developed factors in Aristotle's conception of substance suggests that the factors in question do not offer a conception of being at all.

Such is the essential foundation in experience for the explicitly developed elements in Aristotle's notion of substance. But such is also the context within which the notion of *theoria* in its etymological meaning and the general analogy of seeing and cognizing have their just reference. Whenever the notion of *theoria* is used beyond this context, as Aristotle does when he distinguishes first philosophy from the special sciences and as he would have to do if he were to allow that to which he is sensitive to become explicit within the presuppositions of his form of thought, the metaphor misleads. Thus, for example, the philosophical concern for the universal and eternal leads to questions about the conditions of reflection itself. But the condition of the presence of things to "sight" (or sight) can not itself be "seen" (or seen). Nor can the "seer" "see" himself "seeing." So far as Aristotle clarifies the thought which constitutes philosophical reflection as *theoria* and so far as he treats first philosophy as merely a general descriptive classificatory system concerned with universal features of things which are, so far Aristotle's thought is imprisoned within a mould which can lead—if carried to its limits and purified of contents unintelligible within its strictly conceived purview—only to science, not to philosophy.[12] And yet, despite the element of the scientist in Aristotle and despite a form of thought which would seem to indicate a totally scientific bent, the scientific is not the

[99]

moving force of Aristotle's thought. The conceptions of purpose
and of wonder, of activity in distinction from movement, and of
spontaneity of natural movement, serve among others as aspects
of Aristotle's explicit thought which perhaps more adequately
reflect the concrete significance of the being of things; at least
they constitute foci for experiential reflection which could suggest
that to which he was sensitive and was attempting—though in an
essentially abstract way—to remain faithful.[13] However, it is
rather those abstract elements constituted by the concept of substance and the notion that philosophy is a theoretical science—or,
to put the two together, by the notion that the task of reflective
understanding is a description of what is—that have had the most
decisive influence upon the whole course of Western philosophy at
the same time that these signify a fundamental weakness in it.

Let me now pass on to modern philosophy. While the differences between ancient and modern thought are great, there is an
essential continuity, due both to the historical influence of Greek
(especially Aristotelean) modes of thought and to the presence in
modern thought of an analogous tendency exemplifying the same
abstractness. The differences between ancient and the initial forms
of modern philosophy (exemplified in Descartes) lie to a great
extent in movements of thought developing in connection with
the rise of modern empirical science. Some of these tendencies,
manifested for example in Galileo, concern the distinguishing of
the matematically treatable and stable characters of natural things
from other qualities which seem relative to the perceiving organism (secondary qualities, as they were to be called) and which are
not to be accepted as having status in the real world out there. I
assume that the general character of this background is familiar
and therefore want merely to indicate the nature of the thought
of Descartes as it arises out of this background and functions to
provide a metaphysical rationalization for the new science.
Though Descartes misunderstands the nature of empirical science
and of philosophy, his thought sets the essential framework for the
development of philosophical reflection from his time through
much of the nineteenth century.

Descartes seeks throughout his work for an assured metaphysical foundation for all our knowledge. For if metaphysics, the
fundamental science and that upon which the rest of our knowledge is based, is not secure, how can we ever have true knowledge
at all? The form which his search takes is one intimately connected
with his mathematical bent. Mathematics is the paradigm for

knowledge and for the method of obtaining knowledge; for mathematics involves an intuitive self-evidentness in the clear and distinct ideas at its foundations, a certainty in the movement of its demonstrations (moving intuition) and a method that involves resolution of problems to their simplest elements and building up from there. First philosophy or metaphysics, of course, does not deal with number or quantity but involves the same search for what can be made explicit for rational apprehension with certainty. Thus the central feature of the Cartesian way of thinking is the conception of thought in which thought can be analogized to the use of the eyes to see.[14] And only what is so seen or intelligible, fundamentally is.

Within this mathematical and visual model Descartes works out his thought in such a way as to bring the self to the center of the reflective search for being. The ostensible focus of his attention is an existent individual whose existing involves activity of a certain sort (namely, thought or conscious activity within the context of apprehension of an objective content). The actual focus of his attention is the existent individual *taken as* center of thought. Thus while Descartes' concern is with an existing individual, he does not attend, for example, to himself *as such* an individual (as René Descartes) but to himself just in so far as he is *what* he is, that is, just in so far as he who *is acts* (in this case, thinks). In Aristotelean terms, Descartes' concern is with secondary, not primary, substance.

In so attending, Descartes comes to characterize the individual who so acts as subject. For Descartes, the term "subject," while correlative now to "object," still carries with it the connotations which "subject" had in the Aristotelean analysis, where "subject" meant "that which is thrown under" the properties, that is, substance as underlying substratum. But "subject" is now limited to substance as thinking. Nevertheless, the connection between "subject" and "substance" is so close that Descartes carries over without qualms the idea of existence involved in the concept of substance when he treats the existent individual who thinks.

With the above general indication of certain characters of Descartes' mode of thought, let me now center my discussion of the character and the effect of the visual metaphor in his thought on the discussion in the *Meditations*. There, Descartes' thought focuses on the moment of discovery of oneself as existing in an actual doubting. His characterization of what is understood in such immediate and intuitive awareness is: I think, therefore I am.

[101]

Such a moment of awareness is not an awareness of an object by means of an idea (as, for example, in the case of material things) and not an awareness of an object "out there" at all, but rather the awakening to one's own thoughtful ex-sisting: a peculiarly reflexive awareness of a being with respect to his being.

Let us note three elements in Descartes' treatment of this "truth." First, the moment of discovery of my own thoughtful existing is treated by Descartes as an example of a moment of "intuitive" and "clear and distinct" thought, as if these terms had the same meaning as they would have in reference, for example, to geometrical truths and their discovery (where what is known is "outside" and "in front of" oneself). But the existential situation is not visual at all—the seer cannot see himself as seeing but only as seen—but reflexive.

Second, the visually dominated characterization of the being of the thinker involves use of traditional notions themselves originally relevant to objects and therefore only abstractly referent to realities. Thus while Descartes' attempt to talk about the subject as one sort of substance is an attempt to retain it as such (not as object, in the sense in which other things are), yet his is not only a use of abstract concepts essentially relevant to objects but also an abstract characterization of the sense of being an individual in thinking. All thinking is by an existent individual; the subject, however, is the individual who thinks about other things, conceived merely in his role as center of awareness correlative to what is thought of as object. Thus the concept of subject is reached by ignoring (that is, abstracting from) existence and individuality (and thus, activity as rooted concretely in them) and by casting under the manifold objective thought contents and thought activities a center which serves as unity correlative to them. This center—a functional one—is not I *as* an existent but I (who exist) so far as I am conceived abstractly as active in a certain way. Thus "I" refers to the subject, which I am at best in the sense that this constitutes my role. Actually, a subject does not exist,[15] but an individual may, in the existential situation, think reality objectively and—to that extent, simply as thinker—be conceived (although still abstractly) as subject.

Third, what constitutes the experience which is the center for his thought is an actual moment of existing, not something feigned or feignable. Yet such a moment could never be apart from other existent beings with whom the thinker ex-sists. If the truth

Descartes means to hold to is an existential one, the whole situation—including his doubting—must also be one and be recognized explicitly as such. Yet Descartes' attempt to treat this moment within the context of the traditional conception of substance and by the method of doubt prevents him from bringing to explicitness the full existential situation. Nevertheless, the elements of this situation animate his thought behind his back and lead him to retract what he has earlier affirmed, to prove what is only another and ever-present dimension of the actual situation he is in, to pretend he is in a situation he later says he could not be in at all, and so forth. Thus, for example, as Descartes himself recognizes during the course of the *Meditations,* thinking (including doubt) does not take place in a vacuum. There are in fact two (or three, if you count himself) ever-present elements or dimensions of the existential situation of thought which Descartes (at least implicitly) recognizes—and must recognize, if he is to doubt—but which in the course of his doubt he eliminates as contents which he knows with certainty, only to re-establish them later.

The first of these is God (and himself as created by God). Descartes' doubt can proceed only on the basis of deliberately ignoring the dimension of the existential situation that constitutes the very possibility for his doubt itself: the presence of (the idea of) God or infinite perfection, such that he can recognize his own imperfection and can doubt that he has the truth even in those cases where he most surely seems to.[16] Thus the doubt only leads to knowing "myself better" and discovering "more clearly the author of my being." [17] Thus it depends on the ideas of self (as existing) and of God becoming clearer in the course of doubt although they are indispensable in some sense *already* if one is to doubt at all. These conditions of doubt are not themselves dubitable; they actually fall outside the range of doubt, and in so doing are in some sense indubitable. In fact they are dimensions which require clarification but are obscurely present and recognized already.

The second of these is also a condition of existential doubt, but one which Descartes ignores in its existential bearing, since his preconceptions will not allow him to take sensible realities seriously in their being, though he never really doubts that they are.[18] This dimension—that of the reality of sensible things other than himself—Descartes ostensibly treats as the starting point for his doubt. But actually, he never even considers or asks for the being of sensible things, or takes the senses as avenues of access to actualities themselves. Rather, he is already convinced that the being of sensible things lies in their substantiality, that this being lies behind the sensible characters and is not itself sensible (though material in some sense), and that the sensible characters are somehow a product of causal interaction between material objects and, eventually, mind. What serves as foundation for his treatment of the being of sensible things seems to be (a) his scientific interest and knowledge, which led him (and his contemporaries as well) to take what is fundamentally knowable in sensuous realities to be their mathematically measurable characters, and (b) his acceptance (as self-evident) of the Aristotelean thesis (with its conception of independent existence and descriptive nature which constitutes what the substance is as something knowable) that the being of things is to be understood in terms of substance. Given this conviction about the being of sensible realities buttressed by these supporting conceptions, Descartes, who seems to have no counterbalancing sense of involvement with things which give themselves in their sensuous appearing to offset his theoretical bent, never takes seriously the very presupposition and starting point of his doubt, his involvement with existent sensuous realities. In actuality Descartes' doubt about the "existence" of external things (of the whole world, not just of some things) is not really a doubt relative to their existing at all, but a doubt relative to the referability of any conceived contents to a reality outside experience as their actual substratum. This doubt, in the radical form Descartes gives it, is possible only under the assumption of a self-contained mind whose ideas are merely mental contents, that is, only under the condition of ignoring the existential character of the situation of doubt. For existent things must be given in order for a question as to their existing to arise, and, as Descartes admits, this givenness is nothing we really ever doubt. If that is so and if the question as to the being of other things is to be taken seriously, this question ought to be first one in clarification of what it means to be. The being of sensible realities is as much an indubitable condition of doubt as is God and the existence of the thinking being who is created by God.

However, since Descartes does not treat the being of sensible realities existentially and is led to conceive that he might be the only being who existed, he is forced, when he wants to reestablish the "existence" of those things outside himself, to (1) reify being in its universality (that is, to create a God, who is in effect the unity which has to re-enter the picture by the back door when existent beings are treated as substance, that is, as self-contained and not unified) and (2) make this actual individual being other than himself and knowable by himself the basis for accepting the immanent standard of truth (clarity and distinctness) as being really rooted in the existential situation. Then he has to (3) argue from his clear and distinct idea of "material objects" to their actual "existence," by means of the perfection and power of God, together with a natural disposition of man as an embodied being to believe in an external world which is material.[19] Thus the being of external things (their existence, not their objective nature) cannot be established by Descartes purely on theoretical grounds but only with the addition of practical grounds on the basis of an element of man's being as an agent.

What lies behind this whole procedure is Descartes' inability —within the spectatorial framework as he develops it—to take the existential situation seriously (in particular, to remain true to the unity of things as existing, the initial but as yet incomplete unity of a universe) and thus his having to take and mistake certain aspects of it again in order to escape solipsism.

In sum: Descartes introduces as the central conception of the philosophical interpretation of being the subject-object dichotomy, but he does so in the course of reflection which is incapable of making explicit the concrete conditions of the thought within such a dichotomy. When we ask for these conditions and the nature of thinking as a mode of activity rooted in them, we must ask, not about the "subject," but for the existent individual who thinks and for thinking as a mode of activity of an existent individual. And to the questions, "how is he? how does he exist?" we can say that the individual exists not as substance (as continuous self-contained actual substratum) but as ex-sistent among other ex-sistents. This should be particularly clear where the being who exists is said to be essentially thinker or subject, for there is no subject apart from an object and no existent thinker apart from existent realities with respect to which he in some way thinks. Other beings who stand forth to meet the existent human being are presupposed in his activity of thought and function to set the initial worldly conditions under which human activity lies. These beings, however, are not objects nor substances, and their appearing is not a matter of providing "appearances" which fail to convey, and stand in contrast with, their reality as it is "in itself."

[105]

And yet, with all that I have said above, I think Descartes is not at all insensitive to concreteness, and his *Meditations* are not merely a literary form irrelevant to his fundamental concern. Actually his whole analysis is one which is implicitly led by existential considerations, even though it is also one which is explicitly steered by the demand for intuitive clarity and demonstrative certainty that obscures the essential existential clarification of the nature of being and reasonable thought which is actually at stake. The tension between explicit and implicit shows itself in other places: in the pretenses Descartes has to make that God can and must be proven to exist, that doubt can proceed even without a knowledge of God and self which is in some sense indubitable, and so on.

The development of modern thought after Descartes follows a course which, whether in the empirical or rationalist tradition, is determined to a great extent by the Cartesian framework of questioning. This is so even with Kant, whose thought is strongly critical of Cartesian pretensions to rational knowledge of things "in themselves." Kant, particularly in his discussion of the Paralogisms, is critical of Descartes' claim to know rationally (that is, nonempirically) the subject who thinks (the subject of the *cogito*). While doing so, Kant's analysis of the cognitive situation in effect starts from the same situation as the *cogito,* experience being taken to be subjective apprehension of objects. But Kant argues that the "I think" is purely formal, in the sense that the noumenal self is only indeterminately referred to by it, not in such a way that the category of substance, for example, would strictly give knowledge of it. But in making this starting point and in developing his interpretation of it within the context of a belief in the certain knowledge of objects, Kant ignores, much as Descartes did, the concrete conditions of knowing (the existential situation as such) and separates the being of sensible realities from the being of realities "in themselves" in a way just as detrimental to sensible realities as Descartes' procedure and in a way that makes unintelligible any unity of ultimate realities (and in particular the unity presupposed in his own explanation of experiencing).

One of Kant's main reasons for treating the subject formally is to provide some explanation of the universality of claim involved in a cognition of objects. For if anything is object and conceived as such, it is object for any subject. This universality can be made good, Kant thinks, only if the subject as such becomes creative, that is, constitutes the objectivity of objects. Thus man takes his place as the standard for being, that is, as the determiner of the being of objects. But not, of course, of the being of things in themselves. Of their being, man is not determiner; he is not even cognizer.

This problem of the universality of being, so far as being is known, arises also in Descartes, but is placed in a more fundamental context. Descartes also thought that we have an innate idea of material substance (serving as parallel to Kant's categories and forms of intuition) and that our empirical apprehension of objects (for example, the piece of wax referred to in the *Meditations*) is possible only on this basis (that is, only on a basis of judgment in terms of those characters constituting the objectivity of the object). But in Descartes, the mind did not constitute this objectivity but only discovered it. The question is then relevant: how does one know when the mind has genuinely discovered it? How does the universality of claim (for any subject) show and justify itself? To answer this, Descartes ultimately appealed beyond man to God.

However, this appeal was formulated in answer to a question more inclusive than Kant's. For Descartes is not asking merely for the objectivity of objects but—more fundamentally—for the basis on which *actual* and *ultimately real* objects can be brought together with an actual and *ultimately real* thinker. Thus Descartes is asking his question within the existential context, where the existential dimension as such—no matter how misconstrued by Descartes—is relevant. Thus God, who is for Descartes an *actual* and not ideal being, guarantees the objectivity of the object by guaranteeing the clarity and distinctness of the apprehension and —more fundamentally—guarantees the universal validity of what is known in a case where the knowledge is not of things merely in relation to a subject in experience but of the being of existent things in a universe, that is, of things as they ultimately are when created by God, not by man. Kant's forms of objectivity are only forms of a possible world whose actuality depends on the givenness of content by realities which do not *as such* manifest themselves in that world; Descartes' objectivity is claimed as the form of a given actual world in its ultimacy.

Perhaps the similarities and differences in the views of Descartes and Kant on this point can best be seen at this point by noticing the character of the distinction in being (between appearances and things in themselves) which permeates Kant's thought.

The phrase "in itself" initially had its significance within the existential sense situation when existent things are received and taken in a certain way, namely, in such a way that what is known is a distinct objective nature possessed by something which is and is what it is apart from the knower. Thus it actually has no reference to being at all but to things taken in such a way as to abstract from their being. In any case, the contrasting phrase is not "in relation to the mind" but something like "as falsely apprehended" (through subjective distortions or biases, misjudgments or hallucinations). But with the interpretation of the general sense situation objectively (as in Descartes) and with the claim that such explanation is ultimate, the perception of other realities was interpreted as a causal interaction. Then the contents so originated (appearances) became contrasted with the realities which were "really there" for the knowing mind, so that appearances were said not to be (or to represent accurately) things as they are "in themselves." Hence what is "in itself" comes to be taken as reality (in its ultimacy) lying *behind* appearances.

Kant in effect presses this direction of interpretation further: what is "in itself" is not even accessible to reason, thus is not spatial and material (as Descartes held), but is absolutely out of relation to knowledge and mind. Thus in effect all experience and knowledge of the being of objects is illusion so far as any claim it might have to give reality *as such* is concerned. For Descartes, this would have meant solipsism, but Kant partially escapes this by recognizing the "problem of the external world" to be one only within experience. But this is not sufficient as an answer to the question as to the unity of existent beings in a universe, such that for a thinker there is something other and real. Within experience, there is indeed a correlativity of (actual) subject and (actual) object, *given* the modification of the sensibility of an actual being by actual realities. But how is it that actual realities other (not external in space) than man *give* themselves to him? That is, how *are* realities, such that they are so directed as to be able to constitute a unity and thereby so real as to produce (in their activity and interaction) experience by providing a purchase for the mind's activity? Kant can give no answer to this question. All he can show is how a world of objects can arise when other realities modify our sensibility. Descartes' answer (that in effect God unites realities, God being a knowable being for man, etc.) is not open. For according to Kant, the concept of God (as well as of world and soul) is only an idea which functions regulatively. Ideas are only subjective rational demands, which impose no necessity on realities and which function only within the context of experience as already constituted by the givenness of realities and the activity of the mind. Their function is simply to require that the subject bring experience to (or relate it to) totality in some sense. But what constitutes the legitimacy of such demands of reason? What constitutes their relevance to things in themselves, such that we can expect of these things that they will give themselves in such a way as to be so organizable? Descartes would connect reason with an ontological foundation which is knowable; Kant can not. Thus we are left in the dark so far as any reflective answer is concerned.[20]

Kant is making a very important point here: the conditions and nature of the unity of realities as such are not *knowable*. In Kant's terms, what lies beyond the formal (and thus also beyond the material) is what is ultimately real, and this is beyond science or metaphysics, construed as objective knowledge. And yet his way of making the point is criticizable. In the first place the transcendental and *a priori*, so far as these signify the constitutive aspects of the spectatorial mind when this mind is made active and thus essentially a biased and distorting spectator with respect to reality, do not indicate the concrete conditions of thought in the existential situation. Moreover, the placing of reality as such beyond the scope of objective knowledge is not counterbalanced by an appreciation of a mode of concrete understanding in which it is possible to find some purchase within being in its ultimacy that is not just a "rational faith" or a thinking which is no understanding at all. If, as seems to me to be the case, the situation of man is the sensuous one (where sense is receptivity to reality as it gives itself in existing), the philosophical question as to being— what does it mean to be?—must be answered *within* the situation on the basis of the thoughtful clarification of moments in which the sense of being comes alive.[21] If the meaning of being, clarified through reflection on such experience, involves existing, so that being is essentially universal (thus, in some sense relational), there is no justification for a question as to the being of things which poses itself in the form: what are things "in themselves"? The "in themselves" is an abstraction relevant at best to the scientific concern for things and irrelevant to the question of being; just the reverse, in a sense, of Kant's view.

In short, while Kant is explicit in attempting to make agency —as he conceived it (essentially as rational self-determination by finite beings) —fundamental, his conception of it was abstract and distorted by spectatorial assumptions and ideas having their import in a visual context.

4.

In the above discussion of Aristotle, Descartes and Kant, I have tried to suggest one point: that in varying ways the traditional mode of philosophizing (culminating actually in Hegel, not in Kant), when it is concerned with elucidating the nature of being and its relation to thought, is colored by a certain inadequate framework of thought. The thread of continuity I have tried to point out is the subject-object dichotomy, worked out more or less explicitly on the basis of the analogy of spectator and thinker. This underlying framework, I have suggested, is inadequate, mainly for reasons traceable to the inadequacy of the metaphor at its roots. What forms the basis for the inadequacy of the metaphor? Underlying all the particular reasons I have offered in the course of the discussion above, is this reason. Philosophical reflection, in seeking the universal and eternal, seeks what underlies and permeates itself.[22] That is, it is a seeking for being from within being. Man, within being, is agent, and his thought, if it is to reflect his situation as agent and to elucidate his being and that of other beings in the world, must involve the presence of, and remain true to, the sense of being belonging to a being *in* being. For man, this means reflecting from his own standpoint as agent, clarifying his modes of activity (as manners of movement in being with beings, so that being is at stake) in a nondescriptive, nonspectatorial way. Man cannot get outside of his condition to "look at" it,[23] any more than he can get outside being to "look at" it. Nor will "looking at" others allow elucidation of them in their being, for "looking at" involves among other things a presumption of detachment at variance with the manner in which beings exist universally, thus the manner in which the beings I "look at" are essentially united with me in my being.

To affirm the above is merely to sketch out tentatively a warning against certain pitfalls for reflection, as these are exemplified in past thought. The intent in doing this is to suggest the direction of my thought, without attempting to develop it in its

[110]

own form and terms. Enough will be accomplished if this suggestion is conveyed and more than enough if someone is stimulated by what he has read here to think out for himself the character of our past philosophical tradition and its pertinence for us today.

NOTES

1. Also involved, for example, is the fact that the act of reflecting, as an act of an existing human being, grows out of a manifold universality, such as would be involved in any individual's situation as the situation of an active existing human being. See the subsequent discussion of Descartes (on the indubitability of the conditions of doubt) .

2. The manner in which and the extent to which this is so, as well as the manner in which to make a distinction between temporal and historical, is matter for careful consideration. But I can not enter into it in this essay.

3. Despite the parallels, I have not in this essay acknowledged any indebtedness or made much reference to the thought of these men for the reason mentioned in the text; and also because, as I was first developing the ideas expressed here, I was thinking along lines formed in great measure in response to ideas of Professor Henry Bugbee. In addition, I was thinking in almost a vacuum with respect to first or second hand acquaintance with the thinkers mentioned. When I came to read their thought, it was with a sense of fellowship in a common critique, a fellowship of which I had not previously been aware. I have since learned much from them (particularly from Heidegger) , but a discussion of that is beyond bounds here.

4. The phrase goes back at least to Dewey, but my conception of it includes Dewey himself as involved in such a theory.

5. Note that difficulties arise when this independence is questioned by reference to "objective" explanation of the subject. Thus perception as part of a causal process and (in Kant) mind as having an active or constructive role in the production of experience: in both cases, reality as it ultimately is, is inaccessible.

6. See *Metaphysics,* 1051b 24 and 1072b 21–22, for example.

7. To the best of my knowledge touch is never used as if it were by itself a sufficient analogue; it always seems to stand for a partial factor in a knowing dominantly conceived as seeing.

8. This sense of immediacy is integral to Aristotle's conception of knowing and, even without the metaphor of touch, would be suggested if we remember that we "see" in philosophy while in the midst of wonder, which as lovers of wisdom we never escape.

9. An individual is unique, so that there can be no principle of individuation if this be a universal. For what falls under a universal is

[111]

identical with all else that does so as well; something else must "individuate" or distinguish it. As I use the term, "individual" stands for a being, where being, in being universal, is thereby a "principle of individuation" as internally inclusive of infinite beings or individuals. But being is not *a* universal.

10. I use this word deliberately because it serves as reminder of how integral man's position is in being. For "presence" has a fundamental reference to that which a thing is present to, that which can grasp it and see its form (*eidos*—rooted etymologically in a word for vision). This at least reminds us that the reflection of Aristotle does not fully abstract from the human situation as the situation of being, though it leaves open the question of how Aristotle conceives the part which man plays in the being of being.

11. Thus, for example, Aristotle never senses the question as to the existence of things and/or world implied in the question: why is there something and not nothing?

12. Thus there is legitimate reason for calling natural science, but not philosophy, theoretical. If so, the phrase "philosophical theories" is a misnomer. Perhaps it would be appropriate to speak of "philosophical positions," *if* this be taken to refer to the stand man takes as he is placed in being and if philosophical thought be conceived of as required by its nature to reflect (among other things) explicitly the ground upon which and within which it stands.

13. Even in Aristotle's references to sight, there is a suggestion which, when connected with his conception that philosophy begins and remains (as love of wisdom) in wonder, helps to supply the concrete context of the thought he is analogizing with sight. Moreover, as the opening lines of the *Metaphysics* suggest, "seeing," including that caught up in wonder, is something we delight in. These suggestions, however, are easily overlooked because they are subordinated to the essential features of the analogy, features pertaining to sight regardless of whether or not we wonder or delight in seeing. If, in our understanding of Aristotle, we let these latter characters guide our interpretation of the meaning of "seeing" as "contemplation out of wonder," then we not only allow one side of his metaphorical use of sight to submerge the other but we keep ourselves from entering into the situation of his thought so as to be able to understand the limitations of the metaphor (as he uses it) to convey what is at stake in its use.

14. See for example Rule 9 of the *Rules for the Direction of the Mind* and Section 45, Part I, of the *Principles*.

15. Thus the use of "I" to designate the "subject" is misleading, for "subject" does not designate an existent but refers to an existent being who acts subjectively.

16. See *The Meditations and Selections from the Principles of René Descartes* (LaSalle, Illinois: Open Court Publishing Company, 1945), pp. 54–55 and p. 90.

17. *Ibid.*, p. 90.

18. *Ibid.*, p. 19.

19. The "very strong inclination to believe that those ideas arise from corporeal objects" (see *ibid.*, p. 93) seems actually to be the *natural* inclination of the embodied and sensuous creature (pp. 87–88 and 94–95), reinterpreted in terms of Descartes' theory of sense perception in order to fit the needs of Descartes' argument here. I can find no other inclination to which he could be referring: therefore, my interpretation above. If this interpretation is correct, then the following should be noted: the natural inclination is not an inclination to believe in material objects as causes of their sensible appearances (ideas), not even in Descartes' own interpretation of it. Only in a rationalistic-scientific context could it be so reinterpreted. Such reinterpretation is an example of Descartes' failure to stay within the existential context in attempting to understand the meaning of the being of sensible realities as we naturally believe in them.

20. Not even the other critiques can supply any reflective answer which would be concrete. For example, the use of theoretical concepts in respect of practice and the idea of a rational faith in this context seem simply to perpetuate a conception of reason which dissociates it from being in its universality, thus from beings with which man is, and from the context which alone makes the reasonableness of thought understandable.

21. Those moments that Kant comes closest to allowing to be developed in this way—the experiences of beauty and sublimity—are nevertheless restricted in their import by being seen through the framework already established in the first critique.

22. Heidegger is particularly emphatic upon a point analogous to this, namely, that philosophical questioning brings the questioner himself into question. See *Sein und Zeit* (Tubingen: Max Niemeyer Verlag, 1959) pp. 5–8; or *Was ist Metaphysik?* (Frankfurt A.M.: Vittorio Klostermann, 1955), p. 24; or *Introduction to Metaphysics* (New Haven: Yale University Press, 1959), trans. by Ralph Manheim, pp. 4–5.

23. Thus *intro-spection* is not involved in reflective thought.

HENRY W. JOHNSTONE, JR.

REASON LIMITED [1]

I

My fundamental orientation in philosophy arises from a concern
with the nature of philosophy itself. One thing that interests me
about philosophy is the claim that it is a rational activity. I am
convinced that this claim is correct, although I am far from being
able to enumerate the conditions under which I should regard an
activity as rational. One necessary condition, I suppose, is the
possibility of justifying, explaining, proving, or arguing for the
conclusions reached in the course of the activity. Any activity in
which it is recommended that certain conclusions be accepted even
though they are not adequately supported by proofs or arguments
seems to me to be clearly different from a rational activity and
hence clearly different from philosophy. I doubt very much,
though, that the condition I have just indicated is sufficient to
establish the rationality of an activity; for once justifications,
explanations, proofs, and arguments have been worked out, they
can be learned by rote, and when a person produces a reason he
has learned by rote he is not engaging in a rational activity,
especially if he does not understand the statement he produces as
a reason or does not understand why it is a reason. Perhaps my
view of rationality is hypercritical, and perhaps I am being too
finicky in insisting that philosophy be rational within the limits

[115]

I have just suggested. In any event, there are activities generally regarded as philosophical that I am reluctant to consider philosophical. I do not know, for instance, to what extent I would wish to qualify what is ordinarily known as "Oriental Philosophy" as philosophical at all.

Of course, there are other rational activities beside philosophy. In fact, some of these are more clearly rational than anything that I could point to as a definite example of philosophy. If mathematics, chess, and the design of jet aircraft are not rational activities, then nothing is. One sort of evidence for their rationality is that the literature of these activities is clearly justificatory or explanatory in intent and makes essential use of argumentation and proof. A further reason for thinking of these activities as rational is that although the world is divided, the fruits of such activities are not correspondingly divided. There is undoubtedly far more in common between American and Russian jet aircraft than there is different; and what is common is a set of design principles that thinking people on both sides of the world are led to, not as the result of any cooperation, but just because such principles are what anyone must come to if he is to cope with the problem of jet flight. So too, *a fortiori,* for mathematics and chess.

The feature of mathematics, chess, and jet engineering just pointed to is, of course, what has usually gone under the name of the "universality" of reason. To ascribe universality to reason is to assert that to the extent that an activity is rational, it must have the same outcome no matter who performs it. This is, of course, scarcely a sufficient condition for the rationality of an activity. The activity of jumping from a fifteen-story building also has the same outcome no matter who performs it. The crucial question, however, is not whether universality is a sufficient condition for rationality, but whether it is even a necessary condition for it. If an activity cannot be rational unless it is universal, then philosophy is certainly not a rational activity. It is the fact that the results of philosophical activity are not universal which, as much as anything else, accounts for the dividedness of the world. Philosophers disagree in a way in which mathematicians, chess-players, and designers of jet aircraft do not disagree. Jet engineers can disagree over the advantages of one airfoil over another, but they cannot disagree over whether a jet airplane should have airfoils or not. Chess-players can disagree over the value of a certain opening, but they cannot disagree as to the value of check-mating one's opponent. Philosophers, on the other hand, can and do disagree over the most fundamental issues. People who have supposed that only a universal activity could be rational have viewed philosophical disagreement as a great scandal. Descartes, for example, complained that in philosophy "there is nothing that is not disputed and consequently not in doubt." [2] Kant developed this complaint in a well-known passage in the Introduction to *The Critique of Pure Reason*.[3]

Given the datum that philosophers disagree, together with the assumption that universality is a necessary condition for rationality, there are several conclusions that one can choose. The first is that philosophy is not a rational activity. The second is that the observation that yielded the supposed datum is inadequate, for if we look hard enough we shall see that the disagreements of philosophers are provisional, but not final. The third conclusion is that universality is not a necessary condition for rationality at all, so that it makes sense to characterize as rational an activity that need not have the same outcome no matter who performs it, and hence to speak of reason, in its role in philosophy, as limited rather than universal. This is the conclusion that I shall wish to develop and defend.

The first conclusion can be given short shrift, at least within the confines of this essay, because it merely denies what I am assuming and would thus beg the question if used as an argument against my position. My position is that, owing to the occurrence of arguments, proofs, justifications, and explanations in philosophical discourse, that discourse is a rational activity; and it certainly is no rebuttal of my position merely to say that philosophical activity is *not* rational. Of course, one might take the position that philosophical arguments are not real arguments at all, that nothing is proved by a philosophical proof, and so on. Perhaps philosophical discourse is either simply a tissue of logical confusion or simply a species of rhetoric. But such theses are merely hasty generalizations from the fact that *some* philosophical arguments are certainly fallacious or sophistical. Of course, there would be no point in noting the weaknesses of some philosophical arguments unless there were others that had strength. We can be disappointed by sophistry only because we are not always disappointed. And if anyone should tell me that I ought always to be disappointed in philosophical arguments, whether I am in fact disappointed or not, then my reply would be that such an opponent is just not talking about the same thing I am talking about when I evaluate some philosophical arguments as weak and others

[117]

as strong. Just as I cannot talk science with a person who denies the presuppositions of science, so I cannot talk history of philosophy with a person who dismisses that entire history as an error.[4]

The second conclusion deserves closer consideration. It might be said that philosophical disagreement is a necessary but provisional stage of an activity eventuating in unanimity, so that such disagreement is not really an exception to the rule that rational activities must be universal. Perhaps disagreement is among the tests to which a philosophical belief would have to be subjected before its acceptance could be considered rational. Methodological scepticism and the use of Platonic dialectic, for example, both make this assumption. But the fact of the matter is that there are disagreements over the results of carrying out methodological scepticism and Platonic dialectic. Not everyone is a Platonist or a Cartesian, and few Platonists or Cartesians—even the most dedicated—would dismiss those who disagree with Plato or Descartes as merely ignorant or irrational. One might attempt to attribute this disagreement to an incomplete use of the method in question. Perhaps Platonic dialectic could be extended so as to reconcile the differences between Plato and his critics. Perhaps methodological scepticism could be similarly extended. But this attempt is not likely to succeed. For among the objections against the results of methodological scepticism are objections against any results whatsoever that have been obtained by the use of this method, and similarly for Platonic dialectic. But to use a discredited method in the effort to overcome objections to this method is only to beg the question in the most egregious way. My point is just that philosophical disagreements can concern not only beliefs but also methods for testing beliefs. So such disagreement cannot be regarded as any stage of an activity destined to eventuate in unanimity. It is radical, not provisional. Platonic dialectic and methodological scepticism are, of course, merely examples of views according to which philosophical disagreement has a provisional role. But in the nature of the case, there cannot be any view of this sort that is not itself capable of inspiring radical disagreement. Any announcement of a trend toward universality is, at the minimum, sure to be met by a denial of the existence or propriety of a trend in that direction. We are brought back, then, to the failure of philosophical activity to be universal in the way in which other rational activities are universal.

Not only are the major philosophical disagreements not pro-

[118]

visional, but also they are not even expected to be provisional. If it was generally supposed that disagreement prevails only in those phases of philosophical activity in which the ultimate insight has not yet been attained, then philosophical disagreement would surely be regarded as no more than a symptom of misunderstanding among philosophers, and hence dismissed as irrational. No doubt, it is sometimes so regarded. But there are cases in which philosophical disagreement is not thought to be reducible to a mere misunderstanding, and it is in these cases alone that philosophers are doing what is expected of them. It follows that if philosophers disagree at all, then their activity can be thought of as rational only if their disagreements are felt to be genuine.

I think that these remarks are sufficient to show that the second conclusion cannot be maintained. Not only are philosophical disagreements not, in the nature of the case, provisional, but in fact they are not even generally thought to be provisional. Let me turn, then, to the third conclusion, that reason in its philosophical role is essentially limited. It is this conclusion that I favor.

Reason is limited when it is not unlimited or universal; i.e., when an activity in which it is operative does not necessarily have the same outcome no matter who performs it. I take the view, then, that there is an activity that may have different outcomes if performed by different philosophers. Of course, it may be objected that there is no one activity of this kind, that different philosophers are performing essentially different activities. But this objection overlooks the fact of philosophical disagreement. If philosophers were participating in essentially different activities, they could hardly accuse one another of failing to achieve identical outcomes. It might be said, however, that philosophers are in fact engaged in disparate activities without realizing that they are, so that their disagreements are in reality misunderstandings. Over and above what I have already said about the thesis that philosophical disagreement results from misunderstanding, I should want to add only that disagreeing itself is clearly one of the most important aspects of philosophical activity, so that even if philosophers are to some extent otherwise engaged in disparate activities, at least their disagreement is a common activity. I do not mean this in a facetious way. As I shall try to show later, I feel that the only philosophical statements worth making are those that arise from disagreements, so that disagreeing is an activity in its own right, and one that all philosophers must perform. Perhaps the obvious-

[119]

ness of this point would appear if we were to replace the word "disagreement" by the word "criticism"; for the developed and articulate disagreement of philosophers is criticism.

Once we deny that an activity is universal, the only possible remaining reason for regarding it as rational is the occurrence within it of arguments, proofs, explanations, and justifications. It might be asked, though, to what end the philosopher uses arguments and seeks to justify his position. Does not his very effort to convert others to his own point of view constitute a *claim* that his activity is universal? I think not. The claim that mathematics is universal is not accompanied by an effort to convert people. The universality of mathematics consists rather in the fact that people do not *need* to be converted to it; that its truths are what every thinking person would come to if only his thinking were free from error. One can, of course, undertake to free others from error. But such instruction is altogether different from the polemic that must be used to win over minds not merely lacking the truth but rather committed to an alien position. Such polemic need involve no claim that the position it seeks to establish is one that every thinking person could come to merely by dint of thinking.

I have already discussed the view that sees in the philosopher's attempt to convert others nothing but the use of rhetoric. Such a view is false to the history of philosophy, wherein we can distinguish rhetoric from cogent argumentation. It might be said, though, that while cogent, the arguments of philosophers are never more than partially cogent. For an argument is at best a restricted device for articulating that which alone could be totally cogent; namely, reason as unrestricted. Reason limited is, on this position, partial and hence partly irrational. It seizes upon and exaggerates what are in fact merely aspects of a vision of totality, turning them into irreconcilable dogmas, and hence falsifying the vision itself.

The difficulty with this position is that it cannot show why the vision of totality upon which it centers should be regarded as anything more than a vision. There seems no basis for its claim that this vision is tantamount to reason. Why not rather an intuition, an insight, an ecstasy? Certainly, neither of the conditions that I have in this essay associated with the operation of reason is associated with any vision of totality so far beheld: such a vision neither involves the use of arguments, proofs, justifications, or explanations, nor is it the invariant outcome of any human activity. Visions of totality have usually broken down into inarticulate idiosyncrasies. They have rarely served as anything like the instrumentalities of unification they are supposed to be. Universal reason there is, of course, but only as articulate and argumentative, only as manifested on the mathematician's blackboard or the jet engineer's drawing board. These two boards are among the very few things in the world that can withstand protracted public inspection.

But there is a paradox. For if reason unlimited in philosophy turns out to be an idiosyncrasy, so also does reason limited, supposing that its limits are fixed. Philosophical reason is limited because each philosophical point of view—at least in its metaphysical implications—is a definition of reason. There is, accordingly, no standard outside the point of view itself by which its rationality can be tested. Every philosopher has reason on his side. How, then, can any be refuted? And if none can, in the nature of the case, be refuted, what is the point of argument, proof, and justification or explanation in philosophy? Should not the philosopher be content to cultivate his own garden, isolated from all other gardens by what seems to him to be horizons of the world, which are in reality prison walls?

If one mode of reason limited could be criticized only for failure to conform to the standards of another mode, there would be no way out of this impasse. It is possible, however, to criticize a mode of reason limited for failure to conform to its own standards. Indeed, reason in philosophy is always in disequilibrium with its own standards. Critical argumentation has a point to the extent that it articulates this disequilibrium and tends to restore equilibrium. Thus reason limited is open to criticism in that it is subject to revision. It need not stand in solipsistic isolation.

Both the paradox that I have just briefly sketched and my suggestion as to its resolution need illustration. That is the purpose of the following section.

II

For the sake of a concrete example, I shall discuss the relationship between two contrasting philosophical interpretations of the laws of logic. The first of these, which I shall call functionalism, asserts that the significance of the laws of logic is exhausted by the role of these laws in mathematics and other areas where deductive proofs occur. If there are versions of deductive proof calling for alternatives to the usual laws, then alternative logics can exist side by side, none with more right than the others. For in order to establish the propriety of any kind of logic, it is sufficient to show that it has a use in deduction.

Functionalism in this sense would be opposed by what I shall call realism, according to which no logic is ultimately acceptable unless it is intrinsically connected with the structure of the world. Generally, realism lends its support to the so-called "classical" version of logic, although as I shall point out later, it is by no means necessary that it should. Classical logic is characterized by its inclusion of certain logical laws such as the law of the excluded middle, and when realism espouses this version, it may show its interest in the structure of the world by expressing the law of the excluded middle, and other laws that it regards as fundamental, in ontological terms. It may assert, for example, that to be is, *inter alia,* either to have a given property or not to have it— what violates the excluded middle cannot exist. According to realism, the alleged alternative logics lacking the law of the excluded middle are actually only incomplete versions of classical logic, which indeed is presupposed by the very act of interpreting these alleged alternatives. Realism, it will be seen, inclines toward monism, while functionalism is hospitable to a plurality of logics.

I have chosen functionalism and realism in logic as examples because their opposition seems to me to have a structure shared by many other pairs of opposing philosophical positions. According to one member of each pair, the meaning of any experience of a certain type reduces to its form. Thus we have behaviorism, on which behavior has no meaning over and above its form, ethical formalism, according to which the rightness of any act is uniquely determined by its form, and formalism in aesthetics, as well as the logical theory that I have called "functionalism." The other member of each pair asserts that meaning resides in something over and above form; the meaning of behavior, for instance, must be sought in the conscious or unconscious mental activity of which the behavior is merely the expression. What I shall have to say about functionalism and realism in logic, then, would apply *mutatis mutandis* to many other examples of philosophical disagreement.

Let us consider the arguments for functionalism and for realism. The functionalist will point to various types of deduction in which, in his view, various logics are involved. The considerations leading to the development of modal logics are a case in point. The relation between the premises and conclusion of a valid argument is pointed to as a situation in which the classical treatment of conditional or hypothetical propositions falls short. For we do not say that an argument is valid merely because not all the premises are true or the conclusion is true. We say that it is valid only when it is *impossible* for all the premises to be true while the conclusion is false. There is, then, a logic of impossibility, possibility, and necessity, which contrasts with the classical logic of truth and falsity. To say that there "is" such a logic, however, is not to say that such a logic reflects the structure of what exists; it is only to say that there is a domain of deduction that requires it.

Modal logic is an alternative to classical logic in the sense that it involves a supplementation of the classical laws. Intuitionistic logic, on the other hand, represents a weakening of classical logic. Yet the functionalistic argument can be used to defend intuitionism as easily as it can be used in behalf of modal logic; for there "is" a logic without double negation or excluded middle only to the extent that there are areas of mathematics demanding this logic. No doubt a nonfunctionalistic defense of logics that deny double negation or excluded middle is also possible. The Marxist defense is a case in point: in a world of dialectical flux, the negation of the negation is an emergent. This is actually what I have called realism; for it sees logic as the mirror of reality. Modal logic can undoubtedly also be defended on the basis of cosmic necessities and possibilities. For that matter, classical logic has a functionalistic defense; witness the formalism of Hilbert. What these variants show is just that one should not confuse types of logic with interpretations of logic. It is with interpretations that I am now concerned; for it is interpretations of logic, not types of logic, that can collide philosophically.

I have spoken of the functionalistic arguments for various types of logic. The evidence on which such arguments rest is simply the existence of various domains of deduction, each alleged to require the type of logic in question. I turn now to the realistic argument for a logic based on ontology. The evidence here is the world. But it might be objected, for example, that the world does not constitute clear-cut evidence of double negation. What is solid is not liquid, but what is not liquid is not necessarily solid. So the denial of the denial of *solid* is not necessarily *solid*. Supposing that the realist wishes to defend classical logic, he will reply that this objection rests upon a misunderstanding of what it means to deny a term. The real denial of *solid* is not *liquid,* but is rather *nonsolid.* Once this point is cleared up, the formula "For any property P, P = non-non-P" expresses without distortion an aspect of the structure of the world.

But there is something unsatisfactory about both the functionalistic and the realistic arguments that I have outlined. They seem to sidestep issues that one thinks ought to be met head on. They certainly do not meet each other head on. The outlines I have given are, in fact, incomplete; and what is missing will soon be obvious enough. As matters now stand, both functionalism and realism constitute excellent documentation for the statement that every philosopher has reason on his side and none can, accordingly, be refuted. The elaboration and defense of each doctrine is clearly a rational activity. For the functionalist, it is the activity of examining various domains in which deductions occur to see what logics are required. For the realist it is the activity of correcting language so that the ontologically warranted logic can appear without distortion. But no functionalist will be much impressed by the report that there is ontological evidence for the ultimacy of a certain type of logic; the "evidence" shown him is simply not evidence for him at all. Nor does his own report that, for example, certain areas of discourse require a modal logic impress the realist, who is busily occupied in correcting these areas of discourse to make modal logic unnecessary. Each of the two conflicting positions begs the question in attempting to refute the other, for each argues on the basis of premises explicitly denied by the other. It would seem, then, that neither position can touch the other at all.

Yet I have characterized functionalism and realism as *conflicting.* Functionalism is not merely *non*realism; it is *anti*realism, as realism is *anti*functionalism, and the logic of "anti" is different from the logic of "non." Nonobjective art, for instance, is not necessarily antiobjective art. In a treatise on art, objective and nonobjective art can be discussed side-by-side and the contrasts between them made clear. But this is just what could not adequately be done in the case of functionalism and realism. For there is no universe of discourse in which their contrasts can be made clear. Each position claims possession of the only universe of discourse in which comparisons can be made at all. Each compares itself to its rival from its own point of view. To ignore this claim is to disqualify oneself from making any comparisons except those that both of the conflicting positions must disown.

But I still have not shown how positions related in the way that I have maintained that functionalism and realism are related could conflict with each other at all. How can two positions conflict if neither is capable of regarding the other as a challenge? What I have said about the logic of "anti" needs supplementation. Let me return to a previous point. The relation between objective and nonobjective art is one that, conceivably, might be instructive to consider. A person uncommitted to either type of art could be instructed as to the difference. But it could never be very instructive to consider the difference between functionalism and antifunctionalism in logical theory. For, on the face of it, both views are equally arbitrary, in a way in which we would not say that objective and nonobjective art are arbitrary. Functionalism and realism, to the extent that I have so far described them, seem arbitrary because the sketches I have given contain no clue as to the *point* of either position. Why on earth should any sane person adopt either one of them? One does not see the *point* of a philosophical position until he grasps the motivation underlying the position. The descriptions of positions in dictionaries of philosophy are usually inadequate because they omit reference to motivation. But, of course, it is insufficient merely to describe the motives from which a philosophical position is taken, since such motives will themselves seem arbitrary. Suppose we are told that functionalism stems from a concern with deduction, and realism from a concern with ontology. We are tempted to ask, "What on earth is the point of such odd concerns?" The only way to answer this question is to become involved in the differences between functionalism and realism, instead of being content merely to describe these differences. Being involved in the difference, we shall have to be polemical instead of instructive; we shall have to win over minds committed to an alien position, rather than merely to supply the truth to those who lack it. The unsatisfactoriness of the functionalistic and realistic arguments as I have outlined them so far arises from the failure of these outlines to suggest the polemical orientation of the arguments. So oriented, the arguments do not sidestep the issues but meet them, and each other, head on.

Realism cannot refute functionalism by pointing to evidence, for the "evidence" it points to is not such as functionalism can even admit to exist. But the realistic *polemic* against functionalism has little in common with the attempted refutation based on alleged evidence. Polemic, rather than making a point that the position under attack must, on its own principles, ignore, makes a point

that the position under attack cannot, on its own principles, ignore. Thus the full realistic argument against the functionalistic
waiver of double negation would *not* appeal to the structure of
what is. It would appeal instead to the principles of functionalism
itself. But it is necessary to make only a minor change in the word-
ing of the argument in order to implement this major shift in strat-
egy. According to the argument I outlined before, the realist
wished to specify precisely what it means to deny a term so that
symbols might express reality without distortion. Suppose instead,
the realist wished to specify the precise meaning of denial in order
to make explicit a hiterto implicit presupposition of functionalism.
The argument might then run as follows: "Let us grant the functionalist his deviant notions of negation and the queer logics that
he develops from these notions. But he will find that he cannot
even state these queer logics without making use of normal logic
with its customary law of double negation. For if a formula in a
queer logic is *not un*provable, it is provable; if a queer system is
*not in*consistent, it is consistent; and so on. These are relationships
that the functionalist continually relies on in developing his logic."

The realist can also observe that the functionalist is not interested in *all* deductions; he is interested only in *valid* deductions.
Thus the functionalist's investigations do not in fact concern deduction wherever it occurs; they concern deduction only to the extent that it possesses a certain property over and above the mere
stepwise movement from premises to conclusion. But the fact that
this property itself remains invariant as it applies or fails to apply
to every deduction in every domain suggests that the functionalist
is actually guided by an ontological consideration over and above
all the peculiar deductive patterns that he investigates. The distinction between a valid and an invalid deduction is, after all, that
a valid deduction is a real deduction, while an invalid one is only
an apparent one.

Similarly, the functionalist must take the realist seriously if he
is to meet the issue. For example, he may try to show that each of
the queer logics he recommends is implicit in the realistic defense
of an ontologically warranted logic. Validity, invalidity, and inconsistency can, after all, easily be construed as modal properties.
The categories of "theorem" and "nontheorem" are not necessarily
exhaustive, since, in addition to statements that are theorems and
statements that are nontheorems, there may be formulas that are
not statements at all. Indeed, what of statements whose status as
theorems or nontheorems cannot be determined? Of course any

realist whose reply consists merely in citing the law of the excluded middle begs the question.

The functionalist can also challenge the realist's intentions in correcting and purifying language. The realist claims he does this so that the structure of reality can be expressed without distortion. But where does "the structure of reality" really come into the picture at all? If one *defines* "non-P" as "everything but P," then non-non-P is naturally the same as P; but this is certified by the results of deduction, not by ontological insight. It looks as if the real reason why the realist wants to refine language is just that he is interested in deduction.

This much will perhaps suffice as an example of the logic of "anti." I should like to generalize as follows. Suppose there are two philosophical positions A and B such that A is anti-B and B is anti-A. Then there are arguments for A, the propriety of whose premises an advocate of B could not acknowledge; and there are arguments for B, the propriety of whose premises an advocate of A could not acknowledge. Both sets of arguments thus beg the question, and to the extent that the positions rely upon the arguments, they are solipsistically isolated one from the other. Each has reason on its side. But in this situation, not only would it be hopeless for an advocate of A to attempt to convert an advocate of B, or vice versa, but also not even the "anti" would make sense. If A is committed to ignoring all "evidence" for B, and vice versa, then there is no genuine opposition. In fact, however, A and B will both be supported by additional arguments, in terms of which there is genuine opposition. The additional arguments for A will attempt to show that B in fact presupposes A; in other words, that implicit in the very formulation of B are presuppositions acceptable to A but inconsistent with the formulation of B. Similarly, some arguments for B will claim to show that A presupposes what is inconsistent with its very formulation as a philosophical position.

The question arises, however, whether these additional arguments can really overcome the solipsistic impasse that seemed to preclude genuine opposition. Suppose an advocate of A produces a presupposition involved in B that is, in his opinion, inconsistent with the formulation of B. What reason is there to suppose that any advocate of B must agree that there is an inconsistency? If he need not agree, the impasse remains.

Of course, the attacker may be mistaken; perhaps what he takes to be an inconsistency between the formulation of B and the presuppositions of B is not really an inconsistency. The question I am now raising is whether such an attacker must always be mistaken. Is it possible for an inconsistency to develop within a position which, like all philosophical positions, "has reason on its side"? If it is *possible,* that will be sufficient to overcome the impasse.

Let me turn the matter around the other way. In point of fact, there will be criticisms of realism to which the realist must reply. It is difficult to see, for example, how he could avoid the obligation to make some reply to the functionalistic objections I have outlined above. To shed light on the necessity of this reply, let us see what reply is necessitated. Consider the functionalist's criticism that modal logics are involved in the development and exposition of classical logic. The realist could counter that the *development* and *exposition* of classical logic is far different from classical logic itself. While classical logic is, or reflects, the structure of what is, its expositor is thrown upon his inadequate human resources in attempting to express this structure. Who can say but that modal logic simply represents the failure of a finite mind to come to grips with the truth? Perhaps it is the best we human beings can do. Perhaps an omniscient being could do without modal logic.

In replying, the realist has made a distinction. He has been forced to do this by his own failure to meet his own standards of exposition. Thus the distinction he has made was already implicit in his original position, because it was presupposed by the very act of articulating that position. All that the functionalist has done is to call this fact to the realist's attention. He has not sought to impose anything on the realist. He has merely invited him to overcome disequilibrium by revising his own critical basis; i.e., by altering his mode of reason limited. This example, then, shows how an inconsistency can develop within a position that "has reason its side," and how the very reason it has on its side may be forced to undergo revision in the effort to overcome the inconsistency.

There is, however, an objection that must be scrupulously stated and dealt with. I have said that the position of the realist, at least before he distinguishes classical logic from human thought, is inconsistent, and that the functionalist calls this inconsistency to the attention of the realist. Does this not presuppose that the realist and the functionalist both accept the same criterion of consistency? If they do, and if the relation between realism and functionalism is really typical of opposed philosophical points of view, then this criterion of consistency must be universal. For any philosopher who wishes to engage in effective criticism of an alien position will have to appeal to this criterion in order to make his criticism clear. Thus philosophical reason is universal after all, even if it consists solely of a criterion of consistency.

The objection goes on to say: consider the alternative. Suppose there were no criterion of consistency common to two philosophical positions. Then neither could criticize the other. The functionalist, for instance, who thought that he saw an inconsistency in the realist's original position would be met by the reply. "But that is *not* an inconsistency in my terms! If you call it an inconsistency, you are begging the question!"

In assessing this objection, I first want to point out that even if conflicting points of view must share a criterion of consistency, it does not follow that any such criterion is universal. All that does follow is that for every pair of conflicting points of view, there is some criterion or other of consistency—not necessarily the same in all cases of conflict.

Also, it is obvious that different criteria of consistency are operative in different conflicts. Sometimes, for example, positions are condemned as inconsistent when contradictory consequences can be drawn from them. Sometimes the alleged inconsistency is felt to lie in the impossibility of exemplifying a position. Neither of these criteria, however, seems particularly relevant to the issue between the functionalist and the realist. The criterion to which appeal seems to be made here is a pragmatic one: no view is consistent if the truth of the view would imply the impossibility of stating the view. I call this criterion pragmatic because of its obvious relationship to what is called the pragmatic paradox; i.e., the paradox of a proposition whose utterance by certain speakers would be self-refuting.

Indeed, the very notion of a universal criterion of consistency immediately destroys itself, because universal criteria of consistency are among the very things that philosophers argue about. Aristotle attempts to defend the law of noncontradiction as a universal criterion of consistency in Book Gamma of the *Metaphysics*. It is highly significant that Aristotle's defense pivots upon precisely the pragmatic considerations adduced in the last paragraph: when someone ignores or denies the law of noncontradiction, his inconsistency must then consist in a systematic incapacity to state his own position. For such a person cannot legitimately say anything, and so *a fortiori* cannot give articulate expression to any particular point of view.

I do not wish to imply, however, that I regard this pragmatic

[129]

criterion of consistency as having any more of a role in philosophical criticism than any other criterion. Let us consider the role of the criterion of exemplifiability. By this I mean the principle that a philosophical position is inconsistent if the contents of the world cannot be interpreted in such a way as to exemplify the position. The use of such a criterion obviously hinges upon an agreement between critic and defendant to the effect that certain interpretations of the contents of the world are precluded. Consider the realistic polemic against the functionalist claim that all deductions are equally worthy of attention. What the realist claims is that this generalization is too inclusive to have any model. It says too much, and therefore says nothing. The most that one could properly say is that all *valid* deductions are equally worthy of attention. This implies that on any possible interpretation, the world contains invalid deductions as well as valid ones; it is impossible to interpret the world as containing valid deductions only. So the issue between the functionalist and the realist presupposes a common ontological commitment. But from this it does not follow that there is any ontological commitment that is presupposed by all philosophical issues. The fact that there is not is immediately proved by the occurrence of arguments over ontological commitments of all kinds. Even the point on which the functionalist and his realistic critic agree has been denied, e.g., by the philosopher for whom all talk is rhetoric and the distinction between valid and invalid talk is an illusion.

So much for the objection. In the process of dealing with it, I have made use of ideas that can have further utility in connection with the main topic, by which I mean the limitations of philosophical reason. The exercise of reason is limited in philosophy partly by pragmatic considerations and partly by ontological considerations. It is pragmatic considerations that make us avoid uses of reason that lead to infinite regress. We cannot say anything the saying of which would require us to talk forever. We also avoid circular reasoning—not because there is any *logical* difficulty in the notion of a proposition implying itself, but only because there is a *pragmatic* difficulty in the notion of *inferring* a conclusion from premises that have not been *asserted* on independent grounds. Finally, we avoid reasoning that commits us to silence, but not because there is anything inconsistent in silence itself.

Ontological considerations limit reason when the criterion of consistency we are using is exemplifiability, because the only models available to test the consistency of philosophical reason are limited ontologies. This is true simply because there are no unlimited or universal ontologies; i.e., ontologies acceptable to all parties to every philosophical dispute. It is also what we might have expected. Model-theoretic consistency is, after all, not absolute consistency. It is relative to the consistency of the model itself. In logic, the consistency of such models as the series of natural numbers is accepted on intuitive grounds. In philosophy, nothing is universally accepted on intuitive grounds, because for every philosophical intuition there is certain to be a counter-intuition. Whoever says that the actual contents of the world guarantee the consistency of his position is sure to encounter an opponent who will deny that the contents of the world are of this nature at all.

I have related the limitations of philosophical reason to various criteria of consistency. But in point of fact, just so long as we admit that there is *some* criterion of consistency by which the use of reason in the elaboration and defense of a philosophical position could be cogently criticized, it will follow that reason in this use is limited. For whatever can be cogently criticized stands in need of revision. But it is a truism that only the limited can undergo revision.

If reason in philosophy is limited, what limits it? Is it limited by ignorance, for example? Do we accept whatever situation will save the consistency of our position simply because, as finite human beings, this is the best we can do? Do we suppose that if we were to become omniscient, the limits would then fall away? Clearly, no activity carried on as a mere substitute for omniscience could be identified as reason. Such an activity could at best produce prudent beliefs. It could not, on its own assumptions, produce cogent philosophical criticism. Philosophical criticism made as the result of an incomplete grasp of totality could never be cogent, because the defendant would have only to reply, "If you saw the whole, you would not talk that way." (Nonphilosophical criticism, of course, could still be cogent under these these circumstances, because we do not have to see the whole in order to know what is prudent.) Cogent philosophical criticism presupposes the possibility of a critic who can speak with authority about inconsistencies that actually occur. Such a critic no doubt occupies a limited perspective. But unless there can be authority in a limited perspective, no critic can have any grounds for asserting that a philosophical position is *sound.* If a philosopher wishes to share an important insight with me, he commits a tactical blunder if he begins by suggesting that I am in no position to judge insights. What he ought to do is to begin by putting me on the map, i.e., declaring the authority of my own limited perspective.

Not only *can* an authoritative perspective be limited—it *must* be. An individual for whom there are no limitations could not speak with authority because he could not speak at all; he would not know where to begin. He could know where to begin only if his perspective were limited. He could speak to a purpose only if his perspective were limited. If there were omniscient speakers, their speech would be like the babbling of an everlasting brook. There is repose in that, but no authority.

Reason limited is limited, then, because there would be no reason at all if it were not—nothing authoritative could be said, and so nothing possessing the authority of reason could be said. Hence, it is reasonable that reason limited should be limited. But if it is reasonable, then it is dictated by reason. I come to the conclusion, then, that the limitations imposed on reason are imposed by reason itself, in the interest of maintaining itself as a locus of authority in the world.

NOTES

1. I am indebted to Dr. Stanley Rosen for his valuable criticisms of an earlier version. The present version includes some material printed in the *Revue Internationale de Philosophie* for 1961, under the title "Argumentation and Inconsistency." I am indebted to this journal for permission to reprint that material.

2. *Discours de la Méthode* (Cambridge Plain Texts, Cambridge University Press, 1942) , p. 7.

3. *Kant Selections,* ed. T. M. Greene (New York: Charles Scribner's Sons, 1929) , p. 13.

4. Cf. Aristotle *Physica* 185ᵃ 1–5.

HENRY G. BUGBEE, JR.

THOUGHTS ON CREATION

Perhaps in so far as myths of creation tell of special events, they do so almost reflexively. This speaking, this uttering, this primordial thinking of the coming into being of things and of man, this placing of all that is in world: is not this speaking, this uttering, this thinking a participation in the coming to pass of that of which such myths tell? So construed, at any rate, myths of creation tend to disclose that of which they speak; the mists and emerging grandeur of the morning of creation play *in* this very speech. Here speech itself seems to find its origin and meaning, bursting forth decisively. It is not that there is, or once was, creation and subsequently a telling of it, by means of speech imported for the occasion and of an origin extraneous to the occasion told. No; primordial speaking and thinking cannot disavow the origin they would acknowledge in myth of creation. They reflect upon that which they bear witness to, realize, and fulfill. Yet the speaker, for all his part in this, remains anonymous, even though man may appear as in some way central in creation as told.

In narrating a story, myths of creation seem to have to do with events in time, with coming to pass. We have begun by recognizing how they may tell of special events. Yet what seems to be special about these events is that they are world events. In them world is coming to pass, and coming into being is coming to pass. The events narrated seem to yield an appreciation of being in time and of all things implicated in temporal existence. And the point seems to be that being in time somehow "has an origin"—that all things implicated in temporal existence *derivatively* enjoy such being as may be theirs. The being of beings in time is somehow bestowed upon them, and the bestowal of being here in question seems indissolubly linked with the coming to pass of world. World and the being of beings in time thus appear alike as of one and the same origin.

Before turning to the element of origin invoked in myths of creation, let us consider how world is suggested in them. The suggestion, as I venture to read it, is that world essentially can be only in coming to pass; it cannot be conjured with as extant. World is, if you will, always in the building, being forged, to be done; it cannot lapse from dawning and formation. It appears as that which dawns and *is* in dawning. So world does appear as world-without-end, and creation with respect to world is continuous creation. Hence the feel of creation is one of fluency and constancy, one of opening out and opening up, one of the gathering up and growing together of things and events to enter into this ongoing ever-forming of world. Thus, to be in and of the world would be to be in and of continuous creation, and to abide in the world would be to abide in no fixed abode.

Turning now to the element of origin invoked in myths of creation, we have every reason to be especially careful. For what is being invoked is invoked as divine, as birthless and deathless, as the ever-so, the self-same, the fundamental and ordaining power. Here, if I were to say that we are hard put to it to know what is in question, I would think it very reasonable of you to smile—providing you don't smile too sardonically. Yet, is the point that the divine is very, very difficult to know and such that only very, very few come to know what is in question—if, indeed, the invocation of divine origin of creation is not what we speak of today as *merely* mythical? Or is it the very tone of primordial speech of creation that must instruct us in listening to its imagery? Is not the divine more like what is to be discovered in this very act of speech, responsively echoed in the hearing of our hearts? The divine is there, animating that speaking, and to be marked, if at all, in a ring of authenticity and a tone over which simplicity itself presides. That is the divine, inexhaustible in power: unutterably simple, presiding, gathering, disposing, revealing Presence—calling forth the very speech, imparting the very gift of speech, in which the being of beings is consummated, acknowledged, confirmed. Then things

[134]

are the things of the world that is coming to pass and address the hearing heart as divine speech.

Creation is indeed a story to be told, and in the telling of it, it is with reason that divine power is extolled. Myths of creation reflect the fact in the primordial doing of the deed. Where this sort of telling occurs, the reason for it appears in and with the telling. In myths of creation, creation seems to be claiming speech as its own proper and revealing dominion.

But how may things stand with us nowadays in thinking and speaking of creation?

Sometimes it seems to me that to bespeak creation comes so naturally and spontaneously that it is what all naturalness and spontaneity do: Whenever and wherever they occur, they bespeak creation. As we put it, there *is* something creative about them, whether wittingly so or not. And it is, above all, of actions and of people in action that we have come to think when we think of creation. There is even a tendency to think of creation preeminently, though not altogether exclusively, in connection with those actions we typify as artistic. Not too many for whom the meaning of creation has been thus focalized wend their way back—or on—to a renewed or new appreciation of the primordial themes of creation: coming into being, coming to pass of world, and divine origin. I will not attempt here to follow up at all the direction indicated by Whitehead through reflection on "aesthetic experience" to reinterpretation of reality. Nor will I attempt to discuss those great essays of Heidegger's which seem to me to go so far in opening up this direction of thought.

What I wish to do now is to suggest that it is our part in creation which presently calls for reflection and that we may come at this task by reconsidering the possible meaning of *creatio ex nihilo*. What I believe is that we become selves—truly ourselves—in willing participation in creation; that in so doing we discover the meaning of our responsibility in relationship with others; and that we cannot conceive of creation in terms apart from our participation in it. But if this is the story of creation that is ours to tell, we must distinguish the possible senses in which it is a story of *creatio ex nihilo*. It is the *nihil* that establishes this story as essentially pertaining to ourselves, as well as all things, and in a way peculiar to ourselves.

The way to willing participation in creation seems to be a dialectical one. It is not at all a matter of destination and linear movement toward it. Whatever we distinguish as pertaining to this way

[135]

is likely to be implicitly involved with contraries. What has appeared thus, now appears so, and thinking does not necessarily stabilize the shape-shifting countenance that appearance wears. But I will speak of nothingness in three distinguishable senses which seem pertinent to the theme of *creatio ex nihilo;* without suggesting, I hope, that I mean to describe "something having a nature," with fixed and discrete properties to be elicited and recognized as such.

First, there is the nothingness known as such, say, in dread and despair—such as Kierkegaard deals with so carefully. Second, there is the nothingness known to renunciation, so central in Buddhist thought and there called *sunyata.* And third, there is the nothingness of being, in the sense that being is not a being at all, as Heidegger makes the point—so central in his thinking.

Now in entering upon a development of these three senses in which creation seems to involve "nothingness," I believe we must be explicit about the standpoint from which we must think and speak and the language in terms of which our thought can move. There can be no talk, no proper thought, in this matter that does not presuppose the standpoint of care and move in the language of care. Nothing and being obtain for care, and it is essentially being of which care stands in need; and being comes to care as calling upon it. Our lives are in essence vocational, however long we may be in realizing it. Perhaps I could say that it is quite impossible to speak without interpreting at least implicitly what is called for and what it is to be called upon. "Philosophically stated," one cannot help begging the question, and explicitly, when it comes to talking of being and nothing. One can only hope to beg it appropriately. This, I confess, I have no assurance of doing, yet I will do my best, tending to follow my master, Eckhart, in the way the question is begged. That is, I shall speak of creatures and of creaturely being in a way that presupposes that decisive mode of care in which renunciation, or "disinterestedness," is pivotal. Implied in this presupposition is the impossibility of forcing it upon anyone, for care only *is* in this mode willingly, by utterly free consent, and not otherwise. As the *Tao Te Ching* suggests, reasoning in this mode of care, however firm it may be, cannot contend.

As in Hindu and Buddhist thought, it must be an early part of our story to take account of the great illusion into which our senses, intellect, desire, and will are likely to plunge: It consists in taking the ten thousand things as if they *were* in and of themselves. Now of creatures thus construed Meister Eckhart seems to be talking when he says that creatures of themselves are mere nothings. Their really being something, their "suchness," is in their being taken as creatures; I would almost say, in their being permitted to be, in being *as* creatures. Thus the irony of the illusion to which I refer is that, in tending to treat things as if they were beingful in and of themselves, we reduce them to nothings. In a way this is equivalent to washing our hands of them—treating them as if they *had* being and could well enough go their own way without us.

But what is this way of construing being implicit in taking things as if they *were* in and of themselves? Is it not that being and care are in utterly contingent, accidental relationship? Being is independent of care. If so, in what way can care work out the equation of its relation with things whose being appears in the guise of inherent independence of care? It would seem that care must alternate between two correlative positions with respect to things and others: Either it can assert itself and seek to impose itself or it can acquiesce in what may be imposed upon it. Care then takes itself to be free and independent in so far as it has its way with things, and any possible dependence in which it may stand must seem to it a threat to its freedom and independence. And death entering the life of care to qualify it as mortal is all that is needed to lock care in an utter impasse, in that it must come to feel itself as bound to fail. Being must seem to tolerate care and ultimately reject it with inscrutable indifference. Dread anticipates the crisis of futility, when nothingness seizes the heart, and care comes consciously to despair.

But through precisely such happening, and not otherwise, is selfhood potentiated, as Kierkegaard says. And precisely through such happening we are cast out of illusory proximity with things and put in relationship with what-is *as a whole,* or better, *in toto.* A pall of nothingness falls between us and everything; it is our relationship with *everything* that is radically in question. Only in so far as this happens can we really come to put the shoe on our own foot, as it were, and come to realize that *our* being is somehow pivotally in question with the being of all things. "At this point" care is got ready for an examined life, when it feels itself essentially in question even as it questions and lives in question. Care awakens to itself as somehow responsible for its way of taking things and may well be imbued with suspicion that as it takes things, so it has them, yet precisely not in the sense that it can at will confer on things the fundamental aspect which they assume for it. Thus everything about the situation of care tends to a dialectic and irony on which tragedy and comedy alike may thrive. And what do the most trenchant tragic and comic dramas tend to show? Is it not that we are somehow responsible for the way in which things appear to us without being able to determine how things appear at will? Do not these dramas study appearance in intimacy with modes of care? And do they not tend to suggest that care cannot absolve itself of the way things appear to it, so that if appearances come to wear an illusory aspect, as in disillusionment with them, then care must acknowledge its part in illusion and know that part as delusion?

At this phase of our story the situation of care seems to be something like this: The being of things can no longer be dissociated from their appearing and the way in which care discovers them. Care and being have essentially to do with one another. Being is no longer that to which care may take itself to be accidentally abandoned. The questionableness of being is now also the questionableness of care. The meaning of being becomes care's own undertaking. We may say that the stake in the venture is both the self and the world. Thus, as Tillich points out, in so far as self-loss may attend the venture, this is also at the same time world-loss. But in the course of speaking of creation and the story that may be ours to tell of it, we have already said as much: Namely, that the coming to pass of world and our coming to be as selves are essentially related; we participate in this as selves and only as selves. World, in turn, seems to come to pass only through our participation in it as selves, and this is ultimately a matter of free consent on our part, while coming to pass through us.

Can we now say what the situation of care implicitly is, with respect to being? I think we must try, in that the very predicament of the self must implicitly foster whatever, by way of resolution, may answer to it. I would say the situation is implicitly this: Care and being are "promised" to one another. In consonance with being alone can care be confirmed in its being. We become authentically ourselves in the image of the divine and on the strength of the divine. This implies that we come to know ourselves in being ourselves and I think in a very precise sense: We are strictly as nothing in and of ourselves. Of all creatures, we must *know* our creatureliness and accept it in order to be as the creatures we really are. Our true dignity consists in our ability to acknowledge that considered in and of ourselves we are as nothing. Now this means two things: It means that considered in and of ourselves we are of no account and impotent. It also means that we are able to be in the image of being, which is no *thing* at all. The free consent to be as nothing in both these senses is what I understand by renunciation. And what is it that renunciation is renunciation of? Simply of the claim, I think, to be in one's own right. Care cannot entitle itself to be nor can it issue the title of anything to be, no matter how benevolently disposed by inclination care may be. In renunciation, so construed, care is not being "heroic" but essentially matter-of-fact. In so far as care is prepared to give itself up, then it is prepared to receive all things. In doing so, it makes room for things to come into being and does not block the mutual access, so to speak, of things and being, consummated through one's willing participation in this. In thus receiving all things into itself, care recognizes them as divine gifts, for so they are in creation.

If these gifts are not to be disavowed, care must be willing to part with them; they cannot be owned; they cannot be claimed; they cannot be clung to; and when departed, they cannot be sought. The continuity of participation in creation is in uninhibiting restraint, forbearance, a continuing receptivity, an evenness in arrival and departure, way beneath the fluctuating surface of events. Otherwise stated, we may say: Receiving is parting, and parting is receiving; renunciation is the receptivity of care—receptivity, that is, on the part of care. Such is the Valley Spirit of Tao and the poverty of spirit of which Eckhart speaks. There is nothing in all creation to which care may make fast; but in so far as care will agree to this it embraces all creatures as creatures, participates in all creation, and abides in no abode.

There is one parting pertinent to the possibility of participation in creation in our own time, especially here in what we may still call Christendom, and I see it as a parting of special historical relevance to us, nowhere more clearly indicated than in a remark of Meister Eckhart's in which he explicitly speaks of a parting that is last and highest:

> Man's last and highest parting occurs when, for God's sake, he takes leave of god. St. Paul took leave of god for God's sake and gave up all that he might get from god, as well as all he might give—together with every idea of god. In parting with these, he parted with god for God's sake and yet God remained to him as God is in his own nature—not as he is conceived by anyone to be—nor yet as something yet to be achieved—but more as an "is-ness," as God really is.
> (*Meister Eckhart: A Modern Translation,* R. B. Blakney, New York and London, Harper & Brothers, 1941, p. 204.)

[139]

The story of creation is an ontological one; indeed, *the* ontological one. But we may surmise what the discovery, the disclosure of being may presuppose. It presupposes radical and willing acceptance of creatureliness on our part. It demands no less and no more of us than ourselves. Perhaps the blessing of mortality consists in this, that as mortality grows upon us it strengthens in us the intimation of what is demanded of us—no more and no less than ourselves. Perhaps this is the one thing we need to know; somehow, unmistakably, unerringly conveyed with the possibility of being as a self, and it must be conveyed as a demand as inescapable as it is incomprehensible and beyond our capacity to bear. Then, in so far as—in spite of ourselves, very likely—we are led, trapped, surprised into moments of unconditional assent and free consent in a mortal existence, we begin to discover the meaning of creation and of coming into the world as men; and the possibility of our part in this, as agents of creation, dialectically insinuates itself into the human will. Now one lives in question: Who is he, really? Does he really will what, somehow, he knows he must will? Namely, as Kierkegaard suggests: one thing. But what would one will in willing one thing? We might say, with Kierkegaard, the Good; or, with Buber, whatever in fact one is *able* to will unconditionally and with the whole soul, by way of contrast with double-minded, equivocal, and only seemingly decisive, namely, *insistent* willing. But what is it one wills in so far as he wills univocally and decisively? It must be something unutterably simple that one wills in willing one thing, so simple, perhaps, as to seem like willing nothing at all; and that is just being. To will one thing is being patient of creation, to be willing to be with all creatures as creatures, even as the most creaturely of creatures oneself.

One really does not know what is happening, or what he is doing, or where it all will lead. But perhaps it is not necessary to know, any more than it is necessary for us to live forever. What is really necessary is what really comes to pass. And it will come to pass, whether we are willing or no, but not in a sense that we can make out independently of care. For care is what we are, and creation uniquely involves us as agents of creation in what necessarily comes to pass. If, as Thoreau says, we may learn to love the darkness no less than the light, we shall know that we do not live in vain and that what is necessary is not imposed on us as a fate. It is simply and eternally to be done.

DUANE H. WHITTIER

KANT AND THE PROBLEM OF SPACE

The first part of this discussion will be concerned with an exposition of Kant's views on space, with special attention being given to the manner in which they are to be interpreted. The second part will be a tracing out of the implications of the Kantian view of space. I am well aware that Kant's pronouncements on space do not appear to jibe with one another, but I have adopted the following as the most just and, probably, most fruitful working procedure: I shall assume, since Kant's diverse insights all came from the same mind and thus very possibly from the same cloth, that all his insights point in a uniform direction no matter how contradictory they may at first appear. Therefore, I shall be concerned with looking for a way to harmonize his various views, and if such can be found, I shall then consider it to be the true Kantian view. It is not enough to find that a philosopher has failed to establish his point clearly. One must see whether his concepts work out in a lawful way which he perhaps failed to formulate explicitly. Often a philosopher may vaguely but correctly sense the implications of something which he cannot formulate clearly enough to communicate successfully to others. There is no point in merely remarking upon Kant's difficulty in communicating. Our concern is to be clear about what he was trying to say and to judge its worth. Even if we find Kant's arguments defective, we ought to assume the correctness of his conclusions and try to find new premises for them. After all, it is possible for a man to be right even though for the wrong reasons. So much for the justification of what I am going to do.

PART I

1.1   Kant states, "Space is not an empirical concept which has been derived from outer experiences" (*9*, p. 68).[1] And further, "Space does not represent any property of things in themselves, nor does it represent them in relation to one another. That is to say, space does not represent any determination that attaches to the objects themselves, and which remains even when abstraction has been made of all the subjective conditions of intuition" (*9*, p. 71). Now it will be remembered that for Kant the distinction between *matter* and *form* is essential. Matter is given *a posteriori* in sensation, while form (as distinct from sensation) lies *a priori* in the mind. In this connection N. K. Smith points out that Kant has an unexpressed assumption to the effect that sensations have no spatial attributes of any kind and that his first argument on space derives its force entirely from this assumption (*8*, p. 86). Smith complains that Kant assumes this and does no more to prove it than remark that "space is no object of the senses." Smith is quite right that this observation is no proof that an extended object may not yield extended sensations. But *is this* what Kant meant to assert? Smith excites himself thusly:

> Kant completely ignores the possibility that formal relations may be given in and with the sensations. If our sensibility, in consequence of the action of objects upon it, is able to generate qualitative sensations, why, as Vaihinger very pertinently enquires, should it be denied the power of also producing, in consequence of these same causes, impressions of quantitative formal nature? Sensations, on Kant's view, are the product of mind much more than of objects. Why, then, may not space itself be sensational? (*8*, pp. 86–87)

And Smith quotes Riehl:

> Were the contention that the relations of sensations are not themselves sensed correct, the inference to the pure apriority of the form of our perception would be inevitable. For sensation is the sole form of interaction between consciousness and reality. . . . But that contention is false. The relations

of sensations, their determined coexistence and sequence, impress consciousness, just as do the sensations. (*8*, p. 88)

Now it seems to me that what Smith and Riehl have said here is very true, but not applicable to Kant. I think they have made two serious mistakes. First, what does Kant really mean when he holds that sensations don't have spatial attributes? Cassirer exhibits none of Smith's and Riehl's confusion on this matter:

> There are . . . the particular, or specific, characteristics of sensible phenomena, for example, qualities such as green, hot, heavy. That spatial and temporal characteristics cannot be considered to be on a par with these should be evident from the following considerations. If a *sensible* occupies a certain spatial or temporal position, this does not affect it in the material sense at all. . . . if a *sensible* is found in a different place, or at a different time, from the place it previously occupied, or from the time at which it previously existed, this does not alter it in the way in which the adding or taking away of some particular quality would alter it. We are thus obliged to differentiate clearly between the "material" characteristics of the given . . . and its spatial and temporal characteristics. . . . Secondly . . . we must note that while none of the characteristics we have just termed "material" are manifested in any and every sensible phenomenon, all sensible phenomena agree in this, that they present themselves in some place or other, and at some time or other. (*2*, pp. 32–33)

1.2.1 As for the second mistake, what does Kant mean by "space"? Space as a form of intuition is general and therefore unable to give us anything about the extension and shape of any particular object. That we must (because of the *a priori* structure of our minds) perceive things spatially and temporally does not explain why I experience this piece of wood as being so long and as being half that length after I cut it in two. Clearly, it is not possible that general space be *a priori* and belonging to mind, while particular determinations of space be *a posteriori* and determined by the external world. (Unless of course "space" is being used in two senses here, two senses in addition to those of "universal" and "particular.") Space as an *a priori* form cannot account for particular bits of extension, nor can time as an *a priori* form determine the particular motions and alterations that will be perceived. By themselves, these considerations would lead us to conclude that space *is* given in sensation. Yet inasmuch as space characterizes all things indifferently, Kant is led to think of it as a form of appearance; such a form not belonging to sensation, for it does not arise through the action of the object *qua* object and consequently must be *a priori*. Two things should be noted at this point: (1) Berkeley's principle that primary and secondary qualities are "in the same boat" and must therefore be either both objective or both subjective applies analogously here. It cannot be maintained that spatiality is *a priori* while the perception of any given particular determination of space is purely empirical. Yet, as the quote above from Cassirer makes clear, spatial relations *are* independent of (externally related to) materiality. These considerations should make us wonder what Kant means by "space," for the referent of the term is not at all obvious. (2) The fact that space characterizes all things indifferently is no proof that it must be subjective and *a priori*. It is quite conceivable that something characterizing all perceptions is nevertheless objective, for there is no *prima facie* reason for holding that only by virtue of the unity of perception (unity because belonging to one ego) can spatiality characterize everything that appears in perception. Fortunately Kant tries to establish this point in quite another way: ". . . in order that certain sensations be referred to something *outside me* (*that is, to something in another region of space from that in which I find myself*), and similarly in order that I may be able to represent them as outside and alongside one another, and accordingly as not only different but as in different places, the representation of space must be presupposed" (*9*, p. 68, *italics added*). I think this last argument valid *if it is properly understood*. What kind of "space" is Kant talking about? The point I want to make is very difficult. There are three types of *perceptual* space: "location-at-a-distance," surface, and what I call "arena" (these types have nothing to do with typifying space as "physical," "psychological," and "mathematical"). Extension (the spatial *surface* of an object) is distinct from the space *in* which the object exists and which exists *between* it and other objects ("in and between" space = "arena"), for one is "space" as colored surface and the other "space" as external relation. Yet these two types of space also have something in common, else we would not call both of them "space." Now the sense in which surface and "arena" are the same is the space Kant holds to be *a priori*. Insofar as these two are different, that by virtue of which they are different belongs to the matter of sensation and not to the form of sense intuition.

(I shall explain in Part II how this distinction is possible and why it is not a violation of Berkeley's principle.)

1.2.2 Now "space" (in the sense in which "arena" and surface are the same) is related to space as "location-at-a-distance" ("distance" here does *not* refer to any measure of magnitude, either of surface extension or of distances between objects, and "location" does *not* refer to anything determined by coordinates). I am using the term to mean "something being outside me in another region of space from that in which I find myself." "Location-at-a-distance" is here a synonym for "over-againstness." If space is the *a priori* form of sensible intuition, then obviously it has something to do with perceptual consciousness. Let me explain what that something is, and in doing so I shall, if I am not mistaken, explain why space is presupposed by outer experience rather than something that comes in the wake of it.

1.2.3 There is a difference between space as extension and space as location. I stand here and look at a car twenty feet away. My *act* of seeing occurs right here, but what I see is over there (and what I see is extended, has surface). My act of perception and the object perceived are related, but *this* relation is not something that is itself perceived (although the relation of the car to one beside it *is* something given in sensory perception). This is to say, there is a magnitude of twenty feet between me and the car, but this magnitude is not a perceived surface, a set of extended sensory qualities; nor is it a perceived lateral relation between objects in the perceptual field. My mind does not look out through my eyes as we might peer out a window. Nor is there a miniature theatre in my brain that carbon copies the external world and "projects" the results. When I feel pain in my finger, the pain is in my finger and nowhere else, but my *act* of feeling is located where the brain is located, and the "across space" connection between finger and brain is not perceived in experience. Now this ability of consciousness to be here and apprehend what is over there *as over there* is not something learned from experience, but something prior to it that makes experience possible. (It may be true that an act of consciousness here, apprehending something over there *as over there,* is partially a product of learning. We learn to estimate great distances and sizes of objects in terms of cues, i.e., by making inferences. But while *judgment* of distance is one thing, experiencing distance and location in the primitive oppositional form of "here and over there" is quite another. One cannot judge that which is not presented for judgment.) *Certainly consciousness' ability to apprehend at a distance belongs to its structure and is nothing given to it by that which it runs across in perceptual experience.* And thus spatiality of this type is certainly not something given in the wake of sensation. *In part,* space may be considered perceptual consciousness' very mode of operation. Consciousness must operate in this way before anything spatial can be given in experience, *even assuming spatiality to be an objective property existing independently of mind.* Whether consciousness casts things in spatial form or discovers them to be that way will be discussed in Part II, where I shall try to show (1) how this kind of spatiality is the same spatiality that makes synthetic *a priori* knowledge in geometry possible and (2) in what way "space" as *surface* and spatial *relations* (in, beside), which are given in perception *a posteriori* along with sensation, are related to "space" in the *a priori* "location-at-a-distance" sense. What I feel I have here accomplished with this complex argument is this: Kant's first argument for the *a priori* nature of space stands independently of the presupposition attributed to him—that of sensations being nonspatial.

1.2.4 I find it hard to believe Kant ever held the view that sensations are nonspatial. We can know objects only *a posteriori;* objects have surfaces, and objects cannot be built by the mind out of nonspatial sensations simply because no amount of compounding and synthesizing of purely intensive magnitudes can yield extensive magnitudes. Surely these things were obvious to Kant. In spite of them, however, he felt our representation of space cannot be *a posteriori* simply because, even assuming space to be objective, it cannot be received unless the mind is ready for it, and this readiness is determined by the structure of the mind, not by the world that is to be perceived. Kant's first argument is, I conclude, valid; but it does not carry us as far as Kant thought. The fact that space certainly belongs to the mind does not prove that it belongs only to the mind. And it is yet to be proved that the various types of space are all dependent upon one basic type.

2.1 Kant's second argument of space states, "Space is a necessary *a priori* representation, which underlies all outer intuitions. We can never represent to ourselves the absence of space, though we can quite well think it as empty of objects. It must therefore be regarded as the condition of the possibility of appearances, and not as a determination dependent upon them. It is an *a priori* representation, which necessarily underlies outer appearances" (*9*, p. 68). The argument here is that if space is a necessary representation, then it must consequently be *a priori,* for necessity is one of the criteria of the *a priori.* Thus Kant thinks that if he can prove space to be necessary, then he has also proved it to be *a priori.* He thinks it to be necessary because of the impossibility of imagining it as absent, though it can be imagined as empty of sensible content. Thus a representation which it is impossible for the mind to be without is a necessary representation. Since space cannot be thought away as sensible objects can be, it must belong to the organizational structure of the mind. This means that its apriority is psychological in character.

2.2 Now we must become clear about what it means to assert the impossibility of imagining space as absent. First we must distinguish perceptual consciousness from conceptual thinking. If space is the necessary form of all intuitions, then it is also the necessary form of imagination, which for Kant is intuitive in character. Percepts (seeing a pasture) and perceptual concepts (imagining the green of the pasture in "the mind's eye") alike belong to perceptual consciousness. Kant asserts the impossibility of representing space as absent from perceptual consciousness. However, space *can* be *conceived* as nonexistent, and it can also be *conceived* as empty. But here the term "conceive" is being used in the sense in which we say, "it is conceivable that stones have consciousness." And it must be noted that the concepts "pure space" and "nonexistent space" very much resemble the concept "square-circle." One can indeed talk about such things, but one can have no real idea what one means by them if they are uttered seriously rather than with tongue-in-cheek. Kemp Smith sceptically remarks that the whole ground for Kant's second argument is merely the "brute fact (asserted by Kant) of our incapacity to think except in terms of space" (*8*, p. 103). I find no reason to doubt the "bruteness" of this fact, if we keep in mind the distinction I have just drawn between the two types of conceptual thinking.

2.3 Kemp Smith remarks that "Kant offers no proof of his assertion that space can be intuited in image as empty of all sensible content; and as a matter of fact the assertion is false" (*8*, p. 104). It is hard to know what Kant really meant to assert in this connection. His words are, "We can never represent to ourselves the absence of space, though we can quite well think it empty of objects." Did he mean that we can't *imagine* space as absent but can *imagine* it as empty? Or that we can't *imagine* it as absent but can *conceive* it as empty? After all, we can *conceive* it as absent (Kant admits this), and Kemp Smith is correct when he says that "With the elimination of all sensible content space itself ceases to be a possible image" (*8*, p. 105). "Space" is like "beauty." We can think the *concept* "beauty," but to *image* beauty apart from a something that possesses it is impossible. I think it fair to conclude that while space cannot be *imaged* independently of all sensible content, nevertheless all Kant needs to assert is that space can be intuited in imagination independently *of any particular type of sensible content* (see quote from Cassirer, 1.1 above).[2]

2.4 Kant regards the impossibility of imagining space as absent as proof that it originates from within. Kemp Smith rightly points out that "the argument is valid only if no other psychological explanation can be given of this necessity, as for instance through indissoluble association or through its being an invariable element in the given sensations" (*8*, p. 105). In line with my interpretation of Kant's first argument, I think we *can* conclude that the impossibility of imagining space as absent *is* proof that it originates from within. One cannot be conscious without having the representation of space, for it is of the very essence of the nature of consciousness. Without this representation we simply are not conscious. Perceptual consciousness is constituted by the subject-object dichotomy in which the Other spatially stands over opposite. This is integral to perceptual consciousness as such. To deny this, one would have to hold that consciousness has no native structure *qua* consciousness and that any structure it exhibits is that which it has acquired in the wake of experience. But clearly objects of perception do not bring consciousness into being, and nothing can have being without having some determinate nature. Thus consciousness with its structure is prior to experience.

3.1 Kant's third argument states, "Space is not a discursive or . . . general concept of relations of things in general, but a pure intuition. For, in the first place, we can represent to ourselves only one space; and if we speak of diverse spaces, we mean thereby only parts of one and the same unique space. Secondly, these parts cannot precede the one all-embracing space, as being, as it were, constituents out of which it can be composed; on the contrary, they can be thought only as in it" (*9*, p. 69). Again, the only way of meaningfully interpreting this is along the lines used already on

Arguments One and Two. *Space is one because our consciousness is one,* and space is the "operational form" of consciousness. Above (1.2.1) I argued that the unity of perception cannot explain how spatiality (surface, and spatial relations like "beside") can characterize appearances universally, but there is no contradiction here in arguing that it can explain why the one all-embracing space is prior to the diverse spaces (parts) that are *in it* (notice, I say "in it" and not "parts that go to make it up"). Appearances stand in spatial relations to one another, but they also stand in relation ("location-at-a-distance") to a mind. They exhibit spatial relations with one another while standing in the perceptual field of some mind. I do not yet want to argue whether or not that which appears can stand in spatial relations independently of some mind's perceptual field. But assuming spatial relations to be objective, the space of the perceptual field in which they appear belongs to the mind whose perceptual field it is. Kant states, "Space is essentially one; the manifold in it, and therefore the general concept of spaces, depends solely on the introduction of limitations" (*9*, p. 69). The appearance in experience of any particular size and shape of surface standing in a particular relation of distance and direction to some similar appearance is a purely contingent and thus *a posteriori* affair. Thus the limitations which give rise to individual spaces do not belong to the *a priori* form of intuition. If the one all-embracing space is *a priori,* then it follows that it *contains* individual spaces, because it cannot itself be composed of them for *they* are *a posteriori.* This intuition which underlies all external perception must be *a priori.* The parts of space cannot precede the one all-comprehensive space, for they can be entertained (come before mind) only in and through it. That space is *a priori* follows from the fact that representation of space as a whole is necessary for the apprehension of any parts in it.

3.2 In Part II, I shall turn to this problem: How can diverse spaces which arise *a posteriori* be "parts" of a single unique *a priori* space? Here I want to lay the groundwork for that discussion. Kant speaks in both ways, referring to individual spaces as parts of one space and as merely things *in* the one unique space. Space is not the kind of "Whole" that can be literally divided into parts. There is no such thing as a "chunk of space." Space can have things in it, and to appear *in* space is itself to exhibit a spatial relation. The "part-whole" relation applied to space is more a metaphor than anything else. More apt metaphors would be to think of spatiality as a "quality" and that things "partake of it," or to think of space as a "system of relations" in which things "participate." "Partaking" and "participation" have nothing to do with being constituent "parts." Some parts of space can be bigger than other parts only in the sense of some things *occupying* more space than others. Thus ultimately even in terms of the Kantian metaphor, being "parts of" space and being "in" space become the same. Yet something having extensive magnitude, while "in" space, is also itself spatialized. And thus the metaphor of spatiality as a "quality." (But this "quality" is something universally exhibited by phenomenal objects and does not therefore admit of degrees of "partaking"—differences in surface areas not being differences in degree of *spatiality* but differences in amount of whatever that something is which is extended and in space.) "Spatiality" is not, as the grammar of the word implies, a quality. It simply means the ability to appear in space and to submit to measurement. Space itself (that in which things appear) is neither extensive nor intensive, for it does not admit of degrees or determinate size. Either something is in space or it is not (i.e., either it is noumenal or phenomenal). With reference to that part of reality which is constituted so as to have intercourse with consciousness, it makes no difference if we say it appears *in* space because *it* is spatial, or it is spatial because it appears in space. Now spatial relations (e.g., size of surface, distance between objects) are just that—*spatial* relations. Their magnitude, whether great or small, does not in any way alter the fact that they are *spatial* relations or qualities ("spatial" here denotes a *kind* of thing). Not all spatial relations are affairs of measurement, for whether a thing appears or doesn't appear is a spatial affair admitting of no degrees. *There is a difference between the space things are in and the spatial characteristics they exhibit.*[3] But there is also a continuity between these things. This will be taken up in Part II. What we must note here is this: Kant is thinking in terms of Newtonian absolute space in which things happen, space being related externally (indifferently) to that which occupies it. But we must remember that Kant is concerned with phenomenal space, the space in which objects are given in experience. Things are *in* space simply in the sense in which they are *in* the perceptual field of consciousness. The fact that Newtonian space is a conception having little scientific utility in modern times, and thus scorned as a candidate for what is to be taken as "real physical space," is an irrelevant consideration in this discussion. Space as an "empty vessel" has a phenomenological validity that is quite independent of its scientific fate. That Kantian space has no import for modern physics I readily admit. In this paper I am concerned primarily with two things: (1) the accuracy and validity of the Kantian *phenomenology* of space; and (2) whether this view of space explains geometry as Kant thought.

4.1 Kant's fourth argument states:

> Space is represented as an infinite *given* magnitude. Now every concept must be thought as a representation which is contained in an infinite number of different possible representations (as their common character), and which therefore contains these *under* itself; but no concept, as such, can be thought as containing an infinite number of representations *within* itself. It is in this latter way, however, that space is thought; for all parts of space coexist *ad infinitum*. Consequently, the original representation of space is an *a priori* intuition, not a concept. *(9,* pp. 69–70)

This argument seeks to prove that space is an intuition, not a general concept. An example should make this clear. "Color" is a general concept containing *under* it "red," "green," "blue," etc. In no sense are these colors parts of one another in the way that one might consider pink a part of red. Yet "space" contains lesser spaces *within* itself; that is, "spaces" are related to "space" in a very different manner from that in which "red" and "blue" are related to "color." Clearly "space" is not a generic class concept. Kemp Smith complains that this fact does not entail Kant's implied conclusion that space must belong to receptivity and not to understanding. He feels that Kant has not proved that space and time are radically distinct from the categories; i.e., from the relational forms of understanding *(8,* p. 107). In view of the color example above, I see no way in which we can avoid making Kant's distinction between "pure intuition" and "concept." For Kant, space is both a form of intuition and itself an intuition, and there is no contradiction in this, for the *form of intuition* is the system of relations in which appearances stand, and the *content of pure intuition* is these same relations viewed as though they were abstracted from sensible appearances and taken together as forming one individual whole. (I say "viewed as though abstracted," for if we let it read "abstracted," then space as an intuition would indeed be something belonging to the understanding rather than

[151]

receptivity.) But our discussion of the role of consciousness shows that space as a pure intuition is not something abstracted from sensible appearances (see 1.2.1, 1.2.3, and 3.2 above). Space as an intuition must belong to receptivity. The space *in* which lesser spaces dwell cannot be the product of an abstraction, because "in-ness" is not only a relation, but also refers to the fact of being located in a common matrix, and therefore relations like "above" and "beside" presuppose "in-ness," rather than "in-ness" being an abstraction from them. "In-ness" is a different kind of relation from spatial relations like "above" and "beside," and while continuous with them, is not an abstraction from them. "In-ness" is not abstracted from "above," "below," "between," "beside" as their common element, rather they presuppose "in-ness" as their common ground. Abstract the sensible from that which is spatial (e.g., a red surface beside a green surface), and what is left is "surfacedness" and "besideness." But these abstract concepts are not synonymous with "in-ness." And for one determinate space (colored surface) to be beside another space, they must be in the same space and thus be "parts" of it, with it existing prior to themselves. Space as an intuition, as a unique whole, is the space (perceptual field) *in which* things appear. The abstraction of the sensible from the spatial characters exhibited by the sensible (surfacedness, besideness) simply cannot give rise to the "pure space" *in which* particular spaces dwell.

PART II

5.1 In this part of the paper I wish to do two things: (1) show how Kant's views on space imply a theory of perception which, when formulated, illuminates the distinction between noumenon and phenomenon; and (2) show that Kant's account of geometry has not been outmoded by modern developments. I shall argue that Kant, by failing to distinguish two senses of the term "space," was unable to fit together the *a priori* and *a posteriori* aspects of space, and that when we see how this can be done by means of distinguishing these two types of space, then Kant's four arguments treated in Part I become both clear and valid. These arguments, by thus becoming valid, entail a particular view of perception, the nature of which will be discussed. And this in turn will show why Kant's views on geometry are reasonable.

6.1.1 Throughout Part I we noticed the constantly recurring problem: How can diverse spaces which arise *a posteriori* be "parts" of a single unique *a priori* space? This is *the* problem for Kant. He explicitly holds space to be *a priori* and just as explicitly that the inexhaustible multiplicity of appearances can be known only *a posteriori*. Empirical laws, as such, cannot derive their origin from pure understanding. And likewise the matters of fact of experience are through and through empirical. Yet the form of experience is *a priori*. How can form in general be *a priori* when particular forms are *a posteriori?*

6.1.2 Paton shows a full appreciation of this problem. He states:

> It is generally admitted that Kant offers no precise statement as to the reason why one object appears to us as square and another as round; but it is commonly held that all such differences of shape must be imposed *only* by the nature of our minds. The ground for this would seem to be that because space and time are for Kant imposed wholly by the mind, therefore squareness and circularity must be imposed by the mind. . . . This commonly accepted doctrine destroys the distinction, upon which Kant always insists, between empirical and universal laws and between empirical and universal concepts. Only what is strictly universal is imposed by the mind upon objects. (*6*, p. 139)

Paton notes that Kant's argument with respect to space and time as forms of intuition or of appearances

> . . . is not at all that relations as such must be due to the nature of the mind. His argument is that space and time, as the *universal* and *necessary* system of relations which is the condition of the particular relations in which appearances are given, must be due to the nature of the mind. (*6*, pp. 135–136)

In a footnote (p. 136) Paton remarks,

> Kant indeed says that the form in which sensations are arranged cannot itself be sensation . . . but he is referring . . . not to the *particular* relations (or empirical forms) in which sensations are arranged, but to the *universal* forms of space and time, which are the condition of all such particular relations or forms.

Paton sees the problem but has no real solution. Granted that the mind does not "impose" particular spatial relations upon empirical contents themselves, nevertheless it is asserted that what is universal is "imposed" by mind upon objects. But what can be meant by this? Paton wants to sidestep the problem by saying that we must distinguish the logical from the psychological in this matter. But this will not do. In the *Aesthetic* Kant is concerned with space as a psychological *a priori*, as something belonging to receptivity. Thus the problem remains: Space belongs to receptivity and is *a priori*, while particular determinations of space appear in receptivity as matters of fact known *a posteriori*. How is this possible?

7.1 Kant uses the term "space" to cover two closely related but importantly different things: spatiality (surface extension, spatial relations like "beside"), and the space that these things are *in*. He felt these two to be related as parts to a whole. But as I showed above, this relationship is not possible. Spatiality appears in empirical intuition just as any other quality does. Empirical intuition is knowledge which stands in immediate relation to objects. Its content can arise only through the action of some independent object upon the sensibility; i.e., the content apprehended must be sensuous. But phenomenal space, the space that belongs to consciousness as such and in which things appear, is a pure intuition. Space [4] as a pure intuition can be contemplated in separation from all sensation (but separation only in the sense of separate object of focus). The pure intuition of space exists as a state of consciousness independently of any actual object of the senses. This is to say that it is characterized by a quality of its very own. It has an intrinsic content, the quality or property of "location-at-a-distance." The tentacles of consciousness are extended even when not wrapped around anything. (Just look as far as your eye can see. Precisely where is the boundary of your visual field? There is a reaching out even when not to anything in particular.) This prehensive urge is the native (*a priori*) content and "location-at-a-distance" the native (*a priori*) form of perceptual consciousness. Merely to be awake is to have the intuition of space. True, it never occurs that there is space devoid of sensory content, just as it never occurs that there is consciousness that is not consciousness of something. Consciousness is always *consciousness of*. But just as no one would maintain from this that empirical data constitute the wakefulness of consciousness, so also no one should maintain that the intuition of space [5] cannot be distinguished from the sensory content of space. Just as consciousness can be aware of its wakefulness (i.e., "hear its own motor running") only in the presence of sense-data (but any data will do, and wakefulness is not the data nor a property of them), so also the intuition of space can be contemplated only in the presence of the sensible (but any *sensible* will do, for it does not comprise the intuition). It is true that there can be no pure intuition of space, but this does not mean that space and sensible content are not distinguishable *and distinguishable in more than a merely conceptual sense.* [The parallel with "wakefulness" should show how this is intelligible. We can be directly aware of our wakefulness as such (as distinct from its content), and this independently of the concept "wakefulness," even though such awareness can never *occur* in isolation from the presence of some content.] With respect to spatiality (space$_2$) —every separate thing has its own "space" and must be known empirically. Yet with respect to the space$_1$ it is in, nothing has its own private space (save minds). This single unique space belongs to consciousness.[6] To be in space$_1$ is not to be a *part* of space, for no object is a part of a mind (for perceiving a square does not result in a square state of mind). Thus Kant should not have talked of things *in space* being "parts" of space, for in talking this way the problem of relating *a priori* space$_1$ with its particular empirical determinations (space$_2$) becomes impossible of solution.

8.1 Without painstaking and detailed attention to the phenomenology of consciousness and to what Kant's views imply as to a theory of perception, the solution to the problem stated in paragraph 6.1.1 would be unapproachable. There are signs that Kant himself had tendencies toward the theory of perception I am about to advance. He states, "Since we cannot treat the special conditions of sensibility as conditions of the possibility of things, but only of their appearances, we can indeed say that space comprehends all things that appear to us as external, but not all things in themselves but whatever subject they are intuited, or whether they be intuited or not" (*9*, p. 72). Kemp Smith remarks that Kant here "propounds for the first time the view of sensibility as a limitation. Space is a limiting condition to which human intuition is subject" (*8*, p. 116). And indeed Kant did go on to say, "For we cannot judge in regard to the intuitions of other thinking beings, whether they are bound by the same conditions as those which limit our intuition and which for us are universally valid" (*9*, p. 72). To be sure, we cannot judge whether or not there are other beings with sensibilities conditioned otherwise than our own, but this remark of Kant's is no idle thought in passing; rather it is a clue, for it throws light on how he regarded the view of space and perception propounded in the *Aesthetic*. And it is the remark that continues the above quotation that is most important: *"If we add to the concept of the subject of a judgment the limitation under which the judgment is made, the judgment is then unconditionally valid"* (*9,* p. 72, *italics added*) . Here we have the real reason why Kant felt that geometry is a synthetic *a priori* affair applicable to the world of the independently real.

8.2.1   What sort of theory of perception can enable us (1) to relate space₁ and space₂ so that we can explain how space can be *a priori* while particular determinations of it are *a posteriori,* and (2) to explain geometry the way Kant wished to explain it? Space₁ has been shown to be an intuition. Space₂ belongs not to receptivity but to objects and is given in sense experience together with all other empirical characteristics. But how is space₂ related to mind? How can space₂ provide the possibility and basis for applied geometry? Does space₂ belong in any sense to the mind?

8.2.2   I want to put forward here a version of the selective theory of perception. Space₂ is neither objective nor subjective, but both and neither. What can this mean? First let us think of space as the arena or area of interaction between mind and reality.

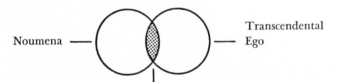

Empirical world of phenomenal space with
its objects and the empirical ego

Space₁ belongs to consciousness as its mode of operation. It is *a priori.* Space₂ belongs to objects, it is their structure insofar as they are presented to us. Where is space₂ presented? In Space₁ of course, else it would not be presented *to us* at all. Space₂ (spatiality) is a universal character of the things of experience, and it is possible that it is an objective characteristic exhibited by much of the reality that lies beyond our perception, but not a universal character of such reality *an sich*. This is to say, perhaps the mind views reality through a "slit." That which fits is let in, that which doesn't is not. On this view the mind admits those sensory data which are congruent with its apprehensive form. The real world, not the mind, is the origin of our sensations. Therefore the mind cannot arrange, cast, or mold sensations in a spatial manner; it cannot constitute the data, and by the same token data cannot cast the nature of mind. This matter of the "slit" is more than mere metaphor. Mind may neither *cast* the world in spatial form nor *discover* it to have that form. It may do both and neither (i.e., there *is* a third possibility). How can that which is objective be subjectively determined while yet remaining objective? This is the problem of how $space_1$ and $space_2$ can interact. This is the problem of empirically determined "parts" of an all inclusive *a priori* space. Let us think about an example. If a piece of wood smooth to the hand and naked eye looks rough under the microscope, does the microscope-eye partnership *create* the roughness? Yes and no. It creates the frame of reference (determines the vantage point of observation), but it does not create what is seen. Does it *discover* the roughness? Again yes and no. It does not create what is seen, but the characteristic seen (roughness) is not a *Ding-an-sich* characteristic. Rather, it is a characteristic that emerges from a relation, the relation being one of selection, not generation. The roughness of the wood is not "put there" by the microscope—it is "objective," yet this objective quality exists only with reference to that which is microscopic, for relative to that which is coarser than itself (my hand) it exhibits the quality of smoothness. Qualities and even "thing-hood" itself are products of relations. This does not make them "subjective." There are no such things as "things-in-themselves" if we take this term to mean something like "windowless monads" or atoms as solid billiard-ball-like entities capable only of external relations. But it is possible and likely that there are "things-in-themselves" in the sense that things that are related to us by way of consciousness may stand in other relations that remain unknown to us. The human perceptual point of view is only one, not a composite of all possible points of view (see quote from Kant, 8.1 above). What we see is as genuine an aspect of reality as any other, but it is only one aspect. What we see is objectively real, but we see only a part of what is real. The necessity to resort to "inferred entities" makes it very plausible that there is much that lies beyond the realm of our perception (although this can never be verified and made more than a reasonable conjecture). On this view space$_2$ is both subjectively and objectively determined. However, there is good reason to place the emphasis, as Kant does, upon the subjective side.

8.2.3 Space$_1$ is the area of contact between the noumenal world and the transcendental ego; thus space$_1$ is the realm of phenomenal objects. Space$_2$ is a featured product of the interaction of these things in contact. Phenomenal objects are not constructed by the mind but are genuinely objective. However, they are subjectively determined (and at the perceptual as well as conceptual level). This is to say that the structure of the mind presents to us a "slice" of the real world in a manner that is metaphorically analogous to the way the penetration of X-rays (shallow or deep) into an object determines what will and will not be revealed of the object's inner structure. Thus phenomenal objects appear in perceptual consciousness as already processed, as products of the interaction of the structure of the mind with the real world. Mind performs this function prior to the level of awareness. This subjective determination is a "slicing" or "penetration" of the world, not a synthesizing of sensations into perceptual objects. This process is "mental" in that it is subjectively determined and registers its import in the occurrences of perception, but in another sense it is not "mental," for the determination is prior to consciousness. But besides *perceptual* consciousness (awareness of the sensible manifold, awareness of *that*), there is *conceptual* consciousness, which is consciousness of meaning (awareness of *what*, awareness of objects in their mutual implications). The first kind of consciousness is a matter of "wakefulness," but the second type is that of conceptual thinking, and only in it does knowledge occur. Percepts must be grasped by concepts before the *that* can become the *what*. The synthetic process that results in knowledge of objects does not literally build objects out of sensations, but rather builds our degree of consciousness of them, our very recognition and knowledge of them. Thus the accounts of space in the *Aesthetic* and *Analytic* are complementary and not competing accounts. There are *both* necessary ways of perceiving and necessary ways of conceiving. Both alike are due to the inherent (*a priori*) structure of mind and consciousness and thus may properly be viewed as essentially subjective. The former limits the range and type of what can be presented for perceptual knowing, and the latter makes conscious knowledge itself possible.

8.2.4 By "space" Kant means both what I have called space₁ and space₂. Only insofar as space₂ enters into space₁ can it become known. Also, space₁ can entertain only those things which have an affinity for it, namely, all that partakes of the nature of space₂. Thus the "selectivity" of perception should be no mystery. What enters perception is provided by the real world, not generated by mind; but the form or cast of what enters is determined subjectively in that only certain types of things can enter—and what these types are is determined by the structure of the mind. Is the mind therefore to be viewed as a filter or screen which sifts the real world, allowing only certain sorts of things to enter? This is my own view, but I do not think it is implied by Kant's assertions, for on my view we perceive things as they really are but only in part. At times Kant talks as though he were willing to admit this possibility, but basically his views point to a somewhat different theory of selective perception, a theory that has a generative element in it. It is possible on a selective theory of perception to hold that some things-in-themselves might very well have spatial properties and other things not, and that while our minds allow us to entertain the one kind and not the other, they do not contribute anything to the constitution of that which they do entertain. But Kant's views in the main imply that without human beings, space and time would not exist. Thus what man perceives in consciousness is the character of his relationship to the real world. An illustration will make my meaning clear: it is as though a chemical substance were conscious, and could perceive only the products of its interaction with those particular things for which it had an affinity due to its and their particular valences. But regardless of which selective view we take, the element of subjective determination is there, and it is this that is important for Kant's view of geometry. As Kemp Smith states,

> Pure geometry presupposes only that space is an *a priori* intuition; applied geometry demands that space be conceived as the *a priori* form of external sense. Only in reference to applied geometry does the Critical problem arise: —viz. how we can form synthetic judgments *a priori* which yet are valid of objects; or, in other words, how judgments based upon a subjective form can be objectively valid. (*8*, p. 112)

The fact that space is the form of all outer intuition explains why we can make *a priori* judgments which apply to the objects of experience. Applied geometry is possible simply because the range and style of what can be presented to perception is determined by an ultimate matter of fact—the structure of mind. There may be real entities that stand in relations other than those of space and time and therefore cannot conform to the requirements of perceptual consciousness. If such exist, then due to the structure of the mind they can never be exhibited to us. And since consciousness' very mode of operation is spatial, everything that is to be experienced *must* exhibit spatial characteristics in order to be experienced. Nothing phenomenal can ever be *more* than spatial-temporal or *less* than spatial-temporal. And nothing will ever enter experience and surprise it by departing from this, because consciousness has a determinate nature and such a surprise for it could occur only if it changed its structure and ceased to be. But that which has ceased to be cannot be surprised.

9.1 What is to be said of geometry when viewed as synthetically *a priori* in both its pure and applied forms? Kant's position is that geometry is axiomatic; i.e., the axioms of geometry are genuine axioms, propositions that are self-evident and do not and cannot stand in need of proof. This contrasts with Leibniz' view that geometric axioms are propositions whose demonstrations have not yet been found, but which can be proved. Now Kant, in adopting this very view, had adopted geometry as synthetically *a priori*. And his view rests upon reducing analytic judgments almost exclusively to tautologies (an "analytic judgment" being one capable of proof from the principle of contradiction alone, while a synthetic one cannot be). I do not wish to discuss the question of geometry in terms of axioms, because axioms can be conceived both as insights into the essential nature of space and also as free postulates, and contemporary work in the field forces us to conceive them as the latter. I wish to discuss the Kantian view of geometry as synthetically *a priori* solely in terms of geometry's constructive character. The term "construction" does not mean "geometrical drawing" (for Kant argues that a circle drawn on the board is not a circle, etc.). Construction belongs to intuition and, when advanced as a requirement, it "limits the definitions which are possible in themselves to those whose concepts have objective reality" (5, p. 22). Drawing exact circles and actually constructing thousand-sided figures is not the point; it is rather that we have available the schema of the construction. The intuitionist school founded by Brouwer has followed Kant in admitting as legitimate (in the full sense) only those mathematical concepts that can actually be constructed (the nonintuitionists holding to the contrary that these concepts need be no more than free from contradiction). The Kantian view that geometry is intuitive in nature means only that geometry is limited to objects that can be constructed. Martin presents the whole matter clearly when he says,

> Kant . . . denies the mathematical existence of a closed figure composed of two straight sides; it is indeed logically possible because it is free from contradiction, but it cannot be constructed and given in intuition. Kant's conception of non-Euclidean geometries in general has to be understood in the same way. Non-Euclidean geometries are logically possible but they cannot be constructed; hence they have no mathematical existence for Kant and are mere figments of thought. (5, p. 24)

So much for the Kantian position as Kant saw it. But as Martin goes on to observe, while it is no longer tenable in *this* form, it can be reformulated in modern terms and found *to be still an open question*. He states,

> It seems to be the case that there are ways in which non-Euclidean geometries can also be constructed, by purely analytical means or by constructing Euclidean models of non-Euclidean geometries, and certainly Kant's assumption that non-Euclidean geometries could never be used in physics has proved too narrow. On the other hand we should have to formulate the problem differently today and ask whether Euclidean geometry does not have a feature which distinguishes it from all other geometries, and this is a problem which we are as yet quite unable to solve. We know that there are Euclidean models of non-Euclidean geometries but we cannot yet survey the connections between all possible geometries. Is one geometry perhaps, and presumably then Euclidean geometry, distinguished by being the foundation of the other geometries, or by being the only way through which we can reach the other geometries? (5, p. 25)

9.2 On the Kantian view intuition is not an additional source of knowledge for geometry, but rather it is that which limits the wider field of "logical existence" (that which is thinkable without contradiction) to the narrower field of "mathematical existence" (that which can be constructed). On this view the judgments of geometry are synthetic *a priori* because they are capable of construction in pure intuition. What is interesting here is the idea of intuition as a source of limitation (in the sense of selectivity). Only certain things can be entertained in intuition just as only certain things can be entertained in perception. Both exhibit a determinate character which must be recognized and appreciated in its full significance.

I think constructive criticism is the best way to come to close grips with a philosophy, and in this paper I have tried to support Kant's position by attempting to find ways to harmonize his diverse views. I have not, I think, been guilty of forced interpretations, but rather I have attempted to make those interpretations which seem the most reasonable and which place Kant's views in the best possible light.

NOTES

1. References quoted in this essay are listed below.

2. The space that can be so intuited is "location-at-a-distance" space, the space *in which* things are. Spatiality ("surfacedness" and relations like "beside") is distinct from this kind of space and cannot be intuited but only conceived as empty of sensible content.

3. Something is either *in* space (location) or *has* space (extension). There is no such thing as being a "part" of either kind of space.

4. "Space" as "phenomenal field," the space things are in. The empirical intuition of "extension" always finds it qualified (colored if nothing else). Extension devoid of quality is merely a concept and nothing belonging to receptivity.

5. Henceforth in this paper $space_1$ = phenomenal space that contains appearances and $space_2$ = surface extension and position relations.

6. Kemp Smith sees clearly that this is Kant's view when he states: "Throughout the *Critique* Kant insists that space is a form of receptivity. It is *given* to the mind. It has nothing to do with spontaneity or understanding, and therefore cannot be acquired by reflection upon any activity of the mind. But neither can it, as *a priori*, be acquired from without. Consequently it cannot be acquired at all. But if *given*, and yet not acquired, it must as a representation lie ready in the mind from the very birth of consciousness. Constrained by such reasoning, Kant views it as given in all its completeness just as truly as is a sensation of color or sound" (*8*, p. 92).

REFERENCES

1. Caird, Edward   *The Critical Philosophy of Kant,* Macmillan, N. Y., 1889.

2. Cassirer, H. W. *Kant's First Critique,* Allen & Unwin, London, 1954.

3. Fischer, Kuno *Commentary on Kant's Critick of the Pure Reason,* Longman's Green, London, 1866.

4. Gotshalk, D. W. *Structure and Reality,* Dial Press, N. Y., 1937.

5. Martin, Gottfried *Kant's Metaphysics and Theory of Science,* Manchester University Press, 1955.

6. Paton, H. J. *Kant's Metaphysic of Experience,* Allen & Unwin, London, 1936.

7. Prichard, H. A. *Kant's Theory of Knowledge,* Oxford Press, 1909.

8. Smith, N. K. *Commentary of Kant's Critique of Pure Reason,* Macmillan, London, 1923.

9. Smith, N. K. (trans.) *Immanuel Kant's Critique of Pure Reason,* Macmillan, London, 1933.

10. Watson, John *The Philosophy of Kant Explained,* Maclehose & Sons, Glasgow, 1908.

HENRY A. FINCH

THEORETICAL FRUITFULNESS AND THE MEASURE OF CONCEPTS [1]

"Our starting point is the question whether there is a connection and as it were a mutual partnership between objects of reason and the things of nature, or there is none, but the two are, so to speak, separated, though they cooperate somehow to make up the whole of reality. It is, at all events, more reasonable to suppose that there is a connection and that the universe is not a mere series of episodes."

—Theophrastus, *Metaphysics* I, 2.

I

From the substance of the considered reflections advanced in the most recent and responsible symposia [2] and, quite plainly, from all the findings and theory of the case,[3] the creative skills of mind remain performances whose necessary *and* sufficient conditions are—at least presently—unknown. Whether this deficiency of human insight is transformable into a comprehensive, resigned "postulate of impotence" is a question, I am convinced, which may be profitably argued only if the attempt to answer proceeds with scrupulous attention to the discovery of acceptable rules for the logical addition or compounding of necessary conditions into conjunctions of conditions which are either exact equivalents of, or converging approximations to, really sufficient conditions. A *perfect* command of the conditions which are both necessary and sufficient for any natural or cultural or moral property, character, event or production is, to speak with sobriety, an ideal never possessed but capable, nonetheless, of endlessly progressive approximation.[4] I am confident that the nonavailability of perfect control at every moment of time is derivable from the defining features of experimental inquiry for which completely isolated systems are and must be forever an ideal and never a present possession.

Every reasoned hope for the understanding of the creative skills of man's unconquerable mind turns, therefore, upon the coherence of the unattainable ideal of perfect control of production with the active cultivation of enhanced powers of invention during an endless convergence toward that ideal. The arresting diagnosis of man's condition attributed to Alcmaeon [5] in antiquity, namely, that man cannot (I take it, by additions, compoundings or sequential deeds) join together "beginnings and ends" still can evoke for us distressing images of the baffled resolve of Sisyphus or of the paltry prizes which may well have been involved in Prometheus' rather quick reconciliation with cruel and oppressive powers.[6] For the reflective modern intellect—which ought, of course, to be distinguished from momentary distempers—there is, of course, nothing whatever in the nature of infinite sequences which implies either cyclical repetition of defeat, or incapacity to maintain an approach to a limit-ideal within any degree of approximation.[7] Were this an occasion for the exploration of instructive collateral issues, I should like to assess critically the intellectual fallacies as well as the obstructive pseudo-technologies of prudence and consolation engendered by the (often obsessive) belief that both necessary and completely sufficient conditions of valuable states or outcomes "must" have been available in the finite past, or "will" be available in a finite future or "are" available at present, to at least one person.

II

To my mind—and I surely do not stand alone—the pioneering explorations of Spinoza and Kant in experimental teleology, as well as the related, rigorously conceptualized experimental teleology of E. A. Singer, Jr.,[8] together with the information-entropy conceptualization [9] of order and organization by Boltzmann, Shannon and Wiener, are revolutionary in their import for the understanding of creativity. Telic systems and mechanisms can be coherently conceived—this is the essence of the suggestions and models I refer to—as open and, hence, replaceable and *improvable* subregions of "closed" natural systems. Improvement in design for productive subregions of nature is logically and technically consistent with growing proficiency of productive action in widening ranges of environments. Natural necessity includes in its texture open systems and their productions, and thus shows a visage of realizable opportunity which cannot indeed long sustain the improvident or the witless, but which can be the permissive framework for that growing technical process which even so conservative a thinker as Burke perceived to be uniquely characteristic of man's nature in his memorable comment, "Art is man's nature." [10] One must also insist, especially in the current climate of querulous literary misunderstandings, that the rationale of technical aptitude now conceivable in experimental terms is not at all limited to physical technology nor restricted to mechanical causation.[11] The folk-mind and its philosophical proponents—a larger group than is usually suspected—find it increasingly difficult to reserve any experimentally definable desirable outcome as inaccessible to perfectible control and facilitations for the alleged reason that the decisive powers are "spiritual," "transcendent," "beyond mechanical design," "incalculable" and the like.

Without forgetting for a moment the magnificent and indispensable contribution of the Democritean tradition to the achievement of a rational philosophy of technology,[12] I am quite content to follow Descartes' recommendation to philosophers not to overlook the so-called "details" of "mere" technology.[13] I find it, indeed, to be inductive evidence rather than willful desire which strongly indicates that the best chance of converting inscrutable or oppressive powers to the status of being humanely and effectively disposable is the discovery that the appearance and determinate modes of action of "powers" depend upon conditions expressible by mathematical structures. Consider some impressive illustrations: from mana and "virtues" to energy; from chemical "affinity" to valence; from the goddess Fortuna to calculable probability expectations; from intuitions of intrinsic value to proposed measurement thereof, e.g., by Duncan-Jones; from "mother-wit" and "mind" to factors of mind enumerable by matrix algebra; from the qualitative causal heuristic of Bacon and Herschel to Fisher's design of experiments; from the "feel" of correct craftsmanship to quality control of manufacturing; from the "sense" of a behavioral or cultured environment to its topological or correlational trait analysis; from T. H. Huxley's almost pathetic sentiment that our opponent, nature, "wishes us to win" to the meticulous development of the metricizable conditions for matching or exceeding in flexibility the strategies of a possibly hostile nature. The foregoing illustrations are but part of a long list which any thoughtful observer may extend. In every instance, an enigmatic "power" has been revealed to have at least necessary conditions for its appearance and specifiable modes of action, which are stateable, controllable, testable, and perfectible because of the successful interpretation of a pertinent calculus, often enough a metricized calculus. To be sure, I cannot here enter into any precise or detailed appreciation of the reasons why the intellectual and instrumental skills of experimental science succeed *only through confirmed and interpreted calculi* in extending man's ability to depict and transform experience's "tossing tides of chance and pain." [14] As Laplace and Hertz among others having a clear right to a judgment noticed, a calculated consequence is a *sine qua non* for an effectively producible consequence. All metaphysically resourceful irrationalists, I have long observed, are prepared, logically enough, to challenge the possibility of effective calculability.[15] And no wonder, since men of calm judgment even when engaged in classifying "mysteries" will admit at least this in mitigation of overwhelming enigmas: "As soon as we understand how a (natural) thing is produced, it is no longer impossible for us to produce it."[16]

III

I hasten (now, I trust, with some philosophical justification) to my own illustration of the indispensable assistance of calculation and measure in the endless but imperative task of diminishing the suffering dependence of a rational being and its values and purposes upon unmanageable powers.

Just about as mysterious a "power" as one is likely to recall in the presence of those devoted to the sciences is the *comparative power* or *capacity of concepts to generate informative, verifiable, theoretically organizable laws applicable to a domain of objects.* Much contemporary methodological literature is once again aware of the issue of the comparative fruitfulness of concepts and conceptual schemes. There is a definite prospect that the issue may be susceptible of formulation and improved consideration by modern analytical and logical methods not in the possession of such earlier philosophers of science, e.g., Whewell [17] or Duhem, as were especially and alertly concerned with the fruitfulness of concepts. Professor Norwood Hanson's recent *Patterns of Discovery* is an instructive, bravely-sustained confrontation of the problem of inventive thought in physics which stresses the "instantaneous" information by the physicist of integral conceptual schemes. As in the writings of Watson and Toulmin one notices a reluctance in Hanson's pages to search for the isolable determinants necessary for the appearance of integral conceptual schemes. So judicious a beginning in sensitive heuristic calls, nevertheless, for completion in an inevitable direction, for Professor Hanson will certainly not dispute the existence of necessary conditions for any type of process whatsoever; [18] nor would he wish to contend, I am sure, that creativity cannot be enhanced and cultivated.

It is indeed surprising still to find in so prudent and competent a philosophical writer on science as Norman Campbell [19]—and in many others, not to speak of the views entertained by numerous working scientists—invocations of creative "genius" incapable of factorization into any controllable parameters, so vague and so desperate as to recall the poet Edward Young's remark, in his over-influential conjectures concerning "originality," that genius works by "invisible means." One outcome is quite certain: "invisible means" inaccessible to experimental observation and treatment can never receive designed improvements, a criticism I should not hesitate to direct against Professor Ryle's near-mystical theory of skill.[20] An inescapable consequence from all such mystical assessment of creativity is that one must more or less simply wait for it, without responsible intentions. For consolation, the best action one could consider would, on the whole, be the impassioned recital of Dante's hymn to chance,[21] a hymn which I, to speak frankly, deem to invoke a superstitious mood, despite its very moving ancestral memories.

Steadily persuaded that the enhancement of creative production requires the isolation and compounding of its necessary conditions, I propose for your consideration the perplexities of an inquirer who confronts a finite universe ⊔ of objects whose size N may be as large as you please, provided it be finite. Our inquirer's commendable ambition—it is an ambition which may well yield clues to the feasibility of more daring ambitions in the forbidding presence of time and infinity—*is to find and state and axiomatize laws of the form,* all β's are α's or, precisely r of the β's are α's where $0 < r < 1$. That this enterprise is an instructive paradigm for the better comprehension of scientific inference has been concisely and attractively argued by Braithwaite, e.g., in his British Academy Lecture, "The Moral Basis of Inductive Policies." Assuming as we must that the symbols β, α correspond to or, if you will, form non-null sets of the individuals in our universe, our inquirer has a decision to make; namely, which of all the possible candidates for β should he select so that his choice is one intelligently governed by considerations of maximum fruitfulness? The possible candidates for β among available non-null sets are equal in number to 2^N-1, N being the size of ⊔ . It is a staggering thought to become distinctly aware of the abundance of candidates from which β is to be chosen as N rises through any moderately high values. *Among all these β's (each β denotes a subset of ⊔) is there one β of determinate measure or a single-valued metrically determinate family of β's which has maximal nomothetic power, i.e., maximal capacity to generate the largest number of distinct laws of which β is the logical subject, each law embodying a maximized cognitive content? Could a β so determined also be characterized by theoretical fruitfulness in the additional but related sense that it is maximally effective in forming axioms from which the laws into which β enters are deducible?*

By now my reader will have surely noted with suspicion a failure upon my part to refer to "concepts," "meanings," "intension," "sagacity," "serendipity" and the like among my inquirer's resources in his search for laws. My critic is alert, but I counter that my purpose is just that of showing how a helpful indispensable measure of the nomothetic power or potentiality of β can be developed solely from the size or measure of β's extension, without reliance upon any rules for "meaning" or intension beyond those determinable extensionally, e.g., "Sets differing in extension must differ in intension." [22] My procedure is simply prudential and, once more, an application of the logic of necessary conditions; the fruits of extensional analysis are capable of cultivation while one awaits better experimentally controllable conceptions of "intension." I am impressed by the disposition to reserve definite proposals concerning a calculus of "meaning," among masters of symbolic logic such as Church. Whatever the future may bring forth in the way of intensional calculi, some helpful heuristic hints *are* developable meanwhile *from the fact that concepts, at least first order concepts, imply, i.e., necessarily presuppose, extensional sets whose members meet the conditions expressed by the concepts.*

That the size or measure [23] of β (mathematical measure coincides with countable extension in finite sets) is pertinent to its nomothetic or theoretical power even the ordinary judgment of the plain man can surmise without the assistance of logical science, although such judgment is characteristically incapable of discriminating the exact form and force of pertinent factors. Overspecification and overgenerality are plausibly to be avoided in a choice of fruitful β, even for common sense. To say very little about a great many things is no more commendable to the plain man's intelligence than to say a great deal about very few things. Generalizations based upon a small β are less valuable than generalizations over β with respectable scope. Nevertheless, a large β, say near or at the extreme measure, measure of $\beta = N$, deprives β of, or strongly diminishes in β, its capacity to convey or indicate discriminating information. (I am willing to impute to the plain man's judgment a latent desire to discover an optimal combination of scope and information-content in generalizations; but he needs assistance from the logician.) Even these common sense desiderata for fruitful β presently lack a satisfactory rationale and cannot secure one in classical logic unless such supplementary measure-theoretic concepts are introduced as make possible the development of metricized probability and information theory. The neglect of the cognitive content of statistical generalization with β as logical subject is particularly noteworthy within classical logical science.[24]

My explication of nomothetic or theoretical fruitfulness of concepts corresponding to the set β recognizes the following postulates of adequacy, some of which have already been acknowledged as implicit in prescientific sagacity. Postulate I: The nomothetic power of β to generate universally quantified laws of the form all β's are α's is to be weighted higher than its power to generate statistical laws of the form r of β's are α's, since universal generalizations involving the same β are (a) characterized by higher colligating power than statistical generalizations, (b) involve less

[171]

(indeed minimal) risk in the foresight or production of α from β, and (c) are theoretically more important in accordance with the requirement of the modern conceptualization of telic systems that provides for open systems to be embedded in closed ones, the latter of which are subject to universally quantified laws and the former of which are subject to statistical regularities. Postulate II: The power of β to generate statistical laws by its proper subsets is part of the nomothetic power of β. Postulate III: A set β is not an optimal set nomothetically if it generates distinct universal laws each of which is less than maximized for cognitive content, i.e., economy of laws is a theoretically justified demand if and only if it is compatible with maximally instructive distinct laws. Postulate IV: Nomothetic powers of β must stand in some definite relationship to theoretic power in the axiomatic sense, i.e., the most nomothetically powerful β ought to function most effectively in any axiom set from which the laws of ⊔ are deducible.[25]

IV

I come directly to my proposal for measuring the colligating power of concepts from the measured extension of their corresponding sets and for measuring the colligating power of laws stateable in terms of concepts possessing colligating power. The principle that an event's happening conveys information measurable by −log of the prior probability of the event's occurrence is familiar in information theory and now quite rigorously conceptualized.[26] Professor Putnam has utilized this principle in his own investigation concerning a topic related to our own.[27] I think it helpful to emphasize in our independent investigation that a *true judgment* expressing a law is, indeed, *itself an event* having a "prior" probability of occurrence. It is also necessary to recall, from the deep background of Boltzmann's ideas, that *degree of organization is measurable by the probability that it would be attained by a summation of random processes.* What indeed do the pair of concepts β and α express in a true law of the form all β's are α's or r of β's are α's? Organizationally *they express a structure of the extensions of two sets,* i.e., total or measured partial inclusion of the members of one set in those of another. It seems quite plain to me that a mind which possesses the concepts β and α entering into the statement of a true law possesses *infallible* [28] formators of sets extensionally related by inclusion precisely as the law asserts. If concepts function as infallible formators, i.e., the right sets are formed by concepts in true laws with probability of success equal to 1, with what random process ought one to compare these infallible formators of sets in order to measure the colligating power of concepts as formators of sets? I answer that if the possession of the concept β, where β's extension is measurable by a finite number $m(\beta)$, enables the possessor to form infallibly the extensional set β in $m(\beta)$ steps, *the colligating power of β is properly measured by $-\log$ of the probability that a random selector of objects from* ⊔, *possessing no concepts other than that defining objects in* ⊔ *will form the extensional set β in precisely $m(\beta)$ steps.*

It is indeed a pretty, if elementary, proof [29] which shows that, for any set β whose measure is $m(\beta)$, the probability of β's extension being formed by random selection in $m(\beta)$ steps is exactly equal to $\dfrac{1}{C^N_{m(\beta)}}$, a result from which we can readily find an optimal β.

V

I shall now outline, in sufficient detail, proofs that a set β, single-valued in measurable extension, can always be selected in finite ⊔, such that this set is optimally fruitful both in the formation of distinct generalizations of maximal colligating power and in the logical axiomatization of those generalizations. Results are collected into numbered theorems; brief lemmas of philosophical import are appended.

Theorem (1a). Any measurable set β, whose measure is $m(\beta)$ will allow the formation in ⊔ of $(N - m(\beta))$ distinct generalizations implying that all β's are α's, whenever $m(\alpha) = m(\beta) + 1$. (By a set of distinct generalizations I mean a set such that no one of the generalizations could be deduced from any conjunction of the others). Proof: $\beta \equiv \alpha_1$ does *not* qualify as a distinct generalization, for it cannot be excluded that α_1 is included in α_2, $m(\alpha_2) = m(\alpha_1) + 1$, so that all β's are α_2's will become a theorem dependent upon $\beta \equiv \alpha_1$, and lose its status as a distinct generalization. All generalizations from all β's are α_2's up to all β's are

[173]

$\alpha_{N-m(\beta)}$'s are necessarily distinct so long as the measure of each α is equal to m (β) + 1; sets differing *inter se* in one element and of the same size are distinct, i.e., incapable of any relationship of inclusion. Evidently, $(N - m(\beta))$ is a maximum under these conditions for any m (β).

Theorem (1b). The colligating power of each distinct generalization of the form all β's are α's, m (α) = m (β) + 1 is equal to

$$-\log \left[\frac{1}{C^N_{m(\beta)}} \cdot \frac{1}{C^N_{m(\beta)+1}} \right] \quad \overset{\text{(1b)}}{} C^N_{m(\beta)}$$

being read, of course, as "combinations of N individuals m (β) at a time." Proof: As shown above (see note 28) a random selector of individuals from $\cup$ will form the extension of β in m (β) steps with probability of success equal to $\frac{1}{C^N_{m(\beta)}}$; the application of the proof to α's extension whose measure is m (β) + 1 is plain and the product within (1b) justified, since the random selector without benefit of conceptual insight must form his sets independently.

Lemma 1. Concepts in true statements assure, with probability of success equal to 1, the formation of sets in their correct extensional relationship. *Since the logarithm of the probability of the chance that the sets have been correctly formed is a measure of entropy and ignorance, true concepts function to diminish entropy and ignorance to zero, i.e., they assure a maximal information gain.*[30] *Colligating power is the cause of information gain and measurable exactly by measuring information gain.*

Theorem (1c). The total entropy of all the distinct generalizations involving β as subject is measurable by $(N - m(\beta))$

$$-\log \left[\frac{1}{C^N_{m(\beta)}} \cdot \frac{1}{C^N_{m(\beta+1)}} \right] \quad \text{(1c) since each distinct generalization has}$$

its own entropy.

Theorem 2. From theorem (1b) it is clear that maximization of the denominators will determine the optimal β. Simple combinatorial considerations [31] will show that the measure of β which corresponds to the size of the *modal* class or classes in $\cup$ is the measure of β which will maximize colligating power of each distinct universal generalization into which β enters as subject.

Measure of modal β in is indeed equal to $\dfrac{N}{2}$ so that there exists at least one, and at most two, measures of β (differing by one unit) from which optimal m (β) can be selected; when N is odd the requirement to maximize $(N - m(\beta))$ will indicate the choice of the lesser size of m which is equally modal; *in any case, m (β) is uniquely determined.*

Lemma 2. The effective calculability of an optimal set β in terms of its measure is, for infinite $\cup$, a problem in its own right. I have not given up hope that for sets of positive measure in infinite $\cup$ a method for *estimating* colligating power may be developed, but this is a reserved theme.[32]

Theorem 3. β is capable of generating statistical generalizations, since it has proper subsets. Let x be a positive number ranging from 1 to m (β) $- 1$. Then for each value of x, β will be capable of generating $(N - m(\beta))$ $C_x^{m(\beta)}$ distinct generalizations each of calculable colligating power. For example, if $x = 1$, the corresponding colligating power for each generalization of the form $\dfrac{1}{m(\beta)}$ of β are α will be $-\log \left[\dfrac{1}{C_1^N} \dfrac{1}{C_2^N} \right]$. Proof: Each proper subset of β can be treated as a set in $\cup$, capable of inclusion in sets of measure greater by 1 than itself.

Theorem 4. The axiom $\beta \equiv \alpha_2 \ \alpha_3 \ \ldots \ \alpha_{N-m(\beta)}$ (4) is, when m (β) is optimized by theorem (2) the most powerful axiom for logically deducing all distinct universal generalizations involving β,[33] for the reason that this axiom will most effectively minimize the maximum entropy of the deducible universal generalizations involving β as subject. Proof: The generalizations, β is a proper subset of α_2, β is a proper subset of α_3, etc. have in theorem (1c) above been shown to have conjunctively a measurable entropy. But the statement β is a proper subset of α_2 implies all β's are α_2's as does the statement β is a proper subset of α_3 imply all β's are α_3's, etc. Consequently, the probability of the random formation of the set of generalizations of the logical form all β's are α's, from α_2 up to $\alpha_{N-m(\beta)}$ is at least as great as the probability of the conjunction involving the term "proper subset" which implies it. An implied statement cannot therefore have greater entropy than the statement which implies it.[34] Hence, the maximum entropy of the generalizations all β's are α's, when freed of reference to "subset," i.e., *when logically expressed,* is the quantity stated in theorem (1c). But the logically expressed distinct generalizations involving β are patently also deducible from axiom (4) ; therefore, the entropy relative to this axiom has a new maximum, namely $-\log\left[\dfrac{1}{C^{N}_{(\text{modal }\beta)}}\dfrac{1}{C^{N}_{(\text{modal }\beta)}}\right]$, which is less than the entropy stated in (1c). The only other axiom which could serve in place of axiom (4), namely β is included in $\alpha_2\,\alpha_3\,\ldots\,\alpha_{N-m(\beta)}$ has colligating power at most equal to that of axiom (4), since axiom (4) implies it.

Lemma 4. The function of axiomatization viewed information-theoretically is to reduce the entropy or ignorance or uncertainty of a system to that of the axioms by adjoining axioms to the system.[35] It remains to be seen what light can be thrown upon the ideals of simplicity, completeness and decidability by this conception of axiomatization. Clearly, however, *the truth of axioms will secure enormous information gains by diminishing the entropy of highly organized theorems to zero.* Whether this finding contributes, as I believe it does, a new understanding of "novelty" in logical inference also deserves further study.

Theorem 5. For each of the distinct proper subsets of β, there will be a most powerful axiom of the form r of β are α_{11} $\alpha_{111}\,\ldots\,\alpha_{N-m(\beta)}$, where r ranges from $\dfrac{1}{m(\beta)}$ to $\dfrac{m(\beta)-1}{m(\beta)}$. Proof is similar to that of theorem (4) .

Theorem 6. Axiom (4) in theorem (4) maximizes colligating power at the same time as it maximizes the minimum number of independent conditions [36] which could be met by any individual which met conditions for being in the β set.

Lemma 6. *More colligating power or information content in the sense of more surprising outcomes is therefore compatible with a variety of distinct items of information in the outcomes.* Inference can, I have no doubt, rise beyond the trivially tautological in many ways to decrease ignorant uncertainty and impotent amazement, the latter of which is, alas!, so often even deliberately confounded with the victorious wonder of instructive foresight. Most assuredly, the cognitive content sought by rational and experimental inquiry is precious not only for the achievement of unexpected structure but also for the character and variety of the structural components.

Now, at long last, a comprehensive admission which from the

outset I well knew I was obliged to grant, having the choice only of a more favorable moment. I fully understood that concepts serving in laws can unquestionably be conceived as determining corresponding sets but that sets of themselves do not invariably correspond to concepts or conditions "interesting" enough to enter into authentic laws.[37] Nevertheless, it remains incontestable that the exploration of indispensable extensional prerequisites for genuine laws can call attention to whatever can or should be added to the extensional frames for potential laws in order to actualize laws from the frames.[38] As always, the imaginative projection of optimal performance can best arouse clear-headed inventive effort when the projection is preceded by a survey of measurable potentiality. I concur unqualifiedly with Whewell, whose appreciation of the colligating power of true concepts is so early, so discerning, and so calmly courageous: "The modes of generalization of particulars in science are all of them genuine and indisputable lines of union and connection, by which the mind of man and the facts of the universe are bound together; by which the universe becomes a sphere with intellect for its center; by which intellect becomes in no small degree able to bend to its purposes the powers of the universe." [39]

I have done what I was able, in a simple case that may be instructive for the deeper comprehension of the theoretical fruitfulness of concepts, *to diminish the enigmatic character of colligating power itself,* by an application of the intelligible clarity of measure.

NOTES

1. This essay was first read in a symposium on empiricism and the nature of theories organized by Section L (Philosophy and History of Science) of the American Association for the Advancement of Science, Denver, December 1961.

2. F. N. Furness, ed., *Fundamentals of Psychology. The Psychology of Thinking* (Annals of the New York Academy of Sciences, Vol. 91, Art. 1, pp. 1–158), New York: 1960; especially Part IV on creativity and thinking.

3. In addition to Norwood Hanson's *Patterns of Discovery*, I have found the following works especially noteworthy in the recent revival of attention to heuristic: R. Taton, *Causalités et Accidents de la Découverte Scientifique*, Paris: Masson, 1955; J. S. Brunner, J. J. Goodnow, G. A. Austin, *A Study of Thinking*, New York: Wiley, 1956; Sir Fred-

rick Bartlett, *Thinking*, London: Allen and Unwin, 1958 (a study of the highest quality and interest) ; G. Polya, *Mathematics and Plausible Reasoning* (two volumes) , Princeton: Princeton University Press, 1954; G. P. Thomson, *The Inspiration of Science*, Oxford: Oxford University Press, 1961; M. Millikan, "Inquiry and Policy: The Relation of Knowledge to Action," in D. Lerner (editor) , *The Human Meaning of the Social Sciences*, New York: Meridian, 1959.

A history of heuristic is sadly needed; a contemporary reader may secure a glimpse of some past treasures from W. Whewell, *The Philosophy of the Inductive Sciences* (two volumes) , London: J. Parker, 1840, Books XII and XIII.

4. E. A. Singer, Jr., *Experience and Reflection*, Philadelphia: University of Pennsylvania Press, 1959; See also C. West Churchman, *Theory of Experimental Inference*, New York: Macmillan, 1948. I like the support of philosophic traditions for modern ideas; see the remarkable passage in Ockham which assesses the aptitude of the mind to depict by the ideal standard of perfect producibility of the depicted object. Ph. Boehner, ed., *Ockham's Philosophical Writings*, Edinburgh: Nelson, 1957, p. 41.

5. "Men perish because they cannot join the beginning to the end," fragment 2 of Alcmaeon; see K. Freeman, *Ancilla to the Pre-Socratic Philosophers*, Oxford: Blackwell, 1948. That the commentators have interpreted this fragment overliterally goes without saying.

6. L. Sechan, *Le Mythe de Prométhée*, Paris: Presses Universitaires, 1951; a judicious and charming book which fairly states, without adhering to the conclusion of G. Thomson, that peace came to Zeus and Prometheus as a consequence of Hera's satisfaction with Hercules as a son-in-law, a marriage which composed her jealous quarrels with Zeus. I note, however, in consonance with my own reverence for Prometheus, that the Athenians knew how to combine in their festivals a very proper homage to love as well as Prometheus but without subordinating the renewing fire of the latter. See the discussion of L. Duebner, *Attische Feste*, Berlin: Akademie-Verlage, 1956, pp. 211–212. The obsessive adoration of Sisyphus in agitated literary metaphysics can be challenged by the calm and lucid analysis of unattainability in terms of convergence offered by E. A. Singer in his "On a Possible Science of Religion," presidential address to the Eastern Division of the American Philosophical Association, collected with other essays in his *On the Contented Life*, New York: Holt, 1936.

7. On the definability of ideals in terms of limits for converging series see C. J. Keyser, *Mathematics as a Culture Clue*, New York: Scripta Mathematica, 1947, pp. 24–28.

8. Singer, *op. cit.*, chapters 17–23.

9. For T. H. Huxley's characterization of nature's play against man as "always fair, just and patient" and as that of a "calm strong angel who is playing for love, as we say, and would rather lose than win," see his *Science and Education*, New York: Appleton, 1895, pp. 82–83. To be compared with Huxley's near sentimental view is the sober account of Braithwaite (who is always aware of the philosophical im-

port of statistical science) of the ways in which men playing against nature can by randomized choice of strategies indefinitely multiply available strategies against an opponent who if not hostile, as Wald was disposed to assume, is at least such that no assumptions concerning his knowledge or intentions are required for prudent action on the part of men. Cf. R. B. Braithwaite, *Scientific Explanation,* Cambridge: Cambridge University Press, 1955, particularly chapter 7.

10. In the school of Anaxagoras, who himself was among the very first philosophers to appreciate man's constructive hand, one finds a remarkable and hitherto neglected, and I think graceful, observation that Zeus works by intellect and Athena by technics, as if to say that the latter is no mean offspring. My attention was called to this observation, attributed to Metrodorus of Lampsacus, by the instructive essay of C. J. Herington, *Athena Parthenos and Athena Polias,* Manchester: Manchester University Press, 1955; see pp. 53–54.

11. See Churchman, *op. cit.,* chapter 12 on nonmechanical concepts.

12. De La Mettrie very nearly grasps the idea that mechanical explanation is compatible with the recognition of functional classes, i.e., that an individual may have a productive and creative history not reducible to but presupposing a mechanical structure, in his *L'Homme-Machine,* pp. 106–107, which I am citing in the edition of Solovine published in Paris, 1921, by Bossard.

13. Descartes, *Regulae Ad Directionem Ingenii* (ed. G. Le Roy), Paris: Boivin, n.d., regula X in particular, which reads with my own italics: "Ut ingenium fiat sagax, exerceri debet in iisdem quaerendis, quae jam ab aliis *inventa* sunt et cum methodo etiam levissima quaeque hominum *artificia* percurrere, sed illa maxime quae *ordinem explicant* vel *supponunt.*"

14. Myths are generated by the mismanagement of equivalence relations; tests avoided by failure to specify definite consequences; comparisons prevented from being expressed in true ratios, etc., etc.

15. Consider for example the following passage in my own translation from Heidegger which I could supplement with many others in the same dark vein: "Calculating thought cannot suspect that everything calculable in calculation is already a whole antecedently to any momentarily achieved sums products and that [this whole] as a unity surely belongs to the incalculable, and that this enigmatic character slips away from all the devices of calculation." Since I find here only punning wordplay and some pained reminiscences of school arithmetic, I will transcribe the passage in the original for the unprejudiced judgment of the reader. "Das rechnende Denken kann nicht ahnen, dass alles Berechenbare der Rechnung vor den von ihr jeweils errechneten Summen und Produkten schon ein Ganzes ist, dessen Einheit freilich dem Unberechenbaren zugehört, das sich und seine Unheimlichkeit der Griffen der Rechnung entzieht." *Was Ist Metaphysik* (5th edition), Frankfort: Klostermann, 1949, pp. 44 ff. Immediately after the passage I have quoted, Heidegger draws the expected conclusions: the freedom of thankful sacrifice is to supplant the intention to control.

Those who truly think and guard being do not seek support in the beings of the world: "Das Denken des Seins sucht im Seiende Leinen Anhalt."

16. J. G. Sulzer, *Versuch einiger Moralischen Betrachtungen uber die werke der Natur,* Berlin, 1750; especially the sixth consideration on the mysteries of nature, pp. 77 ff.

17. W. Whewell, *op. cit.,* II, 201 ff. "We may apply the term *colligation of facts* to every case in which by an act of the intellect we establish a precise connection among the phenomena which are presented to our senses."

18. A magnificent acknowledgment of the importance of the care for necessary conditions is to be found in Plato *Gorgias* 507. See Hanson's more recent paper, "Is There a Logic of Scientific Discovery?" pp. 20 ff., in *Current Issues in the Philosophy of Science,* ed. by Feigl and Maxwell, N. Y., 1961, for a convincing challenge of the view that the creativity of scientific genius eludes rational analysis.

19. N. Campbell, *What is Science?* London: Methuen, 1921, especially chapter 4, *ad finem.* I have been careful throughout this essay to adduce wherever I can support from authors who cannot readily be "dismissed" as "mere" pragmatists, Baconians, naturalists, materialists, etc; I therefore take particular pleasure in citing the following from Bishop F. J. McConnell's *John Wesley,* New York: Abingdon, 1939, pp. 158–161. "This . . . was Wesley's definition of 'enthusiasm' —the search for ends without the use of means. . . . He defined enthusiasm as seeking the ends without using the means that would lead to the ends."

For a reasoned view that the productive imagination of the fine artist is not beyond experimental understanding, see the magistral exposition of M. Nahm, *The Artist as Creator. An Essay on Human Freedom,* Baltimore: The Johns Hopkins Press, 1956. Nahm's essay is very helpful for comprehension of the discussion by philosophers of the relationship between human and divine art.

20. G. Ryle, "Sensation," pp. 427 ff. of H. D. Lewis, ed., *Contemporary British Philosophy; Personal Statements,* London: Allen and Unwin, 1956, especially pp. 440 ff. on "technique" and "skill." It is plain that Ryle believes that once causal prerequisites, physical or physiological, are secure, the logic of necessary conditions does not massively enter into teaching or acquiring skills. If so, we may ask, why is the rate of invention so slow, and the growth of human skill at supreme levels so obstructed? Skill *as such* has its conditions and limits; what are they?

21. Dante, *The Divine Comedy,* "Inferno," Canto VII.

22. An elementary but thoroughly rigorous introduction to the theory of sets which is perfectly clear on the distinction between a set and the conditions which are met by members of the set, without any introduction of "metaphysical" disputes, is R. R. Christian, *Introduction to Logic and Sets,* New York: Ginn, 1958; this helpful book is quite accessible to serious beginners.

23. Those in search of a first orientation in measure theory may

read with profit S. M. Ulam, "What is Measure?" in *American Mathematical Monthly*, 1943, 50: 597 ff.

24. Cf. H. A. Finch, "Validity Rules for Proportionally Quantified Syllogisms," *Philosophy of Science*, 1957, 24: 1 ff.

25. Conditions for being a nontrivial deduction are stated in Kleene, "Finite Axiomatizability of Theories in the Predicate Calculus Using Additional Predicate Symbols," in *Memoirs of the American Mathematical Society* (No. 10), Providence, 1952, p. 28.

26. A. I. Kinchin, *Mathematical Foundations of Information Theory* (translated by R. A. Silverman and M. D. Friedman), New York: Dover, 1957; pages 2 to 30 in the first paper are about entropy and probability. An excellent monograph which is divided into an informal and a rigorous mathematical presentation is Y. S. Touloukian, *The Concept of Entropy in Communication, Living Organisms, and Thermodynamics*, Purdue Engineering Experiment Station, 1956. A very careful and pellucid account of entropy and uncertainty is to be found in R. T. Cox, *The Algebra of Probable Inference*, Baltimore. Johns Hopkins Press, 1961, chapter 2. On Boltzmann's epoch-making contributions to the conceptualization of entropy and information, see the admirable book by E. Brode, *Ludwig Boltzmann, Mensch, Physiker, Philosoph*, Vienna: Deutsche, 1952.

27. Cf., for independent treatment of related themes, H. Putnam, "Formalization of the Concept 'About,'" *Philosophy of Science*, 1958, 25: 125 ff., and N. Goodman, "About," *Mind*, 1961, 70: 1 ff.

28. I reluctantly set aside here any consideration of the opportunity to characterize measurable degrees of clarity of concepts in terms of less than complete elimination of entropy.

29. The chances of forming a preassigned set of m members by random selection of individuals are expressible by the product $\frac{m}{N}\left(\frac{m-1}{N-1}\right)\left(\frac{m-2}{N-2}\right)$ to the mth term. This product is equal to the inverse of $C_\beta{}^N$, after multiplication by $\frac{(N-m)!}{(N-m)!}$

30. For an explanation of the decrease of entropy from an initial to a final value as a measure of information gain, see Touloukian, *op. cit.*, p. 16.

The relevance of information gain or decrease of entropy in confirmation and inductive procedures has been explored by us in a study "Confirming Power of Observations Metricized for Decisions Among Hypotheses" in *Philosophy of Science*, 1960, 27: 293 ff. and the same journal, 27: 391 ff.

31. W. A. Whitworth, *Choice and Chance* (reissue of 5th edition), New York: Stechert, 1934, chapters 1 and 2.

32. I favor strongly explorations along the lines proposed by J. Rothstein, *Communication, Organization and Science*, Indian Hills, Colorado: Falcon's Wing Press, 1958. The essays collected in the foregoing reference are very stimulating and worthy of the closest attention on the part of methodologists of science. Chapter 6 on organization is

outstanding in richness of ideas. I was very much encouraged to find Rothstein sensitive (see p. 56) to the type of logical organization I am studying in the present paper. His treatment of skill in chapter 8 can be profitably compared with that of Ryle.

33. This axiom meets the conditions for nontrivial deduction in Kleene, *op. cit.*

34. Kinchin, *op. cit.*, pp. 6–9, on conditional entropy. I have appropriated Kinchin's analysis for my study simply by employing the axiom, well-known in inductive logic, that an implied proposition has a dependent likelihood equal to 1, relative to the proposition which implies it.

35. Cox's study, *op. cit.*, of the entropy of systems is restricted to inductive systems. Among philosophers I can presently name only L. Apostel and his associates as seriously attentive to the information—theoretic appreciation of deductive systems. See L. Apostel, A. R. Jonckheere, B. Matalon, *Logique, Apprentissage et Probabilité*, Paris: Presses Universitaires de France, 1959.

36. This maximum is not dependent upon any assumption of simple predicates or atomic states, which seems to me to deprive the Bar-Hillel—Carnap concept of "semantic" information of much pertinence to such cognitive content as is actually attractive to scientists.

37. It will never be considered that, e.g., the generalization, all the oranges on my breakfast table are either oranges or dishes, is of great importance toxonomically, not to speak of its infinitely low status as a "law." One must be careful, however, not to succumb to the rigidities of common sense judgment which is always overastonished that a so-called miscellaneous set can be conceived integrally in a novel fashion. In recent chemistry, for example, the term proton donor has with good reason been applied to substances that yield either hydrogen *or* ammonium ions in solution in order to reconstruct the concept of acid.

38. It is a perfectly fascinating question—indeed an analogue of Plato's problem of participation and the problem of universals of the schoolmen—why the divergence in natural system between the number of distinct mathematical combinations of individuals and the number of species in a universe occurs. B. Mandelbrot has, in a masterly paper, treated the facts of the "natural" distribution of species size in Linnean systems of classification to some extent thermodynamically. See his paper "On the Language of Taxonomy" in C. Cherry (editor), *Information Theory*, London: Butterworth, 1956. Estimation of the number of species from random samples of animals has been studied by Sir Ronald Fisher, *Contributions to Mathematical Statistics*, New York: Wiley, 1950, p. 43.

39. W. Whewell, "On the Influence of the History of Science upon Intellectual Education," E. L. Youmans, ed., *The Culture Demanded by Modern Life*, New York: Appleton, 1898. For some definite anticipation of the relevance of extensional set-theoretic analysis for the undertaking of law-like organization in finite universes, see C. S. Peirce, "The Order of Nature," *Chance, Love and Logic*, New York: Harcourt Brace, 1923, pp. 106 ff., especially 108–115.

DONALD KUSPIT

WHITEHEAD'S GOD AND METAPHYSICS [1]

Of import to the interpretation of any philosopher is an acceptance of his modes of language. It does no good for the critic to cas-
tigate the thinker for lingual foibles—especially when the thinker
is as thoughtful about his expressions as Whitehead is. The point
of such a caveat is that we aim to trust the language to expose a
concept implicit in him—trust the language to make explicit an
idea central to divinity. Here we are Whiteheadian; we seek concepts presumed in philosophical practice but ignored in a sche-
matic acknowledgment of that practice—concepts presumed but
not consciously presupposed by the thinker.

> The final chapter of philosophy consists in the search for
> the unexpressed presuppositions which underlie the beliefs
> of every finite human intellect.[2]

Our concept is central to our thinker's thought. It is the crux
of the point [previously discussed], namely, the intimate relation
existing between the categories of existence and the category of the
ultimate—the question [previously raised] is not of the existence
of the ultimate, since the ultimate is presupposed, but of existence's ultimacy, an ultimacy in which the actual entity God shares,
and of the *how* of ultimacy's existence, which introduces the need
for the concept God. The hidden concept—exemplification—is the
crux of the issue of God's existence since it implies the tie to the

categoreal scheme of any entity. Exemplification bridges the speculative consideration of the world in the categoreal scheme and the experienced entities of the world.

> God is not to be treated as an exception to all metaphysical principles, invoked to save their collapse. He is their chief exemplification.[3]

This asserts: God exemplifies metaphysical principles. The dilemma arises: how tie principles to entities without denying one or the other? Now it is easier to see the origin of the dilemma: metaphysical principles are generic to philosophy, as Whitehead conceives philosophy—but so are actual entities generic to the world, as Whitehead conceives the world. How then have philosophy tie to the world if both the world and philosophy are sustained on distinct conceptual grounds? Clearly, metaphysical principles are not actual entities—but they are in some relation to these entities, if philosophy is "about" the world. How is philosophy "about" the world? Traditionally, philosophy "explains" the world. For Whitehead, philosophy "describes" the world. Metaphysical principles describe actual entities. We contend that the meaning of such philosophical description in Whitehead is centered in the term "exemplification." We must determine the precise philosophical meaning of this term to clarify Whitehead's assertion that God is the chief exemplification of metaphysical principles. To do this we must trace Whitehead's employment of the term "exemplification" —a simple task, since the term recurs consistently and deliberately in his works. Then we are faced with the more speculative task of formulating a precise sense of the concept exemplification and attributing this concept to Whitehead's conception of description. Finally, we must return to Whitehead's assertion that God is the chief exemplification of metaphysical principles—and understand it.

In *Science and the Modern World* Whitehead speaks consistently of facts or things, or both, exemplifying general principles or general conditions. In other words, entities (the categories of existence in *Process and Reality*) exemplify general ideas (the metaphysical principles of the categoreal scheme in *Process and Reality*). "Geniuses such as Aristotle, or Archimedes, or Roger Bacon, must have been endowed with the full scientific mentality, which instinctively holds that all things great and small are conceivable as exemplifications of general principles which reign throughout the natural order." [4] General principles "reign" throughout nature by means of exemplifying themselves in nature's entities, which are then spoken of as "exemplifications." Initially, exemplification might be spoken of as a relation holding between general principles and natural entities, and as a name for natural entities when they are involved in this relation. Thus nature, as philosophically conceivable, is "explicable" in terms of general principles and the exemplifications of general principles, the two connected by the relation of exemplification. Clearly, this relation has its source in some feature of the general principles. They, as reigning throughout the natural order, are conceptually prior to the things of the natural order. That is, they are philosophically more significant or important than these things—which is not saying that the general principles are more "substantial" or "ultimate" than the things of nature. In fact, we might note here, looking ahead, that the critical ground for Whitehead's dualism of the world and God in the final interpretation of *Process and Reality* is in the long run traceable to Whitehead's scruple about attributing to nature any single ultimate substance. In other words, Whitehead's scruple about attributing to nature Aristotle's "primary" substance as an ultimate ground for all other entities and activities in nature is the final reason Whitehead consistently holds a dualistic conception of the universe, a conception moving through a dialectic of creativity/ existence, organism/environment, mental/physical, through to the final interpretation's ideal opposites, God/world. We contend that the motive force behind this dialectic, that which makes for a "shift" from one level to another, a shift which Whitehead calls in his theory of prehensions a "transmission," is exemplification —but this is our conclusion, and we have only begun.

It is clear, from the above citation, that things exist in nature, whether or not they are exemplifications of general principles. It is clear that things are transmuted into exemplifications only when we want to conceive them philosophically—when we want to "explain" them. In other words, in philosophy, we have things as exemplifications; but in the world, things are things. One might legitimately ask: why not let things remain things rather than turn them into exemplifications? Why adduce general principles for nature?

> . . . the greatest contribution of medievalism to the formation of the scientific movement. I mean the inexpugnable belief that every detailed occurrence can be correlated with

antecedents in a perfectly definite manner, exemplifying general principles.[5]

General principles in relation to the things of nature are initially conceived in science. The scientist aims to correlate the things of nature—to understand their relations. If the relations between things are understood, nature is seen to be definite rather than indefinite, as it is seen by the world. Through science we see the things of the world to be definite, whereas in the world its things appear to be mere things, indefinite—because unrelated, apparently. The implication is that the discovery of the relations between things is the aim of science—and of philosophy, insofar as philosophy gives science its general principles. The term "exemplification" has been modified slightly by this citation. It is now the case that things are not exemplifications merely because they have the relation of exemplification to general principles, but that when things, or detailed occurrences (this distinction becomes in *Process and Reality* the distinction between actual entities and actual occasions), are seen in relation, then and only then are they exemplifications of general principles. In other words, things in relation are exemplifications. Things *per se* are not exemplifications. Also, things in relation are "definite" by virtue of being in relation. From this, we can see that when a thing is an exemplification it is something definite—or, in the terminology of *Science and the Modern World,* "concrete" and, in the terminology of *Modes of Thought,* "important."

Exemplification initially seems to have two references: (1) to entities in relation, definite by virtue of that relation, and (2) to the relation holding between these entities in relation and general principles. Exemplification is the name of a class of things. The class, apparently, has two differentia; namely, the things in the class must be related to each other, and the things in the class must be related to general principles. Things are things in the world, but general principles are—what? where?

> . . . the function in thought which is performed by pure mathematics. It is a resolute attempt to go the whole way in the direction of complete analysis, so as to separate the elements of mere matter of fact from the purely abstract conditions which they exemplify.[6]

Comparing this citation with the above citations, it is clear that the nature of the relation holding between "mere matter of fact" and the "purely abstract conditions" which these matters of fact exemplify is the same as the relation holding between "things great and small" and the "general principles" of which they are the exemplifications. In both cases the relation is exemplification. Obviously, pure abstract conditions are the same notion as general principles. This similarity is made more explicit by the following citation: "Whatever falls within that [aesthetic] relationship is thereby exemplified in that [unity of one] occasion, whatever falls without that relationship is thereby excluded from exemplification in that occasion. The complete pattern of general conditions, thus exemplified, is determined by any one of many select sets of these conditions." [7] Whitehead is here telling us how the relationship exemplification *operates*. What interests us, for the moment, is that the "general conditions" are seen to be in the same relationship to occasions as general principles are to things and as abstract conditions are to matters of fact. We conclude that the terms general principles, general conditions, and abstract conditions, are equivalent in reference though different in that they emphasize different aspects of the idea of generality and the idea of principles. What these aspects are will become clearer.

It is clear that general principles are conceivable as abstract conditions when they are regarded as the object of analysis. General principles become abstract conditions when the entities which refer to them in terms of the relationship of exemplification can no longer have this relationship to them. In other words, general principles are abstract conditions when general principles are not exemplified by existent entities. The "whole way" in complete analysis is just this separation of existent entities from general principles by denying the relationship exemplification between them. In this case, the effect of such denial is worth noting. The general principles become abstract conditions. This is to say that they do not have the relationship of exemplification to existent entities. Without the relationship of exemplification, principles become conditions, and the general becomes the abstract. In other words, for general principles to be general principles they must necessarily be exemplified. *Exemplification is then essential to the definition and meaning of general principles. Exemplification is at least a necessary condition for general principles. But we might conclude that exemplification is as well a sufficient condition for general principles, since the denial of exemplification destroys the character of general principles.* When general principles cannot be exemplified, they are neither general nor principles, but abstract and conditions. Their character is changed. They are not themselves. Further effects of denying the relationship of exemplification between general principles and existent entities can be noted. The existent entities become mere matter of fact. We cannot predicate of them that they are existent or that they are entities. We are reduced to the minimal assertion that they are there—but not philosophically conceivable. They have fallen from the scrutiny of philosophy to take their obscure place in the world. It is clear that the denial of the relationship of exemplification makes for obscurity and strangeness so far as the philosophical enterprise goes. Without exemplification we cannot speak of existence or of entities—the world becomes obscure, incomprehensible. Without exemplification we cannot speak of generality or of principles—philosophy becomes strange, impossible. Obviously, exemplification is *the* important concept in Whitehead's philosophy of organism, important not merely for its "activities" in the philosophy, but because it permits Whitehead to begin to philosophize. In a sense—the sense with which the concept of exemplification is the ground of philosophizing— the various fallacies and errors which Whitehead attributes to scientists and realists, so far as their general conception of the world goes, are all reducible to a denial of exemplification. Whitehead, in other words, is saying that to speak of empty space or to misplace concreteness is to deny the undeniable, namely, exemplification.

The last two citations make it clear that there are patterns of general conditions, thus implying different kinds of exemplifications. The relationship of exemplification is a constant holding between all sorts of entities, attributing to them their existence; but, because they are different sorts of entities, they, as existences —or exemplifications—are different. It is clear inasmuch as the names for things change when they are exemplified—they are spoken of as exemplifications—that existence is an attribute which is an effect of the relationship of exemplification. The thing then, might be said to go through two stages of character before it becomes an existence, before it can be characterized as existent. First, the thing exemplifies general principles. When it exemplifies general principles, it becomes conceivable, or it gains its first philosophical nature. Second, as it is conceivable, as so exemplifying general principles, it is an exemplification. As an exemplification it is definite, though in relation to other entities. The relationship of exemplification makes clear this very relation, since it alone makes the thing definite *as* related. The thing, defi-

[188]

nite as related, is an existence and an entity. Also, since it is one sort of thing and there is more than one general principle, an existence and an entity are necessarily limited—only certain principles are exemplified by certain things. "The key to the patterns [of totality of general abstract conditions] means this fact:—that from a select set of those general conditions, exemplified in any one and the same occasion, a pattern involving an infinite variety of other such conditions, also exemplified in the same occasion, can be developed by the pure exercise of abstract logic." [8] Thus, though each existent entity is an exemplification of a select set of general conditions, it implies all the other general conditions, also exemplified in the same occasion, though exemplified by exclusion, or what Whitehead calls "negative prehensions" in *Process and Reality*. Why does it imply these other conditions? The only possible answer is because the relationship of exemplification holds exclusively as well as inclusively. That is, principles are exemplified or not exemplified, but in either case there is a reference to the concept of exemplification. Such a reference clearly leads us to the infinity of general conditions. Thus, Whitehead tells us that though general principles can be turned into abstract conditions when the general principles are not exemplified, this very denial of exemplification nonetheless implies the general principles, admittedly in the form of abstract conditions, but also because there is something denied, something that was after all operable until it was denied. There is then in Whitehead, if not a priority of "substance," a priority of exemplification. Such a philosophical priority, such a ground principle solves the dilemma of the relation between principles of any sort and entities of any sort.[9] It assumes that the principles and entities are *given* in relationship, the relationship of exemplification; that the entities do exemplify the principles and that this is the very character of the world; and that the relationship between principles and entities is only denied at some later stage of philosophizing, when the philosopher has moved beyond the given and is busy explaining it—or explaining it away, namely, denying the togetherness of principles and entities, which is presupposed initially, or metaphysically given, as Whitehead speaks of it in *Process and Reality*, or as real, in the terminology of the post-*Process and Reality* books. We have here also the hint as to why Whitehead wants to describe the given rather than explain it. Traditionally, explanation (at least as Whitehead sees the tradition) means denying exemplification, denying that things exemplify principles, and then paying attention only to the principles. But if philosophy is to do justice to the world it cannot deny what is given in the world, namely, things exemplifying principles. It cannot pay court solely to principles if it is to honor the world, which is what it is presumably "about." Moreover, philosophy cannot claim to be merely a matter of principles, cannot simply put the things of the world aside, since, as we have shown, the very sense of principles is exemplification—principles are only principles insofar as they are in the world. "Explain" only principles and you must also speak "about" the world. Principles without things are impossible. Any statement of principles is a statement "about" things—this is the ontological principle of *Process and Reality*. Whitehead's exemplification clearly denies the philosopher his unworldly abstractions in their pristine detachment. Clearly, Whitehead's concept of exemplification is the ground of any naturalism—any conception of organism.

Clearly, things and principles presuppose each other—the "how" of such presupposition is exemplification. Exemplification means that the principles, in their guise of conditions, determine things. This is not to deny the givenness of things prior to their determination—Whitehead nowhere asserts this. For instance, in *Process and Reality,* the categories of existence emerge as the ground of the categoreal scheme, while the categories of explanation and the categoreal obligations, which determine the categories of existence, are dispensable if demonstrably mistaken. Conditions, functioning as determinate of things, are qualified as laws. "Nature exhibits itself as exemplifying a philosophy of the evolution of organisms subject to determinate conditions. Examples of such conditions are the dimensions of space, the laws of nature, the determinate enduring entities, such as atoms and electrons, which exemplify these laws." [10]

In *Adventures of Ideas* Whitehead explicitly asserts the point we have been demonstrating, that every principle is exemplified by a thing, so that the conception of exemplification dominates every effort at interpretation or, in more traditional terminology, of understanding. "The first step in science and philosophy has been made when it is grasped that every routine exemplifies a principle which is capable of statement in abstraction from its particular exemplifications." [11] The fact that the particular relationship of exemplification holding between certain principles and certain things can be stated abstractly, that is, without stating the particular things which exemplify, in nowise denies the prime relationship of exemplification. On the contrary, it is clear that exemplification dominates *every* interpretation of principles. The statement in abstraction from the unique interpretation is important for scientific statement—but that is only one sort of statement. The importance of the statement in abstraction from particular exemplifications is that it allows an intellectual scrutiny of the conditions of the generality of general principles apart from their tie to active things. "Finally they [ideas] pass into exemplification in action." [12] The ideas in action are enduring facts of existence. Exemplification means, in a sense, a putting in action. We can understand then why Whitehead names his philosophy a philosophy of organism rather than a philosophy of things. An organism is always in action, while the notion of a thing implies a static, neutral being. All existents are beings, implies Whitehead, all act, and in acting exemplify the general principles which determine them. Whitehead is consistent enough to attribute mentality to every existent—to apparently inanimate matter as well as to conscious, experiencing beings—admittedly different grades of mentality. Thus, "No fact is merely such-and-such. It exemplifies many characters at once, all rooted in the specialties of its epoch. . . ." [13] For any fact to be a such-and-such would be for it to be a thing, and to have only one character. The fact, as having many characters—as exemplifying many general principles—is an organism. It is clear from this citation that the general principles are in a sense also organic. That is, they are not merely such-and-such, but also tie to a sort of fact, namely, an epoch. The general principles then necessarily express the principles of what Whitehead calls in *Modes of Thought* a civilization. It becomes clear, then, that metaphysics is not "up in the air" but is dependent upon a particular organization of society. Only within a scan of an entire civilization can there by a metaphysics, and that metaphysics is a means of clarifying the character of that civilization. For instance, "The three phases [of Christianity] are bound together as intellectual discovery—then exemplification—finally metaphysical interpretation. The discovery and the exemplification are historically independent." [14] "Discovery" here means the formulation of the general principles of Christianity. "Exemplification" here means the determination of particular facts of actual Christian life. "Metaphysical interpretation" here means the study of the character of the relationship of exemplification holding between Christian principles and Christian facts in civilized life. By asserting the historical independence

[191]

of Christian principles from Christian facts Whitehead does not assert the philosophical priority of the principles to the facts, but rather that the relationship of exemplification is a process, that the principles, in a sense, develop into facts with the passage of time—though this development is not necessarily so. In other words, Christianity need not have come into being—principles are not automatically exemplified by the organisms of an entire society because they are principles. But to be principles there must be some organisms which necessarily do exemplify them. Also, it is clear that "metaphysical interpretation" here means something similar to our previous citation's "statement in abstraction" from exemplifications. In other words, the statement of a principle in abstraction correlates with the study of the relationship holding between principles and facts—a study which, incidentally, Whitehead assumes occurs at a late stage of civilization.

We have set forth, by an examination of some of the contexts in which the term exemplification occurs in *Science and the Modern World* and in *Adventures of Ideas,* the central meaning of the concept of exemplification and some of its applications and influences. It is clear that exemplification is a full-fledged conception—that is, a conception central to an understanding of Whitehead's philosophy of organism. While our ostensible purpose in revealing this hidden concept was to get at the meaning of Whitehead's idea that the chief exemplification of metaphysical principles is God, we are also interested in making clear the full ramifications of the idea, so that no single sense of "God" or His relation to "metaphysical principles" will escape us. Thus, we will continue to trace the term through Whitehead's major work, *Process and Reality,* to demonstrate that it is a conception central to Whitehead's thought by the fact that it occurs in every context of thought Whitehead presents—occurs in his conception of the categoreal scheme, occurs in his discussion of the applications of the categoreal scheme, occurs in his conception of the theory of prehension or feeling, occurs in his conception of the theory of extension or physics, and, lastly, occurs in his final interpretation of the philosophy of organism, his discussion of God and the world. We have clearly shown that the conception of exemplification is central to the final interpretation; but we need trace it through the other contexts of Whitehead's thought to show its consistency as a concept and its consistent usage. Such a demonstration will allow us to introduce the concept as a necessary presupposition of Whitehead's philosophy without any quibbles or caveats.

The absoluteness of exemplification for the metaphysical principles is insisted upon at the very start of *Process and Reality*, before the categoreal scheme of metaphysical principles is offered to us. "The metaphysical first principles can never fail of exemplification. We can never catch the actual world taking a holiday from their sway." [15] That is, every metaphysical principle must be exemplified by the actual world; otherwise it is not a metaphysical principle. From the side of the world, it seems to be under the "sway" of the principles—a phraseology reminding us of the remark in *Science and the Modern World* already cited [16] where the general principles are spoken of as having "reign throughout the natural order." Clearly, while *Science and the Modern World* is concerned with the philosophy of nature, *Process and Reality* is concerned with a cosmology. The application of the concept of exemplification is now on the most universal scale. Not merely is nature under its sway—"sway" and "reign" are complementary terms—but the entire actual world. Also, it is clear that with respect to a philosophy of nature principles are merely "general," whereas with respect to a cosmology principles are "metaphysical." In other words, Whitehead introduces new names for new contexts of thought and new names for greater universality of implication and meaning. We might almost stop at the beginning of our demonstration of the importance of the concept of exemplification for every context of Whitehead's thought, since we are assured that exemplification is complete for the entire actual universe from the first assumption of that universe.

We have already spoken of the various fallacies Whitehead introduces as due to the assertion of principles as abstractions, as without exemplifications. Obviously, the importance of such an assertion is that it forces philosophy to be necessarily general— at least to have an awareness of the whole of thought from which it draws particular conceptions. Whitehead is not denying it its right to examine specific conceptions. But he insists that such an examination necessarily involves a reference to the exemplifications of the conception—necessarily, because the conception is "about" the exemplifications. Thus, true philosophy is an examination of particular conceptions in their more general setting, namely, in their reference to their exemplifications, and against the background of the full ramifications of these exemplifications, ramifications which go beyond being referenced by any one conception. Moreover, philosophy is then fundamental to any special discipline—science, religion, art—in that it is able to see the whole of the relationships holding between the particular exemplifications any special discipline is "about." In fact, one of Whitehead's notions of the tasks of philosophy is this harmonization of various conceptions by relating the various exemplifications they are "about." Philosophy, in other words, makes peace between different disciplines. But for our purposes, this digression is only of worth if it makes us see the universality of exemplification—though it by no means harms our minds to have us know exemplification is the means of harmonizing what abstraction dissembles.

The "fallacy [of misplaced concreteness] consists in neglecting the degrees of abstraction involved when an actual entity is considered merely so far as it exemplifies certain categories of thought." [17] Why is it a fallacy to neglect such abstraction? The answer: because when an actual entity is seen as exemplifying only certain categories of thought, its concreteness as an exemplification, that concreteness whereby it is related to *all* categories of thought, is denied. And such denial is a denial of the actualness of the actual entity—because that actualness depends on the full generality of the entity. The entity, when it is absolutely general—in relation to every other entity—is most actual, is most concrete, is most enduring. Abstract from it one relation to another actual entity, and you have "lessened" its actuality as well as its generality—you have made it less concrete. And its relations to other actual entities are presented in formulations of categories of thought: so assert one category of thought over another, or relate an entity to only some of the categories of thought which determine it, and you have denied the full concrete background from which the actual entity originates and which determines its actuality. You then, in so dealing with only a few of the categories of thought determining the actual entity, are misplacing the concreteness of the actual entity and unwarrantably limiting its exemplification. Such a misplacing of concreteness is the major sin of thought for Whitehead—it does injustice to both principles and facts, the former by limiting their application, the latter by limiting their determination.

We have also asserted, along the way, that Whitehead aims to replace explanation by description, regarding the former as doing injustice to the entities of the world. While he retains the expression "explanation" in his categories of explanation, it is clear that these categories offer us ways of describing entities. They are not true explanation because they do not aim to "reduce" the entities to any common principle of determination. On the contrary, the most important category of explanation for the purposes of relating entities (namely, the ontological principle) asserts that all searching for reasons—the business of explanation—is no more than a referring to other entities. Reasons refer to entities but not vice versa; reasons linguistically offered are dispensable once the entities they refer to are identifiable. Such a referring is clearly no different from description—we will point this out more carefully later. "These [ill-defined and ambiguous verbal expressions] are not premises to be immediately reasoned apart from elucidation by further discussion; they are endeavors to state general principles which will be exemplified in the subsequent description of the facts of experience." [18] And that "subsequent description" is *Process and Reality*.

In other words, the description of the facts of experience is the very nature of the exemplification of general principles— describing the facts of experience is exemplifying general principles. And from the side of the general principles, their exemplification allows the philosopher to describe the facts of experience. The general principles are, so to speak, the "tools" by whose means the facts of experience are described—general principles are the means of description of the facts of experience. It is clear then that "description" is the full meaning of the concept of exemplification. The concept of exemplification, for the practical purposes of the philosophy of organism, broadens into a method of describing experience. This point was partially implied in our citation on Christianity,[19] for there it was clear that the phase of exemplification, as it is put, is a historical phase—a phase putting forward the actual facts of experience. Combining this point with the point we have made about the purposes of exemplification for description, we might conclude that the exemplification of general principles determines that which it aims to describe, namely, the facts of experience. It is clear, then, that determination is a sort of description—the determination of givenness is its description as existent entity. To describe the facts of experience is to determine or characterize them. That this is so will be made plain later. We might at this point merely remark, apropos a common sense approach to this notion, that it makes sense if we understand the determination to be philosophical. That is, Whitehead is concerned to determine the facts of experience for the purposes of thought. They are apparently best determined for the purposes of thought, according to Whitehead, when they are described.

We can adduce another citation demonstrating the universality of exemplification in any determination and functioning of actual entities. "But, though there are gradations of importance and diversities of function, yet in the principle which actuality exemplified all [actual entities] are on the same level." [20] The being "on the same level" of all actual entities means that all actual entities are necessarily exemplifications of general principles. This citation shows us the perspective in which actual entities, insofar as they are philosophically demonstrable as actual, necessarily are in relation to general principles. We cannot conceive of any actual entities without the principles which they exemplify. Without their exemplifying a principle they are neither actual nor entities. Here we have another instance of the operation of Whitehead's dualism, general principles/actual entities. One term is inconceivable without the other—which is to say that either side loses all of its attributes stripped of its relation to the other side.

I want to offer the following citation as a sort of *apologia pro arbitur,* a citation which offers us nothing especially new about the concept of exemplification, but which is, on the other hand, not a digression. I have, as this work progresses, used terms terminologically different from the terms Whitehead uses in *Process and Reality,* his central work. My reason—this is perhaps the best place to mention that reason, since it is prior to my introduction of different terms and since it is in the context of a discussion of perhaps the most scholarly and generally philosophical important point of my work—is offered by Whitehead himself: "But such terms present great difficulties to the understanding, by reason of the fact that they suggest no particular exemplifications. Accordingly, we seek familiar terms which have about them the suggestiveness of familiar fact." [21] It is my special contention that the terms I will later introduce to replace and accompany, at least in the context of the discussion of description, Whitehead's terms "actual entity," "eternal object," and others, are more suggestive of familiar fact than Whitehead's own terms. That is my only excuse for taking such philosophical liberty. I think I am not distorting Whitehead, not doing him an injustice, but rather improving him on his own grounds of principle. Moreover, the new terms I introduce to replace Whitehead's technical terms have the advantage of being consistent with each other—they are all variations of the term "interpretation"—and of being terms which in fact Whitehead uses in his important later works, *Modes of Thought* and *Religion in the Making*. Thus they have the advantage of being in fact Whitehead's terms and at the same time terms which allow me to understand Whitehead more carefully and to show him to be more consistent in his arguments and theories than perhaps he himself thought. What more can a critic do for a thinker than to tell him he thought better than he knew?

The last quotation from Whitehead is important also in that it permits us to emphasize anew the intimacy of the relationship between principles and their exemplifications. The very language in which the principles are formulated must be the language in which the exemplifications are asserted to exist—that, in practical effect, is what we do have in the philosophy of organism. A single example of this should suffice. "That *how* an actual entity *becomes* constitutes *what* that actual entity *is;* so that the two descriptions of an actual entity are not independent. Its 'being' is constituted by its 'becoming.' This is the 'principle of process.' " [22] This is the ninth of twenty-seven categories of explanation. It is clear that the *statement* of the principle is a *description* of process. The explanatory language is the factual language. The facts of any special process are describable in terms of the general principle of process. The terms "how becomes" and "what is" apply in every description.

The quotation prior to the last also implies, indirectly, the limiting civilization of any metaphysics. Why is the language "familiar"? Obviously, because it has long been given currency in some society, because it is so much a part of some way of life, so common to certain sorts of activity. We may expect that the concepts which will be named by the familiar terms are also familiar, since the familiar terms are taken for their suggestive exemplifications—exemplifications which are of concepts—and implying, since the concepts are less difficult for the understanding when they are offered in familiar terms, that the understanding has been "nourished" on familiar things, things necessarily familiar because they are in the world from which the concepts are drawn. Familiar language, then, ties concepts more closely to things and ties both things and concepts more closely to their world—or shows them to derive from their world.

[197]

We have remarked that for Whitehead reasons are ultimately other entities. It would make sense, therefore, to regard general principles, which are reasons, as ultimately other entities. That is, general principles refer to entities—for every principle there is a certain kind of entity. Clearly, since the Whiteheadian dichotomy is of general principles/existent entities, we might suppose that the general principles refer to existent entities, and we might suppose that exemplification, the means of relating general principles to existent entities, ultimately relates different sorts of existent entities. To say that general principles are exemplified by existent entities is to say, since general principles are general only insofar as they attribute existence and entities to the universe, that existent entities are in certain sorts of relationships. In other words, exemplification is the most general name for the different kinds of relationships holding between existent entities. The philosophical concept of exemplification is the general expression for the experience of the relations of entities. "In such a philosophy [of organism] the actualities constituting the process of the world are conceived as exemplifying the ingression [or 'participation'] of other things which constitute the potentialities of definiteness for any actual existence." [23]

These "other things which constitute the potentialities of definiteness for any actual existence" are what Whitehead calls "eternal objects." Whitehead says in this passage that actual entities exemplify the participation of eternal objects in the process of the world. On the face of it, this seems to assert something quite different about the character of exemplification from what we have previously asserted. But this is so only if we forget that ultimately—"ultimately" meaning when we forget that there is philosophy—there are not only actual entities in the world, but other sorts of entities, eight other sorts Whitehead says, with six of these eight being composites of two of the others, i.e., actual entities and eternal objects. There are in the active universe no general principles which are entities—general principles are only apparent, only "exist," in philosophy. There are, however, relations in the active universe—relationship is in fact the very ground of its activity, the very meaning of action, asserts Whitehead. Ingression or participation is one sort of relationship. So that when we speak of an actual entity as exemplifying a relationship we are not using the term "exemplify" in any obscure sense. We are saying that an actual entity is an exemplification of a relationship. And we are saying that exemplification also has its other sense, of relationship—ingression is one sort of relationship. In Whitehead's initial formulation this assertion might be rephrased: actual entities exemplify the general principle of ingression of eternal objects. What is important to note here is that actual entities retain their role as exemplifications and that the general principle is specified. We have been speaking all along of general principles/actual entities without specifying the former. We have made clear that there are different kinds of general principles. One kind is the ingression of eternal objects. This quotation does not deny our conception of exemplification; it exemplifies it.

By and large we have spoken of exemplification with respect to its relevance to actual entities. While we have never explicitly asserted that exemplification is finally, after the application of the ontological principle, a concept expressing the universality of relationship and relations between actual entities, we have constantly implied that general principles are expressions for the functions of actual entities, so that exemplifications, rather than the tie of exemplification between general principles and actual entities, are more "important" for Whitehead. It is clear, however, that Whitehead does not mean his general principles to be mere illusions. While the world may exist *per se,* it does not so exist for the mind. The mind can approach the world only through principles—principles alone make the world self-evident. What, then, is the point of speaking of actual entities exemplifying general principles, with respect to the general principles? Is there any philosophical reason for speaking of such an exemplification, other than the simple expression of the mind's understanding the world?

"This ideal realization of potentialities in a primordial actual entity constitutes the metaphysical stability whereby the actual process exemplifies general principles of metaphysics, and attains the ends proper to specific types of emergent order." [24] Whitehead calls it "metaphysical stability" that the "actual process exemplifies general principles of metaphysics." Correlative with this "metaphysical stability" is an actual process and an emergent order. The actual process is itself this emergent order insofar as it has ends. The realization or completion of potentialities or eternal objects in the actual entity "constitutes" this "metaphysical stability." Now we have seen that any realization of an existent entity is an instance of exemplification. For a realization to occur, some general principle must be exemplified—such exemplification is the completion of the entity doing the exemplification. Thus, it is clear that the completion of actual entities by the ingression into them of potentialities is an illustration of the general way exemplification operates. But such an illustration has an added significance: because of the fact that an eternal object—a category of existence—is exemplified, the general character of the concept of exemplification is grounded or made stable or "justified," which for Whitehead is to say that the universe, in its very essence, metaphysically, exhibits exemplification. Thus all general principles are "justified" by virtue of the ideal character of the realization of potentialities. They are justified because there is no greater "depth" to the universe than its potentialities and because these potentialities, as completing an actual entity, exemplify that actual entity—thus showing the presence of exemplification in the very "depths" of the universe. The realization of potentialities is not one more illustration of exemplification, it is the chief illustration of exemplification. "Metaphysical stability," as constituted by the realization of potentialities, asserts that our general principles are *necessary,* are truly descriptive generalities, since the most important of the general principles (the principles describing the very making of actuality, the actualizing of its potentialities) is self-evident. In other words, Whitehead is here arguing from the part to the whole, from one principle's self-evidence (to himself) to all principles' self-evidence. He grounds his argument on the assumption that the actualization of potentialities is the most general principle, all other principles being in some sense modeled after it. That he holds this principle of actualization to be the most general principle is clear from his frequent statements that actual entities and eternal objects are the basic stuff of which the other entities in the universe are made. It is also clear that Whitehead's part—one principle—is actually a whole, since it is the ground or type of all principles, underlying their generality. This will be further clarified in additional quotations. "It [the principle that, so far as physical relations are concerned, contemporary events happen in *causal* independence of each other] receives an exemplification in the character of our perception of the world of contemporary actual entities." [25] It is obvious that this very special principle, which Whitehead says "lies on the surface of the fundamental Einsteinian formula for the physical continuum," [26] refers to the actual world and its perception. These are grounded on the general principle of actualization of potentialities, since any reference to the actual world, in terms of a principle, is incoherent without an application of the ontological principle to determine the entities referenced—always some sort of eternal objects, whatever the relation of these eternal objects to each other. This principle becomes clearer from Whitehead's discussion of the extensive continuum. "All actual entities are related according to the determinations of this continuum; and all possible actual entities in the future must exemplify these determinations in their relations with the already actual world." [27] In other words, any reference to general principles, any exemplification of them, is necessarily grounded on the actual world, which in turn is a function of the extensive continuum. And in itself the extensive continuum is nothing but real potentiality—eternal objects. "Thus in itself, the extensive continuum is a scheme of real potentiality, which must find exemplification in the mutual prehension of all actual entities. It also finds exemplification in each actual entity considered 'formally.' " [28]

We have come full circle, by a sorites, to conclude that exemplification always means the actualization of potentialities. General principles are potentialities for actual entities by virtue of their generality, which offers the necessary grounding for any activity—here the activity of actualization. General principles are important in that exemplification originates as a functioning of their actualization of entities—exemplification is the "means" of this actualization. We should not, however, confuse the particular instance of the exemplification of eternal objects in actual entities with the widest sort of generality implied by the actualization of potentialities. We will henceforth make this linguistic distinction which we held in abeyance. The ingression of eternal objects into actual entities is only one instance of the actualization of potentialities wrought by exemplification. The distinction between the two is that the former instance is a *particularizing* of actual entities, while the latter instance is a *generalizing* of general principle. The two are related in that both particularizing and generalizing are ways of characterizing. And finally, Whitehead is concerned to show how each thing in the universe has the character it has, and how it can change character; thus his emphasis on perishing.

Our final formulation of the concept of exemplification can be stated: that general principles exemplify actual entities means that actual entities gain their actuality and generality, expressed by the single term rationality, in relationships with other entities.

This rationalizing of actual entities is their exemplifying general principles. Actual entities are final because they exemplify the generality of general principles. Actual entities are fundamental because they exemplify the "principleness" of general principles. For Whitehead, a principle is metaphysical—that is, grounded in the categoreal scheme. Thus actual entities are metaphysical, which means that they are describable by the categoreal scheme. The concept of exemplification serves a dual purpose in Whitehead's philosophy of organism: (1) it allows us to describe any actual entity by means of the categoreal scheme; (2) it assures us that any description of actual entities is justified. This, incidentally, constitutes Whitehead's apologia for speculative philosophy and his correlation of it with naturalism. Whitehead's naturalism—his conception of actual entities as the ground of the universe—is necessarily speculative since Whitehead wants to describe the entities. All description in Whitehead is clearly a form of "speculation." By this we do not mean to imply any indefiniteness by the term speculation. We mean that the philosopher speculates just to determine the definiteness of actual entities—speculation means the relating of any actual entity to any other, necessarily. Necessarily, since the determination of any actual entity's definiteness is an effect of its character as an exemplification in some speculation.

We are now prepared to return to our original statement as to God's being the chief exemplification of metaphysical principles. However, before doing so, I feel compelled to complete my task by bringing forward a number of other quotations employing the term "exemplification," simply to show that their sense is derivable from our formulation of Whitehead's hidden concept of exemplification and to fulfill our original purpose of showing the concept's thoroughgoingness in Whitehead's philosophy of organism by showing its utilization in every part of that philosophy. We have already shown, partially, its application in Whitehead's examination of the applications of the categoreal scheme. Continuing further with this application, Whitehead remarks, "But the general principles of physics are exactly what we should expect as a specific exemplification of the metaphysics required by the philosophy of organism." [29] Clearly, the general principles of any special science are exemplifications of metaphysical principles in that they treat of special sorts of relations holding between entities, physical relations. General principles can be exemplifications of other general principles because general principles refer to actual entities, so that the initial set of general principles is a set of entities in disguise. Also, we learn more clearly from this quoted passage that any exemplification is necessarily a "limiting" of general principles—a completion of them which transforms their generality into the definiteness of the entity determined by them. In other words, any exemplification is built on the base of a generality broader than itself. This is not to say that it is not general by virtue of its relations to other entities, but that its generality takes the form of its being definite— definite, as we shall see, for some sort of description by some sort of discipline. Thus the generality of physics is grounded on the generality of metaphysics, which is wider than it and which has the additional *power* of determining entities—a power derived from the category of the ultimate, the category attributing creativity to the nature of the universe. Thus metaphysics has a twofold importance for Whitehead: (1) it guarantees the generality of any special description of actual entities; (2) it guarantees the determination of actual entities. Thus metaphysics in terms of its second characteristic means creativity or rather, more precisely, the acknowledgement of the creativity of the universe. Metaphysics is more general than any special science of study of the universe just because it can acknowledge the most general truth about the universe, namely, its creativity. Generality, then—and this is a conclusion to which we have been driving all along in our remarks on the transforming of generality to character and in our remarks on the making definite or determining of actual entities, both saying in effect that actual entities are novelties— is a reference to the creative nature of the universe. To say that a principle is general is to say, according to Whitehead, that actual entities are created and creative novelties, by virtue of their relations, enduring and perishing. Thus another aspect of the concept of exemplification becomes clear: to say general principles are exemplified by actual entities is to say that actual entities are created by virtue of the metaphysical character of creativity in the universe. "Thus the 'production of novel togetherness' is the ultimate notion embodied in the term 'concrescence.' " [30] The point to note at present is that the concept of exemplification is the connection between the ultimate and the existent, between the creative and the actual. Exemplification shows how the two interrelate to define organism.

Whitehead makes more of this connection—it is perhaps the central definition of exemplification—in speaking of the meaning

of actuality, of stubborn fact, of a common world, all special instances of determined organism, all definite forms of actual entities
in relation, together novelly. "The canalization of the creative
urge, exemplified in its massive reproduction of social nexus,
is for common sense the final illustration of the power of stubborn
fact." [31]

Societies exemplify the creative urge; which is to say that the
creative urge determines societies; which is to say that societies
are given their definite form by the creative urge; which is to
say that the creative urge describes the character of society and
ascribes to it its generality. In this passage Whitehead emphasizes
the determinate aspect of exemplification. But the determinate
aspect of exemplification is more clearly rendered in the notion
of composition or realization. " 'Actuality' is the fundamental
exemplification of composition. . . ." [32] Clearly, then, composition
is a general principle—which is to say that the composing of an
actual entity by actualizing its potentialities is the carrying out
of exemplification or the making of actuality. Moreover, the composition, once completed or realized, is the constitution of the
actual entity, and from this constitution the everyday actual
world derives—by analysis of the entities involved in the exemplification. "It follows from the ontological principle, thus interpreted, that the notion of a 'common world' must find its exemplification in the constitution of each actual entity, taken by itself
for analysis." [33]

Whitehead in this passage says the actual entity is a general
principle for the common world—which is to say, following out
the meaning of exemplification, that it determines the common
world, grounds its generality, and characterizes it as novel. It
should be clear from these quotations pertaining to Whitehead's
application of the categoreal scheme that exemplification is,
so to speak, the cement holding the bricks of the philosophical
building to the foundation of the world. Exemplification makes
for the very nature of things and for their necessity and continuity.
"The oneness of the universe, and the oneness of each element
in the universe, repeat themselves to the crack of doom in the
creative advance from creature to creature, each creature
including in itself the whole of history and exemplifying the
self-identity of things and their mutual diversities." [34] Clearly,
"exemplification" could entirely replace "relation" in the philosophy of organism. Things can be spoken of as in relation or as

exemplifying each other. The meaning is the same; the emphasis, however, is different. To say that things are in relation is not to show the thoroughgoingness of the relationship—that in relation things penetrate one another. But to say things exemplify each other is to show that things are so intimate with one another that to deny the exemplification of one by the other is to destroy the existence of both. Perishing is the loss of exemplification. For the purposes of the philosophy of organism, "exemplification" is the preferable term. It is new, it is not cluttered with the meanings of another terminology such as "relation" is, and it makes distinct that for Whitehead the essence of the universe is that peculiar togetherness of things whereby they are able to exist definitely and be novel.

In the theory of prehension or feeling the concept of exemplification also has an important place—for feelings are basically a matter of actualization and are the smallest units wherein concrescence occurs, wherein realization is rooted, wherein potentialities actualize. "From each physical feeling there is the derivation of a purely conceptual feeling whose datum is the eternal object exemplified in the definiteness of the actual entity, or the nexus, physically felt." [35] This quotation is similar to an earlier one [36] concerning which we remarked the metaphysical stability afforded by the actualization of potentialities. Plainly, feelings depend on prior exemplifications of potentialities. Actual entities are the general principles for physical feelings—physical feelings exemplify actual entities—and physical feelings are the general principles for conceptual feelings—conceptual feelings exemplify physical feelings. Moreover, conceptual feelings are the general principles for eternal objects—eternal objects exemplify conceptual feelings. The term "datum" makes clearer that things are given prior to any exemplification. But they are not given, unless exemplified, in any definite, determinate existence or form, whether that of actual entities or physical feelings or conceptual feelings. Again, exemplification, in its broadest sense, is seen to underlie any special theory of the universe.

In the theory of extension or physicality the concept of exemplification also plays a central role, again by virtue of its referencing the basic entities and/or contrast of the philosophy of organism, namely, general principles/actual entities. The terms in the theory of extension are the terms used to describe concrescence and its ground concept of exemplification. Thus

Whitehead tells us that, "A feeling in which the form exemplified in the datum concern geometrical, straight and flat loci will be called a 'strain.' " [37] Geometrical, straight and flat loci are the general principles for the actual entity called a strain. A strain exemplifies such loci. In the more general context of the theory of extension the basic terms of the philosophy of organism are introduced to ground the entire theory. "An eternal object considered in reference to the privacy of things is a 'quality' or 'characteristic'; namely, in its own nature, as exemplified in any actuality, it constitutes an element in the private definiteness of that actuality." [38] Here we have a reassertion of the essentials of the philosophy—eternal objects exemplified in actual entities, actual entities exemplifying eternal objects. The particular relation of eternal objects exemplified *in* actual entities is called a qualification or characterizing of the actual entity. Obviously, this takes us back to the very origins of our discussion, the explication of God as the chief exemplification of metaphysical principles. Clearly, an initial meaning is that God is characterized by metaphysical principles. God is described by metaphysical principles. But prior to shifting directly into the final interpretation, after having shown a few instances of the use of the concept of exemplification in the theory of prehension and in the theory of extension, it is necessary that we fix our terminology. It is clear that while the special theories of *Process and Reality* are grounded upon the primary concepts "general principles," "actual entities," and "exemplification," the entire philosophy of organism is much wider than these concepts, since it considers various kinds of general principles, actual entities, and thus has various kinds of exemplifications. We are interested, however, in only one kind of general principle—namely, the metaphysical principle—and one kind of actual entity—namely, God.

And we are also concerned to show the origins of a discussion of God and His relation to the world in the very nature of Whitehead's philosophy of organism. And to do this it would be helpful to adapt a terminology not only as suggestive as Whitehead states a terminology must be but a terminology consistently used throughout the philosophy, throughout *Process and Reality*. Now Whitehead speaks of his philosophy as "the endeavor to frame a coherent, logical, necessary system of general ideas in terms of which every element of our experience can be interpreted. By this notion of 'interpretation' I mean that everything of which we are conscious, as enjoyed, perceived, willed, or thought, shall have the character of a particular instance of the general scheme." [39] And in the final interpretation Whitehead speaks of the final form of these general ideas.

> In our cosmological construction we are, therefore, left with the final opposites, joy and sorrow, good and evil, disjunction and conjunction—that is to say, the many in one—flux and permanence, greatness and triviality, freedom and necessity, God and the World. In this list, the pairs of opposites are in experience with a certain ultimate directness of intuition, except in the case of the last pair. God and the World introduce the note of interpretation. They embody the interpretation of the cosmological problem in terms of a fundamental metaphysical doctrine as to the quality of creative origination, namely, conceptual appetition and physical realization. [40]

Interpretation is the concept common to a consideration of God and of the philosophy of organism. God and the world are the elements of experience interpreted by the final interpretation of the philosophy of organism. If the philosophy of organism can successfully interpret God, it has achieved its purposes of making God an instance of the general scheme. We propose then to replace the word "exemplification" by the term "interpretation." To do this, we must recall our remarks on "description." Clearly, exemplification, if it describes actual entities by means of general principles, also interprets them. From the other side, an interpretation means a description since a general scheme is used to particularize experiences. What I am terming description is what Whitehead calls "symbolic reference" [41]—which, in the account offered of it, parallels the describing of actual entities by general principles.

> Then there is "symbolic reference" between the two species when the perception of a member of one species evokes its correlation in the other species, and precipitates upon this correlate the fusion of feelings, emotions, and derivate actions, which belong to either of the pair of correlates, and which are also enhanced by this correlation. The species from which the symbolic reference starts is called the "species of symbols," and the species which it ends is called the "species of meanings." [42]
> There is no inherent distinction between the sort of percepta which are symbols, and the sort of percepta which are meanings. When two species are correlated by a "ground" of relatedness, it depends upon the experiential process, con-

stituting the percipient subject, as to which species is the group of symbols, and which is the group of meanings. Also it equally depends upon the percipient as to whether there is any symbolic reference at all.[43]

Both exemplification and interpretation involve symbolic reference; it is their common factor. We assert their likeness by virtue of this factor and hold that we will use them interchangeably throughout the remainder of this chapter, whenever one suits our suggestions more than the other. Also it is clear that symbols : meanings :: eternal objects : actual entities :: general principles : actual entities. For purposes of suggestion, we will call the eternal object the interpreted and the actual entity the interpreter— actual entities can be said to interpret eternal objects, and eternal objects are interpretations of actual entities.

We are now prepared to state briefly but surely what White-head means when he asserts that God is the chief exemplification of metaphysical principles. Whitehead means: (1) that God is described by metaphysical principles; (2) that God is an existent, novel entity; (3) that God is determined by metaphysical principles. Correlative to the assertion that God is described by metaphysical principles are the assertions that God symbolizes the meanings of metaphysical principles and that God is an interpretation of metaphysical principles. This last assertion has as a correlate the assertion that metaphysical principles interpret God. Correlative to the assertion that God is an existent, novel entity are the assertions that God is actual and that God is created. It is clear then that God must have two natures, one to account for the fact that He is actual and one to account for the fact that He is created. These are, respectively, the primordial nature of God and the consequent nature of God. I might briefly present the steps behind this assumption: (a) if God is existent He must be one of the eight categories of existence—Whitehead asserts that He is an actual entity; (b) if God is novel He must be "subject" to the category of the ultimate—Whitehead asserts that He is a conjunction of entities. It is clear that the two natures of God will elucidate in just what way God is actual—in what, ontologically, His actuality consists; and in just what way God is created—in what, ontologically, His created being consists. More-over, since according to Whitehead's ninth category of explana-tion, the principle of process, which asserts "that *how* an actual entity *becomes* constitutes *what* that actual entity is," [44] the account Whitehead offers of God as actual must be an account of how God became actual, and the account Whitehead offers of God as created must be an account of how God became created. The "what" of God's actuality is His primordiality; but Whitehead's account of God's primordiality must indicate its "how." The "what" and "how" differ in that the "what" of God is strictly ontological, while the "how" of God is necessarily an account of God's exemplifying. This last is so in that God, as any other actual entity, is in relation to every other actual entity, and this relation is, as we have shown, an exemplification. As primordial, God exemplifies the togetherness of the universe's eternal objects —He assures that every eternal object will ingress in every actual entity, perhaps negatively, but nonetheless in some prehension. Similarly, the "what" of God's createdness is His consequentiality; but Whitehead's account of God's consequentiality must indicate its "how." As consequent, God exemplifies the togetherness of the universe's actual entities, obviously including His own primordiality—He assures that every actual entity will be an objectification of every eternal object, perhaps negatively, but nonetheless in some prehension. Thus, the primordial nature of God and the consequent nature of God account for the togetherness of the universe or for the self-evidence of societies in the universe. To use an obsolete terminology, whenever there are conjunctions there is the hand of God. God, as holding the eternal objects together, as holding the actual entities together, is completing or realizing Himself, just as any actual entity does when it makes decisions as to what it will allow to constitute itself or relate to itself, or what it will exemplify. Apparently, it is God's satisfaction to exemplify in His character everything in the universe. I am by no means, incidentally, using the term "satisfaction" in a metaphorical or non-Whiteheadian way.

Correlative to the assertion that God is determined by metaphysical principles are the assertions that God is conditioned and that God is concrete in proportion to the degree that the metaphysical principles are not abstract. Since the reasons behind any condition are necessarily other entities, according to Whitehead's ontological principle, the conditions determining God are some or all of the categories of existence. Apparently, all the categories of existence are implied by Whitehead, since he speaks summarily of these conditions as the "World." So that the World determines God. God of course determines, as we have indicated in the previous paragraph, the World, by His completion of it. The World determines God by the World's being a datum for God—without the World God has no-thing to complete or realize, so that He Himself is the no-thing. We assert that God is concrete to the degree metaphysical principles are not abstract, to avoid being accused by Whitehead of the fallacy of misplaced concreteness. It is clear that just because metaphysical principles are principles rather than entities they are necessarily abstract—but to forget this abstraction and then see the metaphysical principles as determining any entity, God or otherwise, is to make that entity abstract as well, or to misplace its concreteness. According to Whitehead, we must never, in determining any entity, assume that the principles behind the determination are abstract, for an abstract principle can only determine an entity abstract. But clearly entities are concrete, though we analyze them into abstract pieces. God can, of course, also be analyzed to abstract pieces—that is what we do when we distinguish between God's primordial nature and God's consequent nature—but if we forget that we are analyzing and abstracting we will never be able to get our concrete entities back again into the world. In fact, we won't even be able to get a world—but that doesn't disturb many philosophers. In any case, according to Whitehead there is no getting away from entities and their evident concreteness. Admittedly, we can never finally explain that concreteness—that is why Whitehead calls the entities final, rather than the explanations of them. But we can try to describe concreteness, which is, according to Whitehead, what analysis does. To determine God by metaphysical principles means to try to describe God in as concrete a manner as possible—to try to describe God's being or character, which are synonymous terms for Whitehead, though contextually distinct. That is why, in the very last chapter of *Process and Reality*, Whitehead begins to talk of such outrageous things as God's patience and God's tenderness and other oddities upsetting to the godless realists. Clearly, patience and tenderness are infinitely more concrete than primordiality and consequentiality, both as qualities and as terminologically suggestive. Thus the fact that we as philosophers want to describe any entity in as concrete a way as we can means ultimately—but only ultimately—the abandonment of technical and analytic terminology. Clearly, Whitehead is not contradicting himself in describing God as patient and tender at the end of *Process and Reality* and in remarking at the beginning of *Process and Reality*, "philosophy is explanatory of abstraction, and not of concrescence." [45] Philosophy explains abstraction, but it describes concreteness. It would be absurd to assume on the basis of this quotation that Whitehead says philosophy has nothing to do with concreteness—philosophy just doesn't explain it, it being inexplicable, though self-evident, acknowledgeable. Moreover, Whitehead is not contradicting himself for another, perhaps more important, reason: philosophers are not always talking ultimately—in fact, as Whitehead seems to imply in his upholding of speculative philosophy, they talk so only too rarely. In any case, philosophy for Whitehead is critical as well as ultimate—criticizes itself and all the principles of any special discipline or science or part of itself insofar as they are abstractions—and makes ultimate statements about things other than itself, namely, the nature of things.

On the basis of the principle of process, Whitehead is neither ontological nor logical. He is neither concerned to say what exists nor how we can think of it; he prefers to say how it is. We were therefore only provisional in speaking of Whitehead's ontological approach to God. To Whitehead, the question as to whether or not God exists is a question based on an abstract conception of God, and therefore makes the fallacy of misplaced concreteness, and so is not at all philosophical or even sensible. It is beside the point, for Whitehead, to speak of the what of God's existence as all traditional arguments for the proof of God's existence try to do, since that what is an abstraction and, though it may be philosophically important, is not important for the way the arguers for God's existence want to bring God into existence, as a full-fledged spatio-temporal being with intelligence and moral and intellectual virtues such as you and I have. To show that God is such a being can be done by describing Him. You can argue to doomsday as to whether God exists or not— or for that matter, whether anything exists or not; you will not prove anything, since existence has nothing to do with argument. You had better describe what is self-evident. To Whitehead, God is self-evident, at least to the Whitehead of *Process and Reality* and to the post-*Process and Reality* Whitehead. In *Science and the Modern World*, God is still abstract, a principle rather than an existence. In *Science and the Modern World*, principles were not yet necessary signs of entities—there was no ontological principle. When in *Process and Reality* Whitehead says that God is an entity he is making clear the ground of saying God was a principle of concretion in *Science and the Modern World*. To say that God was a principle of concretion is to say that He is an entity—and as a principle of concretion or an entity of concretion, God clearly makes for the concretion of things. In *Process and Reality* we are told that this concretion means the things together. So, clearly, God's primordial nature and God's consequent nature mean just that—things together.

The point of saying that God is the *chief* exemplification of metaphysical principles is to emphasize that God involves *all* things together, not just this and that thing in conjunction. God makes no negative prehensions. It is just this fact that has disturbed Ely and Schilpp and has set them wondering how moral Whitehead's philosophy was. How can a philosopher be moral if he cannot deny anything, even evil? And clearly Whitehead's God, as we shall see, does not deny evil or even try to avoid being contaminated by it, but takes it up in His own character and makes it good. Clearly, this evil side of God is the *deus absconditus* to Ely and Schilpp. But this is all by the way. The point to hold fast is that God is the chief exemplification of metaphysical principles because of the special sort of actual entity He is, the only one in the entire universe able to realize in His character the entire universe. Let it be noted briefly that this God is not pantheistic for two reasons: (1) the universe is immanent in Him, in His realization; (2) He is only in the composition of each actual entity—that is, immanent in each actual entity—only insofar as each actual entity decides to allow Him to enter its composition. Incidentally, this term "decision," which I have already used once, is also, like the term "satisfaction," nonmetamorphical and strictly Whiteheadian. God would be a pantheist, insofar as I understand the meaning of the term pantheist, if and only if He could get into the constitution of each actual entity whether or not the actual entity wanted Him to be part of its constitution. According to Whitehead, we can do something or not about whether we will allow God to play a part in our lives—except that our lives, whatever we allow to constitute them, whether we allow God to enter them or not, will be, so to say, surrounded by God. We are in God's hands whether or not we will let Him get into our bones. Thus God is not equally distributed through the entities of the universe, as He would have to be were He pantheist. So that all the naïve damnation of the idea of God as pantheistic used against Whitehead is beside the point and unjust, which are the same thing. In any case, I see no reason why it is damnable for God to be a pantheist. As a pantheist, He does not dominate a man's actions but only witnesses them, for the better or the worse. But this is all beside the point. I am merely clearing the ground of Whitehead of its critical weeds. We must hold fast to God being the chief exemplification of metaphysical principles. The term "chief" also implies that God is in some sense "chief" over other exemplifications or actual entities—Whitehead calls Him absolute. Finally, to say that God is the chief exemplification of metaphysical principle is to say that if He were not wherever He is, the assertion that He is the chief exemplification of metaphysical principles would be worthless, would collapse. In other words, because God is the chief exemplification of metaphysical principles, we can self-evidently speak of metaphysical principles, and metaphysical principles are seen to be self-evident by virtue of their chief exemplification in God. God is the ground of metaphysics in that, by virtue of His exemplifying metaphysical principles, He shows their applicability. Metaphysics is the ground of God in that, by virtue of its exemplifying God, it shows God's experienceability. For we must never forget that the original and ultimate purpose of *Process and Reality*, the first and last purpose of Whitehead, is to make apparent or self-evident whatever can be experienced. God, since He is metaphysically determined (that is, determined by the categoreal scheme) and since the categoreal scheme can interpret Him (that is, He exemplifies metaphysical principles), must be experienceable and hence existent. But the experience of God's existence is an affair of each private actual entity, much as the experience of the blue of the Mediterranean is an affair of each private actual entity, an affair of its own self-originating concrescence. Both can be taken or left, positively or negatively prehended. But taken or left both are real, according to Whitehead.

NOTES

1. The author and the editors wish to acknowledge their thanks to Jurgen von Kempski, editor of the *Archiv für Philosophie*, for permission to reprint a slightly revised text of a chapter of the author's book *Whitehead on Divinity*, originally printed in the *Archiv für Philosophie* (11:1–2). The author would also like to acknowledge an especial debt to Professor Theodore W. Adorno, of the Institut Für Sozialforschung, and the Philosophisches Seminar of the Johann Wolfgang von Goethe University, Frankfurt-am-Main, Germany.

2. Alfred North Whitehead, "John Dewey and His Influence," *The*

Philosophy of John Dewey, ed. Paul Arthur Schilpp, 2nd ed. (New York: Tudor Publishing Co., 1951), p. 478.

3. Alfred North Whitehead, *Process and Reality*, 1st ed. reprint (New York: The Humanities Press, 1955), p. 521.

4. *Science and the Modern World*, 1st ed. reprint (New York: The New American Library, 1949), p. 5.

5. *Ibid.*, p. 13.

6. *Ibid.*, p. 26.

7. *Ibid.*, p. 28.

8. *Ibid.*, pp. 27–28.

9. Whitehead writes as though this problem is without precedent in philosophy and, as a result, writes naïvely. His naïveté is perhaps consistent with his reluctance to acknowledge historical sources which, in turn, is due in large part to his ignorance of much of the history of philosophy and, undoubtedly, to his feeling that any elaborate acknowledgment of the background of his thought would digress from its consistency. Whitehead pays passing attention to Bergson, McTaggart, and Bradley—we record them as prime sources. But behind the latter stands Hegel, whom Whitehead no more than cursorily and flippantly criticizes, yet whom he hints may be *the* figure in his philosophical development (Hegel not at first hand, but as the touchstone of both Bradley and McTaggart). Bergson called Whitehead's attention to process, but Whitehead could not stay satisfied with what he considered, unjustifiably, Bergson's loosely rationalized return to naïve concretion. To avoid this conception of naïve concretion, Whitehead turned to Hegel's conception of the concrete as the context and of the abstract as isolation from the context. Hegel's conception is the presupposition basic to an understanding of Whitehead's method of extensive abstraction (*Principles of Natural Knowledge, The Concept of Nature*).

It seems probable that Whitehead read McTaggart's *A Commentary On Hegel's Logic* (1910), and even if he didn't, he admits almost daily conversation with him when McTaggart was working on his study of Hegel (see Whitehead's "Autobiography" in his volume in the *Library Of Living Philosophers*). There are many passages in McTaggart's book which strongly echo Whitehead's language (e.g., the use of "exemplification"), and there are more important passages in which the general rationale of Whitehead's philosophy, at least as it is understood in this essay, is characterized.

Is the Absolute Idea exemplified in any concrete state known to us, in the same way that the category of Cognition was? It seems clear to me that Hegel regarded it as exemplified by consciousness of some sort. In the first place there are the references to personality in the passage quoted above from the *Greater Logic* (iii. 327). The Notion is here, "as a Person, impenetrable atomic Subjectivity." This does not, I think, indicate that the nature of the Universe as a whole is exemplified by personality, since the Universe would never be described by Hegel as impenetrable or atomic. It is, I think, the parts of the Universe which are to be regarded as having these characteristics, and as therefore having a nature exemplified in personality. In the second place, we have the statement that the Idea is its own Object, and again that the Absolute Idea is the truth which knows itself. (Page 309, 1930 edition)

It seems clear to me that the question McTaggart puts is similar in form to the question Whitehead asks as to God being the chief exemplification of metaphysical principles. Moreover, apart from any tie to Hegel and without stretching the imagination, Whitehead's actual entities are intrinsically personalities. The entire scheme of the ingression of eternal objects and of the objectification of actual entities reads like a metaphor for a theory of communication between persons. The actual entity has all the traits otherwise attributed to personality, as humanistically conceived. It conceives itself, it perishes, it inescapably is in the world, with ties to others. Moreover, what Whitehead terms the "real internal constitution" of the actual entity is described in terms of personal feelings. In any case, the similarities between Whitehead and Hegel—Hegel as conceived by McTaggart—are apparent apart from any detailed commentary.

The direct tie to Bradley is more obvious, and we mean only to indicate it generally. In the preface to *Process and Reality*, Whitehead remarks that his conclusions are essentially those of Bradley, though he despairs of Bradley's methods. Bradley's conclusions, as he offers them in Chapter XXVI ("The Absolute And Its Appearances") of *Appearance and Reality*, are that there "is but one Reality, and its being consists in experience" (page 403, the ninth impression) and that "the various aspects of experience imply one another, and that all point to a unity which comprehends and perfects them" (page 414). Now this implication is exactly Whitehead's category of creativity, the category which assures such connectivity. And just as for Bradley all the diverse provinces of the Absolute or Reality are no more than partial aspects of the universe, grounded one and all on their experienceability, so for Whitehead all the dualities of his philosophy of organism, from process and reality to God and the world, are interpretations of the nature of experience.

Our remark about general principles (*deutera ousia*) is more fully qualified by remarking its Aristotelian point, that they are in some way constitutive for *entia* (*prote ousia*). Whitehead takes the trouble to say this is so, as we understand him; but, unfortunately, he does not say how so—though he implies, with his category of creativity, that there is a single general principle which guarantees the singularity of the conjunctions which make for numerous individual *entia*. This aspect of the category of creativity, viz., that it implies this kind of exemplification, is analogous to Duns Scotus' principle of *haecceitas*. In Duns Scotus there are three metaphysical principles, out of which the *ens* is capable of being constituted. They are purely ontological, that is to say, regarded as independent from thought. Here is the prime point of agreement between Whitehead and Duns Scotus, though for Whitehead they are not so independent of thinking. For Whitehead, metaphysical principles are thought. They are generalizations about experience, but, to preserve their ontologicality, they are not regarded as being won through experience. The principles of

Whitehead and Duns Scotus constitute a *res,* or "actual entity" in Whitehead's terminology, and the principles are called by Duns Scotus *realitates siva entitates*—a terminology remarkably similar to Whitehead's insofar as his categories are also real and constitutive for the *res.* But the important point is that Whitehead's principle of exemplification is as much a self-evident ontological principle as Duns Scotus' *haecceitas.* For Whitehead and Duns Scotus, accidents are not capable of explaining the individuality of a *res.* Therefore the *res* reflects its individuation in its substance by mediation of the additional principle of *haecceitas.*

Bradley and McTaggart are idealists, and so is the later Whitehead; the question to ask of Whitehead is how far his idealism influences his philosophy of organism. The great tradition of idealistic thought is German and, by way of the English Hegelians, German idealism settled in England. But in our concern to trace the influence of Hegel's idealism in Whitehead's thought, we are not interested in mere historical precedents, nor do we want to know whether Whitehead consciously took over ideas from Hegel as found in Bradley and McTaggart. Our question rather is to find and, in this small space, simply indicate motifs of Hegel's idealism which Whitehead took over in his own philosophizing. The basic problem of Whitehead's philosophy, to demonstrate the synthesis of subject and object, is the aim of dialectic: the attempt through thought's spontaneity to find a synthesis between subject and object, so as to avoid the isolation of both these moments in reality and knowledge. These moments epistemologically and ontologically belong together, as dialectic and the philosophy of organism claim. However, this togetherness is no mere harmony, but a prime concern of the theory of knowledge: how subject and object connect up, how the object is known, how objectivity is gained.

For Hegel and Whitehead, this "how" is a matter of speculation (*Process and Reality,* chap. i). The nature of speculative thinking "besteht allein in dem Auffassen der entgegengesetzten Momente in ihrer Einheit" (Hegel, *Logik,* Glockner edition, p. 177). "Das ist ueberhaupt das Geschaeft der Spekulation, dass sie alle Gegenstaende des reinen Gedankens, der Natur und des Geistes in Form des Gedankens und so als Einheit des Unterschiedes auffasst" (Hegel, *Vorlesungen ueber die Philosophie der Religion,* Vol. I, Glockner edition, p. 40). Reflection for Hegel means to speak of subject and object as isolated terms, means to separate form and matter. When Hegel speaks of reflection he thinks of the Kantian attempt to reflect knowledge in subjectivity. Speculation, by means of a second act of self-reflection, reduces matter and form to unity. Hegel and Whitehead are concerned to find a rationale for such speculation.

A criticism of positivism is part of Whitehead's assertion that speculative philosophy is *the* method of philosophy. Whereas, in empirical thought, subject and object are regarded separately, they are thought together in speculative philosophy. This is by means of reflection—reflection mediates subject and object. Through this mediation *Geist* itself is achieved. ("Mind" is an inadequate translation of *"Geist";* we prefer the German meaning.) For Hegel, *Geist* exists in the ultimate unity of subject and object (or, as he puts it, in the identity of non-identity) , not in separate subject nor separate object, one of which is then said to bring *Geist* to the mediation. Whitehead's creativity con-sists in a similar bringing together of subject and object in, as Whitehead says, conjunction. Whitehead's universe is a mental poten- tiality. Hence, Whitehead regards God's consequentiality to be physical; but His primordiality (i.e., His mentality) is a potentiality which, when actualized, is physical (viz., the world) . T. W. Adorno in "Erfah- rungsgehalte Der Hegelschen Philosophie" (*Archiv fuer Philosophie* 9:1–2) remarks a similar point when he says (p. 84) that what most shocks uninitiated students of Hegel's *Phaenomenologie des Geistes* is just what is dialectical, that "zwischen den obersten spekulativen Ideen und der aktuellen politischen Erfahrung aus der franzoesischen Revolution und der Napoleonischen Zeit" there is mediation. Here speculative ideas are a kind of potentiality to be realized in actual events in history. Applying this to Whitehead, we might say that the world is the history of God.

It is also important to understand that Whitehead's "emotionaliza- tion" of the universe, his theory that feelings or prehensions are, so to speak, the instruments of mediation, is idealistic. Whitehead's feelings function on the subjective side, or rather in subjectivistic terminology, in the same way as Hegel's Moments. In Whitehead's universe, par- ticulars are mediated through feelings. Separating feelings from one another decomposes the universe or, as Whitehead says, keeps it primi- tive. Feelings build the universe by forming ever more complicated patterns, till the complex feeling called "consciousness" is achieved and held fast, sustained in what Whitehead names "intellectual feelings." Feelings, then, are functions for a whole—they are the bearers of meaning (Bedeutungstraeger) . Or, as Hegel might say, feelings are Moments which are constitutive for the whole itself. In his theory of feelings (Part III, *Process and Reality*) Whitehead attempts, through an "emotionalization" of the universe, to solve the problem of the re- lationship between subject and object, the problem of the theory of knowledge. Despite their separation they are identical, because they synthesize in "feeling" each other. As Hegel says, the object is sub- jectivized in knowledge and thereby becomes a subject in kind. The end result of this process of subjectivization is Whitehead's subject- superject. But this process also objectivizes the subject, which means the subject gains its objective nature as a subject having a definite object—something more than the subject being mere subjectivity. Whitehead calls this process of the reflection of subject and object "interaction."

Another motif of idealistic philosophy to be found in Whitehead is his conception of the actual entity's self-creation. This conception reminds one of Hegel's Absolute Idea—that which by and of itself is capable of becoming an object. Whitehead's conception of self-creation is the theory whereby he explains how subject becomes object; like Hegel's reflection, this conception explains the object's self-production or self-constitution. Self-creation—development—stems from the sub- ject-object structure and means a taking-leave-of, a going-out-from, the self-identity of the being in order for it to develop into an object, since the subject is now free of itself, free of its subjectivity. Whitehead calls such a getting-free-from, subjectivity—the actual entity's lure for feeling into its environment. Such a lure can be regarded as connoting an aspect of Hegelian reflection. The subject must be free of its subjectivity to tie-up and tie-in with the other. But the reverse is also true: to be an object, the being has to be a subject as well. This is what Hegel calls the *Idee*, viz., having this subject-object structure of the being. The *Idee*, a synthesis of subject and object, involving the identity and difference of both, functions like Whitehead's exemplification: God identifies with the world, but He is also different from the world, since He is the chief exemplification of the metaphysical principles of the world.

Hegel's fundamental principle is the mediation of subject and object—that they intrinsically imply one another. Subject and object without this intrinsic togetherness are nothing but abstract generals without any nature, since nature is a determinant of the whole, their relationship. Subject for itself is loosened from the whole; object for itself is emptied of its contents. Object wins its contents only insofar as I can reflect on it, which means only insofar as I enter into it. This means that only through the mediation of subjectivity does the object come to its objectivity. Only through me does the object first become concrete. Subject and object, involved with one another, connect up. Through this act of knowledge—the getting-involved—subject becomes objective subject, object loses its emptiness and indifference and becomes subjective object. Through this process of interaction the general becomes a substantial principle, i.e., becomes constitutive; or, in Whiteheadian terminology, general principles become capable of constituting actual entities, while previously the general principles were mere abstract entities. Prior to interaction general principles are merely dogmatic assertions, positivistic. But a complication ensues, since the dialectician next asks: How is it that we could assert the principles, merely set them down, if we did not know beforehand that interaction between subject and object was implied from the start? Thus the subject-object structure is present even at the extremes of abstraction, at the start of speculation. Thus subject as general and object as general are mutually related to one another to constitute principles. Subject must function in object for object to be objective. Object must function in subject for subject to be subjective. Otherwise subject and object are mere voids, closed-in monads, subject the merest egotism, object the merest abstraction. But Whitehead's general principles are not merely principia, but principiata as well, i.e., only in action are they principles. For Whitehead, any single factum can become a principle to be realized in another interaction. For instance, actual entities are principles for nexus, much as eternal objects are principles for actual entities. Thus, principles are not empty and static, but living—any particular (e.g., an eternal object) reflects itself only insofar as it is in the general (e.g., an actual entity). Through the totality of conditions the general situation—one might say the general is always a situation to be realized—becomes concrete. Reflection, for Hegel, is interaction, not mere connection. We can best say, in the English language, it is connection through opposition and contrariety —a conception fundamentally similar to Whitehead's conception of connection through contrast. For Hegel, and to a certain extent for

Whitehead, this constant compulsion to acknowledge and overcome contradictions brings process (which is itself contradictory) forward, makes process fruitful, and realizes potentialities. Principles are not only constitutive, but new principles are constantly being constituted. The cause, so to speak, is always itself an effect.

10. *Science and the Modern World*, p. 94.
11. *Adventures of Ideas*, 1st ed. reprint (New York: The New American Library, 1955), p. 145.
12. *Ibid.*, p. 71.
13. *Ibid.*, p. 236.
14. *Ibid.*, p. 170.
15. *Process and Reality*, p. 7.
16. *Science and the Modern World*, p. 5.
17. *Process and Reality*, p. 11.
18. *Ibid.*, p. 19.
19. *Adventures of Ideas*, p. 170.
20. *Process and Reality*, p. 28.
21. *Ibid.*, p. 49.
22. *Ibid.*, pp. 34–35.
23. *Ibid.*, p. 63.
24. *Ibid.*, p. 64.
25. *Ibid.*, p. 95.
26. *Loc. cit.*
27. *Ibid.*, p. 103.
28. *Ibid.*, p. 118.
29. *Ibid.*, p. 178.
30. *Ibid.*, p. 32.
31. *Ibid.*, p. 197.
32. *Ibid.*, p. 223.
33. *Ibid.*, p. 224.
34. *Ibid.*, pp. 347–348.
35. *Ibid.*, p. 379.
36. *Ibid.*, p. 64.
37. *Ibid.*, p. 472.
38. *Ibid.*, p. 444.
39. *Ibid.*, p. 4.
40. *Ibid.*, p. 518.
41. *Ibid.*, p. 276.
42. *Ibid.*, p. 274.
43. *Ibid.*, p. 276.
44. *Ibid.*, p. 34.
45. *Ibid.*, p. 30.

INDEX

[221]

A NOTE ON THE TYPE USED IN THIS BOOK

The text of this book has been set on the Linotype in a type face called "Baskerville." The face is a facsimile reproduction of types cast from molds made for John Baskerville (1706–1775) from his designs. The punches for the revived Linotype Baskerville were cut under the supervision of the English printer George W. Jones.

John Baskerville's original face was one of the forerunners of the type-style known as "modern face" to printers: a "modern" of the period A.D. 1800.